ONE FOOT ᴜɴ THE GROUND

BY

HARRY SMITH

CIRRUS ASSOCIATES

PUBLISHED BY:
Cirrus Associates (S.W.),
Kington Magna,
Gillingham,
Dorset,
SP8 5EW UK.

© Harry Smith 2002

ISBN 1 902807 14 6

PRINTED IN ENGLAND BY:
Bookcraft Ltd.,
First Avenue,
Westfield Trading Estate,
Radstock,
BATH,
BA3 4BS.

PHOTO SCANNING BY:
International Graphics Services Ltd.,
24-31 Fourth Avenue,
Westfield Trading Estate,
Radstock,
BATH,
BA3 4XE.

DISTRIBUTORS:
Cirrus Associates (S.W.),
Kington Magna,
Gillingham,
Dorset,
SP8 5EW UK.

COVER: Original photo by Bill Tate, computer-enhanced by Ken Whiteley. All other photos by the author unless specified otherwise.

DEDICATION

Why *"One Foot On The Ground"*?

One day in 1932, Mr B.D. Whittaker, Chief Engineer of the Herts & Essex Aeroplane Club, entered the Clubhouse kitchen and said to the part-time cook: "Mrs Smith! We have an aircraft about to fly on a short test-flight. Would you care for a flip?"

My mother, who had opined on occasion that aeroplanes and motorcycles were all 'inventions of the Devil,' replied: "Only if I can keep one foot on the ground!"

So, in her memory and with regard to my own aeronautical aspirations and experience recounted within, it seemed a good idea to call my book *"One Foot On The Ground."*

Harry Smith
16th March 2002

ACKNOWLEDGEMENTS

I would like to express a few words of thanks to those people who helped in the inception of this book:

To Jim Norris (DH Moth Club member) and Diana Barnato-Walker for suggesting it: to Mike Vaisey and Stuart McKay for proof-reading and putting me right text-wise: to Bruce Bosher for processing the crop-dusting Tiger and burst tyre photos; and most of all to Connie, my wife, for encouragement in many ways.

CONTENTS

PROLOGUE

This is primarily a story of a period of my life in the aircraft industry from November 1940, when I enrolled as a 14-year-old shop boy, until leaving the hangar floor to join the Design Office in the early spring of 1957.

Many authors have written wonderful biographies concerning pilots or top aircraft designers but few have chronicled the everyday dramas, frustrations and humorous cameos of the aircraft industry workshops. I have tried herein to redress the balance a little. Using the premise that it is better to please all of the people some of the time rather than some of the people all of the time, I've endeavoured to balance the technicalities with what I hope are interesting generalities; plus a bit of regard to those who like historical facts by quoting aircraft registration letters and such now and then.

I have been extremely lucky to be involved in the industry during its golden era and to experience such a wide variety of trades and tasks therein. Engineering is a wonderful vocation, and Aeronautical Engineering – in my humble opinion – is best of all: one never ceases to learn something new.

My eldest brother started his own engineering career in the machine shop at Stones of Charlton, near Deptford in East London, where they manufactured ships' propellers. He managed, by study and progressing through various positions, to attain Training Centre Manager status in the Government Training & Rehabilitation Scheme. In this capacity, he associated with other professions and amazed certain colleagues in the medical profession with the learning required for any qualified engineer, Aeronautical, Civil, Electrical, Electronic, Mechanical, Metallurgical, Structural, or whatever, each in their own field, needing to amass knowledge as much as – if not more than – their medical colleagues in order to obtain the appropriate letters after their name. If we revere the doctor, why not the innovative engineer? Sir Roy Fedden, Chief Designer of the Bristol Aero Engine Company, averred that no one should call themselves 'engineer' without the appropriate engineering degree or equivalent in their particular engineering discipline. How sad it is that in Great Britain we now denigrate engineers and regard them as mere greasy-overalled 'yobs.' Ignorant folk frequently refer to fitters and mechanics as mere 'engineers.' How many real engineers, I wonder, have when divulging their profession to someone suffered the response: "Could you take a look at my washing machine" or something similar? Would they ask a brain surgeon to bandage a sore finger?

The Brunels, Cockerell, de Havilland, Fedden, Issigonis, Mitchell, Parsons, Royce, the Stephensons, Wallis, Watt, Whittle, Whitworth – to name but a few – were all real innovative engineers. Through them and their ilk our country gave to the world steam power, turbines, railways, tunnels, bridges, ships, motors, aircraft, television, radar and many other benefits and, thanks to stupid politicians and blinkered bankers, let them all be exploited elsewhere. Why do our 'fast-buck' merchant bankers sink money into overseas bubbles instead of gold mines in their own back yard?

In 1945, Stafford Cripps clobbered Frank Whittle and gave away his gas turbine secrets to America and Russia. Forbidden to continue his Power Jets business in his own country, Frank went to the USA where the Americans properly welcomed him as a hero. Cripps then went on to compound the felony by forbidding all further work on the Miles M.52 and ordered all their research to be handed to the Americans. This was of immense help to them in their X-series high speed research aircraft.

Sir Geoffrey de Havilland once said, in effect, that for a design to succeed, one has to cut and fasten materials. I've cut and fastened a lot of different materials in my working life, prior to attaining a position where I produced designs for others to do likewise. But, in view of my previous remarks and despite retiring with the title 'Design Engineer,' I never obtained a degree or similar, so cannot in all conscience claim to be an 'engineer' in that sense. To quote my hero Henry Royce, I'll admit: "I'm really just a mechanic."

* * * * * * * * * *

I make no excuses for using Imperial weights and measures in the text throughout this book and for reference to pre-decimal currency. Those were used at the time, and that is how I have recorded them. I know that ten shillings equates in some people's minds as fifty pence, but when I started work that sum represented a fair amount of spending power. So to any reader who relates mainly to today's monetary values, I crave indulgence and ask that they merely multiply sums quoted by about 55 to gain some idea of the values then prevailing.

As to measurements, there are approximately 3¼ feet in a metre and an inch is 25.399541 millimetres precisely. A gallon contains 4.546 litres – but of course you know that. When I was a teenager, if someone mentioned metres I would have heard it as 'meters' and thought they were referring to testing and measuring apparatus. Times change!

H.A. Smith, A.M.R.Ae.S.
Welwyn Garden City
16th March 2002

CHAPTER 1
EARLY DAYS

From about the age of three, aeroplanes were an important interest in my life. Our house, a terraced dwelling in Childer Street, Deptford, S.E. London – near Surrey Docks – was hardly conducive to aviation aspirations. However, despite the aeronautically disadvantaged location, my aircraft interest was generated by several factors.

During the Great War, our father worked for Handley Page at Cricklewood, where he was employed installing and testing Rolls-Royce engines for the 0/400 and V1500 heavy bombers. He often entertained my elder brothers with anecdotes of those years whilst I was in the background – 'ear'oles akimbo,' as a certain one-time radio comedian would have put it.

Our mother had a part-time job at New Cross Kinema and from this, plus her time on stage as an amateur concert singer with a fine contralto voice, she had become something of a film buff. She often took me with her to matinée performances and I usually slept throughout, but once or twice stayed awake to take in some of the programme. I remember a scene of an aeroplane flying with a weighted rope ladder dangling to allow an idiot to climb it from a moving car. At home, I re-enacted the adventure by placing an old pram cushion on a pile of newspapers and this became an ideal cockpit seat, but I was not permitted to use Mum's umbrella as a parachute! At other times, two kitchen chairs, one placed on its back on the floor with the other lying on its front, their seats and backs facing one another but slightly staggered and with an old mahogany board placed across the back legs of the latter, became an excellent aeroplane until one day, in his haste to bale out, the 'pilot' put his foot through one of the vertical spokes of the lower chairback; sounds of splitting wood brought the female parent onto the scene in some haste. After that, aircraft manufacture from domestic equipment was firmly discouraged!

Kind people gave me various tinplate toy aeroplanes, and once someone gave me a 'U-Build' kit of a lovely red and silver biplane. Too young to build it myself, the job was sub-contracted to Dad and eldest brother. They somehow misinterpreted the instructions, for both pressed-steel wheels were assembled adjacent to one another under the fuselage centre-line with the axle sticking out a couple of inches on either side. Even to a 3-year-old it looked wrong; what, I wondered, were they thinking of? Later, an indulgent aunt presented me with a fine tinplate clockwork toy of the Schneider Trophy winning S.6B seaplane. When wound and set on a bath of water, its whirring propeller would pull it across the water in a realistic manner. As we had no bathroom at Childer Street, a zinc-plated steel bath had to be brought in from the outhouse and filled with kettles of hot water, but as bathtime preceded bedtime and toys were not allowed in the bath anyway, I do not remember having much fun with my S.6B.

I noted the highly romanticised pictures of first World War air battles depicted in the boys' magazines and re-enacted their violence with plasticine models, to the detriment of the tablecloth. One day a tremendous engine noise aloft brought us all out to the back yard in time to witness a flight of aircraft pass over Deptford. I heard brother Bob say that he thought they were bombers (probably Wapitis).

Mum looked both cross and very worried and kept saying: "Oh dear! Oh dear! How dreadful!"

I remember tugging at her skirts and saying: "But they are *our* planes, Mummy!" At that tender age I had identified the red, white and blue roundels. However, to Mum all aircraft were 'inventions of the Devil' and, as she had endured the Zeppelin air raids during the previous war, that philosophy was at least understandable.

About then the boys, Mum and I journeyed north across the River to see the wonderful 1930 Hendon Air Pageant. Older cousin Ernie, who was in the Royal Air Force, had arranged the visit. We saw him resplendent in his uniform which, in those days, included soft-top peaked cap and puttees; years later he suffered terribly as a POW in Japanese hands. Mum had a pretty thin time, dragging me around in my ancient pushchair over the bumpy, lumpy grass field. I was not all that comfortable myself as the hard wooden arms kept jabbing me in an irritating manner. I remember most clearly seeing a flight of fighters take off (probably Gloster Gamecocks) and noting that the landing wheels were spinning fast as the machines passed overhead, just like the wheels on my clockwork tin toy at home. I was fascinated when a number of white-suited parachutists tumbled off the lower wings of large twin-engined biplanes, and witnessed the spectacular event of an observation balloon being shot down in flames. It was all showmanship, of course, but I was not to know that! Apart from being taken into a large hangar where refreshments were available, and being treated to a glass of milk and some cake, I remember little else of the day's events.

Brother Joe was often detailed to to fetch me from the Rachel Macmillan day nursery school near the Docks. We passed a large toy shop which had pedal motors and tricycles on display out on the pavement. One day, to my immense pleasure, he took me inside the shop so that we could inspect a pedal aeroplane with a propeller that rotated as it was pedalled along. Joe's popularity was greatly enhanced in my eyes, but not in Mum's when I asked my financially hard-pressed parents to let me have such a wonderful machine.

Reference to my nursery school reminds me of the time it was visited by Her Majesty Queen Mary. I recall a lot of bustle and then we were all sat at tables with various toys and simple puzzles put before us. Having finished mine, I looked up and was horrified to behold an enormous phalanx of people approaching like a monstrous tide. Accompanied by the head teacher, the gracious lady paused by me to see what I had been doing; I cannot remember the conversation, but there were smiles all round as she passed on her way. At home that evening, Mum was very excited at the news of the Queen's visit, and it is to my eternal regret that I never told her that Her Majesty had spoken to me. In recent years, when conversion turns to 'royalty,' I say: "Of course, you know, I was once presented to Her Majesty Queen Mary!"

Early in 1931 the family moved from smoky old Deptford to Rye Park, part of the urban district of Hoddesdon in East Hertfordshire. Apart from the clean fresh air, it was exciting to explore the surrounding countryside. Once, when we were walking along by the New River, crickets were chirruping away nineteen-to-the-dozen, but I did not know about crickets and kept looking in the grassy banks for bicycle chainwheels and sprockets which I felt sure were spinning nearby. (Our Dad was once in partnership with his brothers in a cycle shop at Peckham and often repaired bicycles for friends and the family so they were part of everyday life in our household.)

At that time, a housing development firm known as Homemakers was busy filling up Rye Park with masses of semi-detached and terraced dwellings. Their joinery workshop was a short distance beyond our back garden and we were well supplied with joinery off-cuts for firewood. Some of the pieces were ideal for Joe to make into crude aeroplanes for me, using Dad's hammer and some of his odd nails. Sometimes, I 'wallpapered' them with bits of ruled foolscap stuck to the wings with flour-and-water paste to represent wing-ribs.

A family friend came to visit soon after we moved in and brought me an aeroplane toy that consisted of a tinplate tower with a rotating arm, and small tin aeroplanes pivoted on each end. When the device was wound up and set running the arm rotated, allowing the aircraft to circle the tower whilst the motor within made a very realistic aircraft droning noise. By unclipping the the arm, I preferred to wind it up just to make the droning noise. We had a home-made wheelbarrow consisting of a wooden box placed on an old pram axle with a wheel each side. A pair of shafts were tacked onto the sides and it had a single strut at the back to hold it level when being loaded. I soon found that by placing a short plank athwartships at the front, putting the aircraft-noise toy underneath it and sitting on another little board similarly placed at the back I had made a splendid make-believe aeroplane. All that remained was to wind up the toy and persuade my long-suffering older sister to wheel me around the garden whilst it emitted its irritating hollow drone under the plank.

One day Mum returned from the shops and placed the purchases on the kitchen table whilst she dealt with some mundane domestic chore. I noticed that there were a dozen or so clothes pegs of the common torsion-spring type and a couple of steel pulleys for Dad to erect a new clothes line. The pulleys fascinated me in that they were caged to prevent the line slipping off and the cages were mounted on a threaded spindle to be screwed to a post or whatever. Clipping the pegs together, I built up a crude sort of cantilever low wing monoplane and pushed the pulleys into the wing undersides for landing gear. Mum returned at that point and wanted to know what I was doing with her pegs – she was hardly impressed with my efforts.

At that time, of course, most aeroplanes were biplanes and Captain Percival and Fred Miles were only just beginning to produce their famous Gulls and Hawks. Both types of machine were eventually to be cantilever low wing monoplanes with stirrup based single-strut undercarriage legs. I have thought about this 'peg aircraft' many times and wondered if there was a quirk of telepathy between two of our best aircraft designers and an unknown five-year-old! (Well, I can dream, can't I?)

Soon after this I was struck down with a bout of double pneumonia and whooping cough and had to spend many weeks in bed. When able to 'sit up and take notice' I was allowed to have my plasticine on a bed table and intrigued the family doctor with my efforts to build a small air force of plasticine high-wing monoplanes.

Mum had taken a part-time job as cook at the Herts & Essex Aeroplane Club and, not realizing what a profound influence this establishment would have upon my life in later years, sharpened further my aeronautical interest. One day she took me with her when needing to visit for some reason other than to cook, and I saw a brown & orange DH.60 Moth from only ten feet away! Brown & orange were the colours the Club used for their aircraft and later the local residents were alleged to sing the parody: "A-tisket! A-tasket! A brown & orange basket" as the machines took off over their houses.

CHAPTER 2

SERVICE WITH A SMILE

Much family upheaval was generated soon after this when our parents took up positions respectively as cook/housekeeper and chauffeur/handyman to Lady Maud Tree, the well-known theatrical actress.

Much as I enjoy a good play or film, I always speculate as to what the actors and actresses are like in real life. This approach seldom spoils my entertainment but, I wonder, do they shrug off their fictional character like a cloak upon leaving the stage door or studio, or do they carry it on into their private lives to the irritation of friends and families? If you wonder why I think this way, perhaps what follows will provide enlightenment.

When our family moved to Rye Park in the spring of 1931 our Dad was then employed as a chauffeur with Daimler Hire, but he lost his job shortly after we had moved. For a time he managed to find work driving the various company cars of the aforementioned Homemakers. This job folded when the company required fewer cars, and by 1932 it was difficult for any man to get a job and for a 60-year-old practically impossible, despite the fact that he was an excellent driver and first-class mechanic with Rolls-Royce experience.

In the spring of 1933, and after some time making do with a few menial tasks and taking in private jobs rebuilding bicycle wheels and so forth, he learned of the vacancy for a chauffeur and housekeeper to Lady Tree OBE, widow of Sir Herbert Beerbohm Tree, who resided in Hoddesdonbury, a large ivy-covered former farmhouse near Broxbourne Woods; this was, at that time, part of the estate of Major Smith-Bosanquet and leased to Her Ladyship.

Sir Herbert Beerbohm Tree (1853–1917) was a famous British actor-manager. Noted for his Shakespeare productions and founder of the Royal Academy of Dramatic Art, he was half-brother of the writer Max Beerbohm. His widow, Lady Tree, was in her own right a well-known London West End dramatic actress who also sometimes appeared in films.

In a joint interview, Her Ladyship emphasised that she would employ Dad only if Mum agreed to take up the other vacancy of housekeeper/cook/maid, and both would be required to live in; this would pose a major problem for continuance of family life for the rest of us. At that time, eldest brother Albert worked at the Golden Lion Garage as a motor mechanic; he had been trained in the machine shop at Stones of Charlton – famous for the manufacture of ships' propellers – but it was better than a previous job, which had been as delivery boy with Walker's Stores, a large grocer's at Hertford, the only job he could get when we first moved. Second brother Robert was a counter-hand at the Hoddesdon branch of International Stores, whilst third brother Gordon, then aged 14, was an errand boy with a local fishmonger & fruiterer. Sister Hazel (12) was at school and I (6) was still convalescing.

Lady Tree persuaded Major Smith-Bosanquet to lease the nearby North Lodge of Broxbournebury Park to Her Ladyship and allow the seven members of the Smith family to move in.

As mentioned, Mum had a fine contralto voice and, as a young woman, sang in concerts; I have pleasant childhood memories of her singing me to sleep with well-known gentle ballads and lullabies. She started singing at regimental functions for the entertainment of her father's colleagues and families, then when she entered service she kept up her concert performances at various amateur events and this, no doubt, accounted for her enthusiasm for, and knowledge of, 'the theatre.'

The fact that her voice was of good quality had been borne out by a gentleman of music who asked her to let him arrange an audition for her at the d'Oyly Carte Company. At that time she was a junior housemaid for a wealthy family in London but, thrilled with the prospect of a chance to be in 'real theatre,' she approached her employer to seek permission for time off to attend the audition. To her chagrin and disappointment, the lady of the house said "Certainly not!" and added bleakly: "Servants do not have careers!"

Mum should have turned round to the autocratic old besom and told her to get stuffed, but in those pre-Great War days servants had to know their place and keep within its confines. I doubt if she ever quite got over her disappointment.

In view of such theatrical enthusiasm it would have been a surprise if our mother had not done her very best to obtain the job with Lady Tree. Whether she would have been so keen, had she known to what extent her capabilities were to be taxed, is a matter of some conjecture.

Lady Tree employed three people to attend her needs: a live-in house-keeper/cook/parlourmaid/cleaner (Mum), a chauffeur/handyman (Dad) – to live in or not as necessary – and a Mr Jim Leadbetter, the gardener, who attended daily. Hoddesdonbury was a large converted farmhouse with no gas or electricity. Illumination was by oil lamps or candles and a coal-fired kitchen range provided the only cooking facility and heated water for the bathroom. Any hot water for washing-up and staff ablutions was obtained from a large black kettle permanently simmering on the glowing embers. Separate coal fires were needed in bedrooms and dining rooms. These latter, of course, were only required in cold weather but the range had to burn every day. On the whole, I think Dad had the best deal in that, apart from driving, maintaining and cleaning the car, his daily duties only required cleaning, trimming and filling 30 or so large copper oil lamps, lighting and distributing them around the house at dusk, replenishing the coal scuttles, and any other minor domestic repairs or maintenance. Mum, on the other hand, cleaned the house, stoked the fires, attended Her Ladyship, ordered the groceries and provisions, cooked breakfasts, luncheons & dinners, provided afternoon teas and waited at table. For cooking, she wore a white coat & pinafore and for waiting at table was required to change into black dress with white cap & apron.

Although the laundry van called every week, there were still items of washing she was expected to see to, and all this with the sort of domestic equipment that was obsolete at the turn of the 19th century! The concept of a cosy farmhouse kitchen with its stove is all very well in winter, but in July and August it could be an absolute inferno, with Mum bent over this iron monster in high summer – perspiring and red of face – cooking a three-course lunch. The stove consumed fuel at a prodigious rate and had to be raked out and relit each morning in order to heat water for baths and morning tea.

Before the family moved into North Lodge, Mum had to take up residence at Hoddesdonbury and had a small bedroom above the kitchen entered via a steep narrow stairway from the laundry room at the back of the long kitchen. Dad was not required to be on hand 24 hours a day and so was able to cycle home each night to keep an eye on the family. Due to my delicate state of health, Mum insisted I should be with her and I was in residence almost as soon as she was.

Lady Tree always smiled benignly at me but, being cajoled by Mum to be always on good behaviour and to address her properly, I was somewhat scared and kept out of her way. Because I was always present, I heard the conversations Mum had with all who entered her kitchen and learned of the trials and tribulations of service to Her Ladyship.

Even by 1930s standards Lady Tree was a somewhat difficult employer. Someone had hinted darkly to Mum that she had been taken off the books of a well-known London staff agency (patronised by the nobility) due to her attitude to servants. Her actressy moods varied from sentimental generosity to outright tyranny. When 'resting' between stage or film engagements, it was not unknown for her to take to her bed accompanied by a bottle each of Burgundy and Vermouth. These occasional lapses and their aftermath were the worst times for Mother. A battery-powered electric bell installed in the kitchen was operated by a bell-push hanging by Her Ladyship's bed and, summoned to the bedside by its imperious clangour, Mum would be ordered to provide all sorts of delicacies that Her Ladyship's somewhat pickled palate fancied it needed.

Mum was a dedicated and superb cook who took her calling seriously and with enthusiasm. Having gone to great trouble to cater to her employer's whims, it was not unusual for the dish to be rejected after the first mouthful. Once, when Dad had been specially into town to obtain turbot, it was rejected as "disgusting, bad and not fit to be eaten!" Not unnaturally the cook protested and assured her that every care had been taken, but after some argument Her Ladyship turned her wrath on the fishmonger by telephoning him to demand an explanation for supplying bad fish.

Mr Brill (yes, that really was his name!) heard her out and then said: "Well, your ladyship, there are three possible reasons for your dissatisfaction.

One, if the fish was bad, I have been in the wrong trade all my life: two, you have a rotten cook, but if Mrs Smith cannot cook turbot, nobody else can: or, three, your taste buds are affected by alcohol!"

Lady Tree terminated the conversation at that point by saying that she had never been so insulted in her life and would cease to patronize his shop any more. Brill in turn assured her that no insomnia on his part would ensue from such action.

One such inebriated session was terminated by natural bodily functions taking control whilst she slept. Summoned to her bedside, Mum was greeted by her smiling coyly, confessing shamefacedly that she had "had a little accident," and asking her contritely to help in her difficulty. On another occasion, halfway through a 'lost week,' a film producer at Elstree telephoned and asked to speak with Her Ladyship. Upon being informed that she was, at the moment, unavailable, he replied in effect to inform Her Ladyship that a car was on its way to bring her to the studio and would be at the door in half an hour! Always at her best in a crisis, Mum literally dragged her out of bed into a hot bath, dressed her in appropriate finery topped with her best blonde wig (she always wore a wig even in bed and had a selection of varying quality, mostly blonde) and poured into her a succession of cups of black coffee.

When recounting the incident years afterwards, Mum said: "Many a time I felt like strangling the old b****," but on that occasion I felt the utmost admiration; she walked to the car like a duchess and greeted the driver with a regal smile. Yet what she must have felt inside does not bear thinking about!

She might have been feeling somewhat similar on one occasion when Mum realised that she urgently needed some provisions for the family meals and was unable to go to the shops. Knowing that Dad was not too busy, she persuaded him to cycle into Broxbourne for the necessary. Such was her fate that, when he was then required for an errand or some such, Mother had to admit the reason for his absence and suffer the full range of Her Ladyship's displeasure: "How dare you use *my* servants for *your* requirements?" she stormed.

Difficult as she was from Mum's viewpoint, Lady Tree was always concerned for my well-being. Less than two years previously, I had nearly succumbed when struck down with the aforementioned illness, and it was only Mum's devotion and nursing that brought me round. (when thanking the doctor afterwards for his attention, she was told just that by him). Doubtless this intelligence had been conveyed to Her Ladyship and in consequence she considered me to be still an invalid.

She passed on to me some toy farm animals and a lot of lead soldiers that had belonged to her children and grandchildren. Also, a beautifully crafted toy horse on wheels with a little cart that attached with proper scale harness. Mum always ensured that I was kept out of sight whenever Her Ladyship was at home, but on the odd times she saw me she always smiled kindly. Once when she attended a sale at a nearby stately home, I was allowed to accompany Dad in the front passenger seat of the Essex Super Six. Whilst waiting in the car at the sale for what seemed ages, Dad returned, took me to a window where refreshments were served and bought me milk and some delicious bread and butter – apparently at the express orders and expense of Her Ladyship!

An open-sided wagon barn at the back of the house had been converted to a sort of summerhouse. At right-angles to the house, its open front was parallel to a drive that ran from the road to a meadow beyond the garden. Her Ladyship objected to people using the drive as a short-cut to the field and thence to The Pollards – a local beauty spot – especially when she was using the summerhouse with guests or members of her family; so, in order to discourage any such (in her view at least) transgressors she directed our Dad to paint and erect at prominent positions two notices which bore the legend: 'PRIVATE PROPERTY. TRESPASSERS WILL BE PROSECUTED.'

One sunny Sunday, a luncheon party had been arranged in the summerhouse and Maud was well into the aperitifs. Suddenly aware of a couple of ramblers – all shorts and rucksacks – she staggered to her feet, tottered toward them brandishing her rolled-up sunshade and said: "I shay, can't you read? 'Prosecutors will be persecuted.'" Staring at her in amazement, the couple hesitated a moment and then pressed on, barely able to contain their mirth.

One friendly member of the Tree household was Pie, a pedigree brown-spotted Dalmatian upon whom HL bestowed much love and regard. Despite advice to the contrary, she would insist on him being fed large dishfuls of evil-smelling cooked dog-meat. He spent most of his time in the kitchen and there was always an attendant bowl of this meat on the floor in the corner; I still remember the awful pong! Pie would accompany her on walks around the large garden or sometimes along the road a little way in docile attendance. "Come with me, my handsome prince!" she would croon, "my Grandee of Spain!" and Pie, gently wagging his tail in a slightly bemused way, would follow.

One evening, when HL was so engaged, Mum took the opportunity to tidy her room. Glancing out of the window, she was intrigued to observe a young couple strolling in the road – beyond the rather long front garden – with the girl apparently sobbing on the chap's shoulder. Looking harder, Mum realised that in fact she was stifling helpless laughter. Further along was the object of her mirth; prior to her peregrinations, Maude had obviously visited the 'little room' and upon leaving had failed to properly adjust her clothing, so that the hem of her dress had caught in the waistband of her knickers and was therefore displaying to her followers a generous expanse of pink silk bloomers (the finest that Harrods could sell!). Suppressing an instinct to leave her to her fate, Mum rushed in persuit and upon reaching her called: "M'Lady! M'Lady!" At that point Lady Tree turned and, in her best 'Lady Bracknell' style, berated Mum for so startling her. At last Mum was able to hiss into

Maud's ear the reason for the panic, whereupon she at once changed to 'heavy tragedy.' Fanning her hands in front of her shoulders she began expounding on the *shame* and *horror* of it. Resisting the urge to tell her to leave her name and number and not to ring but wait to be rung, Mum at last managed to get her to stand still whilst she straightened her dress; she said many times afterwards that LT acted better off-stage than on.

There was a large apple tree in the garden of North Lodge, and one sunny day during the school holidays we three younger ones were alone on the premises. Joe (Gordon was always known as 'Joe' by the family!) and Hazel had tied an old tennis ball by a long string to one of its branches and began batting it back and forth to one another. I was nearby sitting on my newly-acquired 10th-hand basic fairy cycle (basic insofar as it was bereft of both brakes and mudguards) and enjoying their pleasure by association. Into this idyllic scene intruded a frantic calling from across the way as Mum yelled at us from an upstairs window across the way at Hoddesdonbury, ordering us to see her at once in a tone that indicated 'trouble.'

Once in her presence we were subjected to the most devastating of tirades. I was completely shattered and failed to understand how we had incurred such displeasure. It was much, much later that the reason was divulged; Mum had had a particularly trying day with Maude in the throes of alcoholic withdrawal. Gazing out of her bedroom window across to the Lodge, Lady T. had seen us in the garden and misinterpreted our actions. Summoning Mum, she stormed: "Anna! Stop your children at once; they're knocking all the little apples off the tree in the garden!" Conscious of her need to keep her job for the family's sake she vented her rage on us without waiting for an explanation.

Some years later I heard her recount her version of the incident to one of her sisters. Mum finished by saying: "The very next day, Joe and Hazel took a stick and knocked all the apples off the tree!" and then laughed with a certain amount of pride. I do think that had she kept her cool and quizzed us as to what we were actually doing and then explained to her Ladyship, all would have ended amicably.

Lady Tree's car, an American Essex Super Six 'D'-back saloon of about 1929 vintage, was fitted with wooden-spoked Stepney wheels. With this type of wheel, the main wheel centre was permanently attached to the vehicle and only the rims with the tyres on them were removable. Therefore, it was only necessary to carry a spare rim with the tyre and tube assembled and inflated, ready to change easily in case of punctures. This device, attached to the rear of the car 'twixt folding luggage-carrier and body, was a continual source of friction between Maud and her chauffeur.

"Smith! There are no spokes in the spare wheel!" – this vouchsafed accusingly as if Dad had carelessly lost them. Dad and later, eldest brother, would then try to convey to her non-technical mind the above facts.

This would only lead to the same question again: "But *why* are there no spokes in the spare wheel?" and so on *ad infinitum*.

Later: "'Is that car in front an Essex, Smith?"

"Yes, Milady."

"*That* has spokes in its spare wheel!"

"It is a later model, Milady, with different type wheels."

"Well, if *that* has spokes in its spare wheel, why hasn't *my* car?"

So the whole repartee would start all over again. It says much for my kinfolk's powers of restraint that the press never carried the headline: *"Famous West-End Actress Battered to Death by Chauffeur With Heavy Spanner."*

I loved to be around whenever Dad was working on the car, and for some reason HL (Her Ladyship) took it quite kindly, often instructing Smith to bring his little Harry with him in front for the ride if the journey was of no particular importance. I had several pleasant trips and was quite astonished a year or two later when school friends admitted that they had never been in a motor car. Maybe they thought I was lineshooting.

One day Dad spent a long time cleaning and polishing the vehicle. Every square inch of the dark blue and black paintwork gleamed. All the bright metal fittings sparkled like diamonds. The everyday linen seat covers were removed and the dark blue Bedford cord seats were brushed and speckless. The carpets were removed, beaten and carefully refitted without a dog's hair or whisker in sight. Even the tyres were blackened and polished. Next day Mum, in such exciting an atmosphere, produced Her Ladyship bedecked in a similar state of *concours d'elegance* to attend the Royal Garden Party at "Buck House." Mum was a trifle scandalised though, because in addition to wearing her most valuable jewellery HL had insisted upon a cheap costume item from Woolworth's being pinned to her dress.

". . . and her in Number One tent too!!!" said Mum indignantly.

Although we had the lodge to live in, the elder boys were at work and Hazel was at school, so I spent most days with Mum, either in the kitchen or playing in the yard nearby. Mum obviously had to leave me to my own devices most of the time, and now and again I tended to get a bit bored. I was excited one day, therefore, to overhear HL remark that the children would be coming home to Baas Hill, and would be visiting her. Lady Tree's eldest daughter, Mrs Viola Parsons, lived at the Old School, Baas Hill, at the other side of Broxbournbury Park; she had two sons, David and Denys, and one daughter, Virginia. Viola (also a West End actress) kept her maiden name professionally and later, David, when he took to the 'boards' and the film set, was also known as David Tree. I looked forward to meeting 'the children,' as Maude called them; maybe, I thought, we could all have a game together? As a 6-year-old, I did not know enough about protocol to consider that it was not the done thing for Her Ladyship's grandchildren to play with her cook's little boy. However, when they arrived, to my eyes they were all grown-ups (they were in their teens). Why, I wondered, does she call such old people 'children'? Mum instructed Hazel and me that, if spoken to by them, we were to address them as 'Mr David,' 'Mr Denys' and 'Miss Virginia' and otherwise we should rarely be seen and not at all heard.

The Parsons family drove a Tickford-bodied Daimler tourer and often used the Broxbournbury Estate roads as a short cut from Baas Hill to Hoddesdonbury. It was part of the agreement that we incumbents of North Lodge were expected to open the Lodge gates to any authorised person who wished to pass through. A toot of the horn usually signalled to whoever was at home to run out and open the gate for the Parsons family Daimler.

Rabbits abounded in the Park to vermin proportions. One day, Hazel walked across to Hoddesdonbury, and as she arrived in the kitchen, Mum called out to her to come and see what Miss Virginia was holding; it was a baby rabbit that she had caught in the Park by chasing it off its run. Mum was a little bit scandalised by Virginia's penchant for wearing slacks – in those days such things were considered a trifle *risqué*.

I remember one day, when Dad drove the children back to Baas Hill, David and Denys rode on the running boards and Virginia climbed onto the rear carrier and thence, via the spare wheel (*sans* spokes) to the roof, where she lay prone, holding herself in place by grabbing the windscreen forepeak. My last view of her was a pair of feet waving above the rear window as the Essex rolled out of the yard.

Once, Mum had to prepare a four-course luncheon to be taken across to the Old School for reheating and serving to Viola and her guests. I accompanied Mum and Dad surrounded in the back of the car by dishes and pans full of delicious goodies.

Brother Bob was just 18 and, with dark curly hair, extremely handsome. Whenever he met Her Ladyship he favoured her with the polite deference Mum always insisted we should show.

Maud was quite taken with him. "Your son Robert, Anna: he is so handsome and he has the manners of a prince!"

More than a little gratified, Mum repeated that remark many times. When Bob met Virginia, she was charming to him and, I suspect, he was smitten with her. I have often wondered since if that had any bearing on subsequent events.

Viola was very tall, somewhat imperious and to me a little bit frightening. Things were seldom described as 'good' or 'nice' but always 'too, too, divine'. She also had a dog, a pink-eyed vicious little monster of a bull terrier called Drummond. Once or twice Hazel had to deliver items to Viola at the Old School from her noble Ma, and on one occasion they had just finished breakfast. Hazel was awaiting the reply when Viola waved vaguely to the table and said: "Clear those things away, girl, whilst you are waiting." Such were the times and our fortunes in those days that she meekly complied, but later, when telling Mum, she was boiling with furious indignation.

On another occasion, when arriving at the Old School with a message, Hazel found the whole family busily gathering the crop from the large mulberry tree in the garden. This time she was asked to help in a more friendly fashion. David, eldest of the three children, climbed to the top of the tree and, selecting the biggest fruit he could reach, clambered down again and handed it to Hazel, much to her delight and confusion.

David went into films and at the start of WWII I remember seeing him as an aircraft radio operator in the film *Q Planes* which starred three other well-knowns: Ralph Richardson, Valerie Hobson and Laurence Olivier. Denys became a writer; I have a delightful volume of his in which he skilfully compiled a whole bookful of journalistic misprints woven into a story called *It Must Be True, It Was All In The Papers*.

It was in the year of 1933 that the film *Private Lives Of Henry The Eighth* was released; we all went to see it because Maude played the part of the old Royal Nurse. I enjoyed seeing her in it but was too young to be very impressed with the rest of the film. In later years I saw her again in a film where she was a real gem as Roland Young's landlady in *The Man Who Could Work Miracles*. On another occasion we all dashed across to the Lodge to listen in to *Children's Hour* on our two-valve Kolster Brand wireless set (powered by high-tension and grid-bias dry batteries with lead-acid accumulator connected by a *spaghetti bolognaise* of wire) in order to hear Her Ladyship deliver a talk.

One morning we saw, from the front bedroom of the Lodge, a strange car in the yard at Hoddesdonbury. Frantic signs were made to Hazel and me that we were not to approach as Her Ladyship was in some distress and was being attended by the doctor. Facts came later: on the previous evening, Maud was reading in bed with her usual beverage at her side and failed to observe that a wasp had ditched into her drink, its presence being felt only when the insect stung her tongue halfway between teeth and throat.

Mum later regaled us with the details: "When I went up to her she was standing in the bath in her underwear with her wig askew, frantically waving her arms about and lisping around her swollen tongue: 'Anna! Feth me an onion!' and when I did, she rubbed the wretched thing on her tongue to try to ease the swelling. Of course it did no good, so I rang the doctor, who had an awful job to try to remove the sting from her tongue." Luckily she recovered in a day or so; had it stung her an inch further down she might have choked to death.

Alas, the doctor was not so lucky; a year later he strode out of his surgery in Hoddesdon High Street, straight across the road without looking, and perished under the wheels of a lorry.

Summer of 1933 seemed to consist of days of endless sunshine. Not everything was so sunny in other respects though. Brother Bob had been moody and withdrawn, and early one afternoon the manager of the Hoddesdon branch of International Stores rang Mum to ask if her son Robert was at home. Alarmed, she replied that she hadn't seen him since he had left for work that morning.

"He was here this morning. Don't worry but, if convenient, I would like to come and see you right away."

Bertie Neal was a charming man and, upon arrival, confided that he and Bob had had a blazing row that morning, after which Bob had not returned from lunch. He said that Bob seemed very upset and Bertie was quite distressed that they had quarrelled. Naturally Mum was very worried, but much later that day Bob returned; over a much-needed meal he confided to her that with his mind in a state of turmoil he had travelled to Whitehall and joined the Army. He was already in the Territorial Army and Mum came from an army family (grandfather Ben Walker had been a Regimental Sergeant-Major in the Royal Artillery). Unable to qualify for the Royal Marines – his first choice – Bob settled for an 8-year stint in the Rifle Brigade, 'The Prince Consort's Own.' I wondered if perhaps he had seen in Miss Virginia his dream girl but, realising the impossibility of any such association, had become morose and taken up with his first love – the Army.

Later, Mum confessed she had "wept quarts" when Bob, hitherto a somewhat faddy eater, wrote home to say that he had never felt so fit and had such an appetite that when put on cookhouse fatigues he often gobbled up the leftovers. Mum at once sent him home-made cakes and any other treats she could afford.

Just as the horse-chestnut tree at the end of our North Lodge garden began to drop its crop of conkers, stirrings in the Smith household hinted at a happy new life ahead. Mum had three sisters in Portsmouth and the husband of one, Uncle Wally, a charge-man of labourers in Portsmouth dockyard, had promised that if we were to move to 'Pompey' he would guarantee a good job for Dad and possibly one for Joe. And so, on the day before my 7th birthday, a furniture van arrived at the Lodge and, with our home packed in it, Mum and the dog sharing the cab with the driver and his mate, and Hazel, Joe and myself in the back with the furniture, we all set off to a new life, full of hope and the spirit of adventure.

Lady Maud Beerbohm Tree; an early publicity photo, given to the author by David Parsons, actor grandson of Lady Tree.

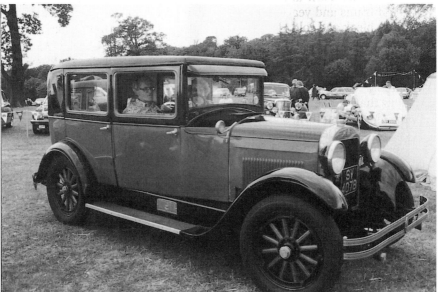

TOP: Side view of Hoddesdonbury showing the kitchen window and the dormer window of Mother's bedroom. The granary steps are seen at the left. BOTTOM: An Essex 'Super Six' similar to the one owned by Lady Tree, seen at Knebworth Park in the late 1990s. (Her Ladyship was a frequent visitor to Knebworth House).

CHAPTER 3

LADY TREE – SECOND ACT

Our hopes for a better life were short-lived. Dad did not travel with us but stayed to finish building a large coal bunker adjacent to the granary. Later, he cycled to the station on brother Bob's new BSA bicycle to bring it to Portsmouth. He may have over-exerted himself for soon after arrival, and when we were in the big rented house in Blackfriars Road, he developed a severe chill which quickly turned to double pneumonia and pleurisy. He was admitted to hospital and was on the danger list for some weeks. This, of course, scuppered any chance of a job at the Dockyard. Furthermore, there was no job for Joe. Soon we had to give up the house in Blackfriars Road and move into a couple of rooms near Aunt Nora and Uncle Walt in Grafton Street. We were practically destitute and Mum eked out a living by taking cleaning jobs. We were, to some extent, dependent upon the charity of Mum's sisters; her other sister, dear sweet Aunt Dais who lived in London, sent us parcels occasionally. Hazel, Joe and I began to feel very much the poor relations.

Many years later, when discussing our time at Portsmouth, Hazel, Joe and I agreed that we all hated the place. I longed for the cheerful vistas of Broxbournebury Park and The Pollards. I began to hate the Corporation buses and trams and yearned to see the friendly red London ones. And it all seemed so bleak and cold and unfriendly (it was October/November).

Albert had left the garage and taken over Dad's job as Lady Tree's chauffeur, and a Mrs Hills was her new housekeeper, a coarse plain cook, noted neither for her *haute cuisine* nor her sweet and genteel manner. I think that Albert, realising the situation we were in at Pompey, intimated to Her Ladyship that, if she wished to rid herself of that turbulent cook, he might persuade Mum to return, albeit on a temporary basis.

Thus early in December she received a letter from Albert which seemed to cheer her up. He often put jokey bits in letters to his intimates; in this one, instead of putting his full address at the top of the letter, which Mum knew anyway, he had put: "c/o Lady Tree, OBE, the cat's in the cupboard and it's done a pee." Although Mum laughed, it was not just the parody of the old nursery rhyme that cheered her. Soon after, Joe left us to join Albert at Hoddesdonbury, where he was allowed to lodge; he had been given his old job back with Mr Brill. (Some years later I was with Mum in Mr Brill's fruiterers and fishmongers in Hoddesdon High Street, and he said that Joe was the best and most hard-working lad he ever employed.)

It was a foggy, and frosty morning when Hazel, Mum and I set out for the station to return to Hoddesdonbury. Brother Bob and cousin George, very smart in their army uniforms, escorted us, carried our luggage and saw us onto the train. Dad was progressing in hospital and was due to enter a convalescent home, expected to make a full recovery. To me, the train journey seemed for ever; when nearing the outer suburbs of London, I looked up to the top of a steep embankment and saw a red double-decker London bus parked. It is difficult to describe the joy I felt at seeing such a familiar mundane object, but I knew we were coming home at last!

Only Mum and I arrived at Broxbourne; Hazel was to stay temporarily in London with Aunt Dais, Uncle George and cousin Betty at their flat in Islington. Lady Tree did not greatly care for girls and so the offer of accommodation was limited to Mum, Joe and myself. In later years, Hazel told me that she had unwittingly overheard Mum confessing to a friend that she herself had little time for girls and much preferred boys; this was borne out later for, when she took in lodgers, she would accept only men. Similar characteristics can often strike sparks, which could perhaps account for the battle of wills 'twixt Maude and Mum. Shortly after alighting from the Green Line coach at Broxbourne, Albert arrived with Lady Tree's blessing and her Essex Super Six. Mum was aghast to see how much much weight he had gained in the three months we had been in Portsmouth, thanks to Mrs Hills' stodgy food which had been heaped upon him in generous quantities. It seemed that when all had dined to elegant sufficiency of her heavy plain fare, there were usually several portions left over, and these were passed to Albert, who lost no time in gobbling them up.

It was very strange at first to see Albert doing Dad's job. He not only coped admirably and efficiently, but took his place in helping Mum to bring me up as well. A nice surprise for me was a supply of discarded toys and pastimes that Her Ladyship had given him for me when I arrived. There was a beautiful little toy model of a coastal defence gun on a rotating base that was supposed to shoot tiny rubber bullets via percussion caps. Sadly, no rubber bullets or caps came my way to put it to test (I suppose these days some woolly-headed do-gooder would ensure such things were banned as dangerous firearms!). There were also the bare bones of a strange construction set called *Kliptiko*, which consisted of different length tubes with 'C'-shaped forked ends made of spring steel that one could clip at right-angles to one another on their round parallel shanks. Pressed steel wheels were included that enabled me to make strange vehicles that only I could see were really cars, buses, aeroplanes and such. Also, I was given the vast tome of *The Boy's Own Annual* for 1927/8; it suffered greatly in my young hands, but I had the coverless bare bones of it until the 1950s – a tremendous book that taught me much. Only recently did I manage to obtain another copy.

Arriving as we did in December, Mum and Albert were soon involved in Christmas preparations. Her Ladyship instructed Albert to devise evergreen decorations for the hallway and dining room. With help from Mr Leadbetter, he gathered a huge pile of holly and some ivy from the front of the house and fashioned it into a large cross for the hall and an enormous wreath for the dining room, each held together with iron wire. No doubt it was very festive and fitting, but I thought it sinister and scary and would have preferred the paper chains and bells we had for our first Christmas in Rye Park.

Despite the fact that only Mum, Albert, Joe and I sat down to Christmas lunch in the kitchen at Hoddesdonbury (after Her Ladyship had been served, of course), it was, to me, one of the happiest days of my young life. Lady Tree had been generous with gifts. I cannot remember what she gave Mum, only that she was delighted with it; Albert had a splendid modern square-faced alarm clock with a £5 note wrapped around it; Joe had some sock suspenders and money; and I was absolutely thrilled to receive a small red leather purse with a whole half-crown tucked inside, till then the largest amount of money that I had ever had. Added to that was the most delicious traditional Christmas lunch. Christmas Day 1933 was a day I remembered long after – even though the family were not gathered in quite the usual numbers. Portsmouth seemed a million miles away.

There was, I think, a certain mutual relief between Her Ladyship and Mum upon her resuming employment as her cook/housekeeper. For Mum it was relief from the worry of how to make ends meet that she had suffered at Pompey; on HL's part it was the realisation that she no longer had to suffer the awful Mrs Hills. ("She was so uncouth, Anna.") HL confessed that when she had suffered a "little accident" in bed one evening, instead of helping her, Mrs Hills had become abusive, calling her rude names and telling her to sort it out herself and not to expect her (Mrs Hills) to do any necessary washing.

"How *can* you be so *crew-ell?*" Her Ladyship was heard to cry. No wonder that she gratefully conspired at Albert's suggestion to reinstate our female parent.

During her time in service where, through various employers, she had risen to be a head parlourmaid, Mum always befriended the cooks. Later she worked as a carver in the kitchens of the Green Parrot in London's West End, learning much from the Chef. It was no hardship therefore (notwithstanding prevailing primitive facilities) to come up with the goods as necessary whenever Her Ladyship had special luncheon or dinner guests. A gentleman of some importance came to lunch one day and Mum had a long discussion with Her Ladyship over the menu; a luncheon resulted that any top hotel would have been proud to serve. With a hint of anxiety Lady Tree confessed that the said gent liked a cigarette after his coffee and brandy and would dear Anna be able to provide any? (Maud was a non-smoker). When she served the coffee Mum placed her own 20-packet of Churchmans No. 1 on the tray. Later, Lady Tree confided that all had been perfect and added that the gentleman had said: "I must congratulate you, your Ladyship; you are very lucky to have secured the services of such a fine chef in these remote parts." I cannot imagine how she managed to cook all that fine food and still find time to wash, change and serve at table.

My own gastronomic education was enhanced during our time at Hoddesdonbury. I learned about such things as artichokes, asparagus, pheasant and game pies. At one time Her Ladyship drank some strange green tea prepared in saucepans and infusers and which, to my young and uneducated nostrils, smelled absolutely revolting! One day, as she passed through the kitchen, I was sitting in my usual place at the small table by the kitchen window, where I had my current playthings. She remarked: "Dear boy! I must get you some dessert." A parental glance indicated that no comment from me was necessary. This cameo was repeated a little later and then, shortly after, she brought me a large plate of assorted fruit: apples, pears, oranges, grapes and a fresh pineapple top. I was overwhelmed; I thanked her as I had been taught and when she returned to her drawing-room I began to attack the goodies with gusto. Fortunately, the maternal restraining hand ensured that no tummy upsets ensued.

Seasonal cold weather meant extra work; fires were needed in Her Ladyship's bedroom and the dining room, and longer hours of darkness meant longer hours of gloomy oil lamps. When first lit, the wicks had to be turned low until they warmed and gradually brightened; turning them too high too soon would make them smoke and, if not immediately lowered, smuts descended in a black blizzard over everything in the room. Both Dad and Albert were at pains to point out this fact to Her Ladyship, but once or twice she raised the wick, with dreadful consequences.

On her days off, Mum would sometimes take me with her up to London to see her sister Daisy and for my cousin Betty and me to play together. We both enjoyed these excursions and sometimes Albert met us with the Essex at the Broxbourne Greenline stop. Once he met us and spoilt Mum's day with the news that Lady Tree had turned up the wick, dropped off to sleep and awakened in a shower of black smuts. It took hours of work to clean the bedroom, soft furnishings and clothes (no vacuum cleaner!).

The very cold weather of January and February also meant extra tasks on the car for Albert; in those days antifreeze was not really an option and he had to drain the car's radiator each evening and refill it with warm water in the mornings. Few cars in those days had heaters, and whenever he drove Her Ladyship into town, there was a large brass carpet-covered hot water container placed on the rear floor to keep her feet warm during the journey; it measured about 24 in x 6 in x 3 in and required several kettles of hot water to fill it.

Lady Tree was a nervous 'back seat driver' due, it was said, to her once being involved in a car crash. Whenever my big brother felt she was being more than a little difficult, he would zoom up behind a slowing lorry, braking at the last moment to generate an aristocratic squawk from the rear seat! When Mum found out, she made his ears burn!

Once, Lady Tree appeared in a film where she was supposed to be at the wheel of a runaway car. Instead of using a studio mock-up and back projection, they mounted a rear-facing camera on the vehicle's bonnet, and whilst Maude – with agonised expressions to camera – wrestled with the wheel, the real driver (out of camera range) was steering the car by means of a periscope and another wheel mounted lower down the column. It was a huge success, I was told, but I doubt if such a thing could be done today in a modern vehicle.

Sometimes, certain economic inconsistencies were manifested in orders passed to her staff by Her Ladyship. During a post-prandial chat, a gentleman dinner guest put forward the theory that one could light a fire in a standard fireplace with no paper and only three sticks of firewood, provided that said sticks had been dipped in melted beeswax. Next day Maud directed that, henceforth, such was to be the fire-lighting method and Albert was soon busily dipping short chunky sticks into a saucer of hot beeswax. Mum was no slouch at firelighting, but soon found out how impractical such a method was for the grates of Hoddesdonbury and ruminated on the delightful prospect of using her own method under the nameless gent who purported the theory. Efficiency soon asserted itself however, and Mum reverted to her tried and trusted method. On the other hand, Lady Tree spent pounds on sackfuls of birdseed for distribution around the gardens and yard for feeding the wild birds, much to the chagrin of Jim Leadbetter.

Someone had given me an old popgun and although the cork was missing, I would put granules of maize filched from the granary into its barrel to eject it like pellets, which seemed to please the chickens. Early in that year of 1934, I was engaged in the pursuit of wild animals and crooked gangsters adjacent to the duckpond in front of the haybarn when suddenly I lost my footing and plunged into the murky depths of the pond. I was conscious of the opalescent green fluid before my eyes for a second or two until I surfaced and clung to the bank, shoulder-deep, with my feet sinking in the disgusting slime of the pond bed and yelling blue murder for someone to pull me out. The ducks behind me continued to swim and quack and spatter with total unconcern.

After a minute or two, Jim Leadbetter ran into the drive from the road, his face showing horrified concern; he quickly hoicked me out by the wrists and rushed me to the kitchen, disturbing Mum's afternoon tranquillity. Albert, reacting with the speed of a Brooklands record-breaker, had me towelled down, clean and dry once more and clad in two of his own woolly vests (they reached nearly to my ankles!). Mum poured a hot drink into me and packed me off to bed to keep me warm and avoid the worst effects of shock – I thought it was for being naughty. When Lady Tree heard about it, she chided Mum for not giving me a hot bath in her own bathroom and gave her for me an old Victorian wooden horse pedal tricycle extracted from her big barn next to the garage that contained many treasures. Later, I would pedal it around the yard at breakneck speed.

Next day the pond froze over. Soon the ice was inches thick and Her Ladyship was concerned that the ducks were unable to swim and instructed Albert to break holes in it for the ducks to dabble. I watched Albert and Joe attacking it with pickaxes and was alarmed when a fearful cracking noise caused them to run backwards to safety at a rate of knots; the pile of ice slabs they produced took a long time to melt.

Dad left hospital shortly before Christmas and went to the convalescent home, then he visited us in the New Year and brought me some late Christmas presents. After leaving the convalescent home, he stayed with his sisters in London for a while until accommodation could be sorted out and the family reunited. I enjoyed his infrequent visits, as he was able to spend more time with me due to Mum's busy schedule. Hazel had left Aunt Dais in order to continue her schooling at Broxbourne, and stayed first with the parents of Albert's girl friend, and afterwards with the Leadbetter family.

As winter progressed and the frosty cold gave way via blustery days into the first hint of spring, the locally-based LNER parcels van arrived in the yard one day with my basic fairy cycle retrieved from storage in Portsmouth – the wooden horse tricycle had, by this time, practically fallen apart. Around about Easter-time, another daughter of Lady Tree, Mrs Cory-Wright, arrived to stay, bringing her son Mark and his nanny Miss Scrivener – "Scrivvy." Mark was a year or so younger than me and when the weather was fine we would play together in the yard, me on my fairy cycle and him in a beautiful polished aluminium pedal car; it was a splendid machine with a racing-car style body and perambulator-type wire wheels with thick rubber tyres. I longed to drive it, but no amount of hints or outright cadging on my part could persuade him to let me have a go.

Although we were allowed to play together in the yard and drive, it had to be understood that whilst Mark could wander wherever he pleased, I was limited to the kitchen, yard and drive. If he ran into the garden, I had to stay in the yard, a very tricky situation for a 7-year-old to cope with.

'Scrivvy' was a charming and wonderful lady who appreciated the difficulties Mum faced and helped her by taking me out with Mark whenever a suitable occasion arose. She had a rag-roofed Austin Seven Chummy of late twenties vintage and took us on various little outings. Once we went on a picnic to Broxbourne Woods, and after we had just set out the tea things nicely it started to rain and we had to bundle them into the car quickly to avoid soggy sandwiches; Scrivvy then entertained us with stories and riddles as we finished our tea to the steady drumming of rain on the canvas roof. It was all new and interesting to me.

Sometimes on sunny days we went on walks. On those occasions Scrivvy took a push-chair because Mark, being younger, tired more quickly. Her Austin Seven was prone to tire as well and be a bit temperamental, and somtimes Albert (and Dad, if he was visiting) would be called upon to persuade it to start. Once, we all pushed the thing down the drive and nearly to North Lodge and back without so much as a peep from its tiny engine; the only part that functioned consistently was its burpy hooter.

The big barn adjacent to the road and alongside the drive contained many treasures and theatrical properties, and occasionally, when Her Ladyship asked Mum to help her sort out some items therein, I was allowed to accompany them. I was permitted to wander about this Aladdin's Cave of artifacts on the strict understanding from Mum that I was to "look with my eyes and not my fingers"! Being a bit nearer the floor than the adults, I soon spotted a magnificent toy fire-engine on the ground under one of the racks behind some stepladders and other bric-a-brac and, by laying full length and reaching through, I was able to determine that its steering wheel actually turned the front wheels exactly like the real thing; it was about 18 inches long and had lovely disc wheels with nice black real rubber tyres.

Soon, as they were about to leave, Mum called me; Her Ladyship smiled benignly at me and said that as I had been such a good boy she would like to give me a present. My heart leapt! "The fire engine!" I thought.

"Here you are, dear," she said and handed me a flower patterned milk jug. I caught Mum's look and thanked Her Ladyship properly.

"Tell me, Anna, who is that dark-haired young gel I've seen here once or twice?" Her Ladyship one day asked.

"She is Albert's young lady, Your Ladyship," replied Ma. Lady Tree was not pleased with that intelligence and, although she would not have actually forbidden the friendship, implied that she was not her idea of a good companion for my eldest brother. Secretly, Mum agreed (what mother thinks any girl is right for her son?). I was happy enough to see her again, though, and enjoyed the day she took me for a ride on the back of her bicycle to her parent's home near Broxbourne Aerodrome, where I was thrilled to see a parachutist descending nearby.

Although the second act of Mum's session at Hoddesdonbury was smoother than the first, there were still odd bursts of temperament from her employer that made life difficult. One day in particular, she and Albert were in the kitchen chewing over events that had upset them, and Albert remarked that he supposed that it was due to her being artistically temperamental.

"Yes!" exploded Mother; "fifty per cent temper, and fifty per cent mental!"

From the bathroom above where they were standing, Her Ladyship's voice came through the ceiling to ask: "Anna! Are you complaining?"

"I'm just having a conversation with my son, Your Ladyship!" retorted Ma. I suspect that it was the sort of verbal jousting they both enjoyed.

Soon after, Lady Tree was offered a film part as a somewhat slatternly working-class housewife. She accepted the role with great enthusiasm and put a lot of hard work into rehearsals and learning her lines. When taking in her morning tea one day, Mum was distressed to find her quietly sobbing. In the post that day was a letter from the producer, informing her in the usual polite prose that the part had been given to another actress.

Mum was always a great comforter, and as Her Ladyship dried her tears she quaveringly told her: "Th-they t-told me that I was unable to s-sound c-common enough!"

Although her schooling had been meagre, Mum was far from being poorly educated. Lady Tree had two daily papers, *The Times* (of course) and the *Daily Telegraph*; when Her Ladyship had finished with them, Mum loved to read them in the limited spare time at her disposal, eschewing with scorn the tabloids my eldest brother favoured He used to buy an inflammatory periodical called *John Bull,* and when Lady Tree found out she said: "Anna, I do wish your son would stop reading that *dreadful* rag!"

Although in accordance with the protocol of that time she called him by his surname, sometimes, when in a jovial mood, she would address him as 'Albert.' Once, when he was waiting for her by a stage door, she came into view carrying a cheese roll in each hand. Taking a bite from one she brandished the other in his direction and thence to the car and said: "Come along, Albert!" grinning around the mouthful of roll. He had to suffer a fair amount of chaffing from the other drivers for weeks after and the words "Come along, Albert!" became a sort of catch-phrase with them.

Summer garden parties at Hoddesdonbury included many people from the worlds of theatre and film. In a discussion after one such event, Lady Tree was full of praise for one young guest from the cast of a current West End production in which Her Ladyship was appearing.

"Such a sweet young gel, Anna; very talented. I am quite sure she will go to great heights. We all think a lot of her!"

When asked her name, Lady Tree replied: "Vivien Leigh."

Praise indeed!

Hazel started collecting autographs and Dad, by now back in his capacity as Her Ladyship's chauffeur, spent a fair amount of time at various stage doors and thus obtained some very well-known names for her; Vivien Leigh was an early contributor.

One day early in that year, whilst sitting in the kitchen, Mum was suddenly aware of another presence; she turned and looked straight into the eyes of a large grey Irish Wolfhound that had silently crept into view. As she moved, it timidly backed away but she soon gained its confidence and ere long it was eating from Pie's feeding bowl. Wolfa was her name and she belonged to Lady Tree's daughter, Mrs Cory-Wright, who was on a visit to Her Ladyship. Timid though Wolfa may have been to humans, she was more aggressive to other species. One day she, along with Pie, Drummond and another dog, got out and rampaged through a field of sheep; the farmer was furious and, although no physical damage to the animals was evident, he demanded that all four dogs be destroyed. The ladies were distraught, but the farmer was insistent and the police were involved. Our local police sergeant, Mr Crouch, arrived to take statements from many people, including Albert. I thought it very exciting for a policeman to call but lost interest when he turned up in civilian overcoat and trilby hat. Things looked grim for the dogs as the farmer remained obdurate. I am unaware of the final outcome save that the dogs were eventually reprieved; I believe Her Ladyship intervened by dispensing charm and recompense toward the farmer. Once more dear old Pie was rooting around in the kitchen.

When Her Ladyship was away or attending film studios, I sometimes accompanied Mum around the house whilst she performed her daily chores. Lady Tree slept in a large draped fourposter bed which I now imagine to have been a valuable antique. She did all her writing in her bedroom with goose-quill pens and wrote in large flamboyant style. All her papers were neatly clipped together with bulldog-type clips, decorated with brass facsimiles of elegant ladies' hands. I was quite fascinated with all the different objects, though Mum ensured that I did not meddle! Joe was less circumspect; when in the room one day he picked up Her Ladyship's false eyelashes and stuck them on his upper lip like a Poirot moustache.

"Put those back at once!" Mum cried, and immediately collapsed into helpless laughter.

From this bedroom window, one could see the front garden with the road and spinney beyond and, a little to the left, North Lodge and the elegant white painted Olde English-style five-barred gates of the Park's north entrance. Opposite these was the more mundane gate to The Pollards. Major Smith-Bosanquet's estate manager rode around on a splendid chestnut hunter and passed through these gates without dismounting by hooking open the spring catches with his riding crop and getting the horse to manoeuvre in such a way that he could either push or pull them open and pass through. Closing them was a simple matter of just letting go; they were hung at a slight angle to be self-closing.

As springtime warmed into summer, so the fortunes of the Smith family improved. Joe, in regular employment with Mr Brill, supplemented his income with part-time work at Lamport's Newsagents at Rye Park; this in turn provided me with a regular weekly comic and bar of chocolate. Bob made an allowance of his army pay to Mum, and Dad was reinstated in his post as chauffeur to Her Ladyship. This, of course, left Albert out on a limb but not for long, because Lady Tree exerted her influence to obtain a post for him as second chauffeur to Lord Dawson of Penn, who was at that time doctor to His Majesty King George The Fifth.

Our family rented a house in Walton Road, Rye Park, where Dad, Joe, Hazel and I came together in late summer; Mum stayed on at Hoddesdonbury until autumn and Dad commuted as necessary. A Mr Sanders arrived to make improvements to the kitchen joinery and do some painting and decorating. Clearly, it was therefore prudent for me to be elsewhere. But I soon settled down to life at No. 8; what bliss to once more enjoy electric light! I soon made friends with a nephew of our next-door neighbour and began to catch up with my childhood.

Not long after we had moved into Walton Road, and whilst Mum was still at Hoddesdonbury, she was in the small dressing room that overlooked the yard when, glancing out of the window, she saw a thin wisp of smoke rising from the gable of the hay barn on the other side of the yard nearest the road. Hoddesdonbury was still a working farm and part of the Smith-Bosanquet estate, Lady Tree's residence having been the farmhouse. The large gravel drive was now a dividing line between house and farm.

The barn in question was the largest of a group of farm buildings that consisted of sheep pens, pig sty, wagon sheds, a small building with a brick fire place & chimney that served as a toolshed and tea hut for the farmhands; also a 'Specialist'-type privy. All were wooden-framed and clad with tarred feather-boarding.

Alone in the house except for Mr Sanders the decorator, Mum called downstairs to him to go and investigate why the barn was smoking. Upon opening the door he saw that the large stock of hay was glowing redly, and despite shutting the door quickly, the whole lot blazed. Mum telephoned the fire brigade and then informed the estate manager who swore as only an ex-Army Major can. Hoddesdon Urban District Council's Fire Brigade did their best, but by the time they arrived the main barn was engulfed and fire had spread to the adjoining buildings; all that could be done was to save the granary, the storage barn and the house itself. The duck pond was pumped dry and even the contents of the septic tank were brought into play to quell the conflagration, thus generating appallingly noisome vapours.

Lady Tree's treasures were saved by an alert local bystander who quickly smothered some small flames at the foot of the storage barn where the tarred surface was blistering in the heat.

Her Ladyship, when she returned, was devastated. "Even that dear little lavatory has gone!" she wailed; "however will they manage?"

On the Sunday following the fire, Dad took me on the crossbar of his bike to view the damage; it seemed the end of an era. A solitary brick chimney stood in the middle of half an acre of ashes and charcoal. I was relieved to see that the storage barn had survived, though, if I'm honest, just glad that the splendid toy fire engine had not been lost! A small crowd of Sunday afternoon strollers were viewing the remains, including the fire chief in his summer light grey flannels and short-sleeved shirt, who quickly spotted a thin wisp of smoke curling up from the charred and soggy remnants of hay bales. Supplied with an enamel bucket of water he expertly doused the embers. A grey slime indicated where the duck pond had been but water was already beginning to seep in again.

Soon after this event Mum left Lady Tree's employment, and I accompanied Dad when he brought her home in the Essex, having first taken the replacement cook/housekeeper to her new appointment. Mum was tearful on the journey home. Maybe it was the sight of another woman taking over her domain; or perhaps, just a natural reaction. In any event, we were a family unit once more.

Dad continued to work for Her Ladyship until 1936. At Christmas-time (1934) following Mum's departure, we were again remembered by Lady Tree; she sent presents for all of us, and to me she sent my first-ever electric torch.

CHAPTER 4

SCHOOL DAYS

In due course I attended Rye Park Mixed Junior School, about 100 yards along the road from our house. One day, toward the end of October 1935, a friend and I had to deliver a message to the headmaster and were slightly later than usual going home. Leaving the playground, we and the teachers who were still around at that time were intrigued when a huge RAF twin-engined biplane began to circle Rye Park with our school as its centre point. We pivoted on our heels watching it descend and grow even larger until we could discern the features of the crew. By the time it was on finals, schoolboy radar took over and we made a beeline for the landing ground, which turned out to be what was known locally as "Hundred Acre Field," a generous portion of agriculture bordered on three sides by Ware Road, St. Margarets Road and Stanstead Road. It was the first time I had been really close to a proper aeroplane; I noted the two separate undercarriages, boxkite tail unit, 4-blade propellers on uncowled radial engines and its huge bulbous round fuselage and savoured every inch of the resplendent silver structure with its enormous red, white and blue roundels. A large crowd of locals began to trample over the field around the aircraft. Soon the local constable arrived on the scene, chivvied everyone away and stood guard until the RAF ground crew arrived to take charge. It was, as I learned later, a Vickers Valentia troop-carrier, and it took off next day under its own power with only one pilot and with everything removable stripped from its interior; I did not see it depart but Joe did whilst on his rounds riding his tradesman's bike. We never knew the reason for the forced landing, but a former colleague who diligently researched local history to find a record of the event recently sent me photo-copies of relevant newspaper-cuttings.

Prior to the above exciting event I had accompanied Mum and her friend on a day trip to Southend-on-Sea. Her friend was very indulgent toward me and we gravitated to the children's funfair adjacent to the pierhead. In it was a new roundabout made up of a number of pseudo-aeroplanes suspended on arms. As the machine started, the propellers spun and pulled the aero-cars around, then, as it gathered speed, they swung out and simulated a delightful banking turn. I lost count of the number of goes I badgered from Auntie Alice!

I was very lucky with Mother's friends and came in for some fine 'hand-me-down' second-hand toys. Auntie Alice was more generous than most; one of the many she passed to me was a German-made *Dux* aeroplane construction set. Made of thin sheet-steel pressings and bolted together on the Meccano principle, one could construct low-wing, shoulder-wing and parasol-wing monoplanes with or without its cast lead simulated radial engine; it had hinged ailerons, elevators & rudder and rubber-tyred wheels.

From early in 1936 until late spring 1939 we lived in a small terraced cottage in High Road, Broxbourne, Hertfordshire, about a mile from Broxbourne Aerodrome. The aerodrome was actually just across the border in Nazeing, Essex, but from our house we could see the Club aircraft circling after take-off and prior to landing. Once or twice on summer days, Dad and I would cycle down Nazeing Road and pause by the aerodrome hedge to watch the aeroplanes. I would bombard him with questions and he would struggle to deliver technically viable answers! On Sundays – in order, no doubt, to encourage the young to attend Sunday School and church services – the swings and slide in the adjacent recreation ground were chained and padlocked, but this did nothing to encourage me to Christian worship; instead, I cycled down to the aerodrome gates and watched the flying. Once I was thrilled to see a visiting Hawker Audax prepare for take-off; it seemed huge, sleek and powerful compared to the Club Moths, and the bellow of its Rolls-Royce Kestrel engine and the grass flattened by the slipstream from the Watts airscrew have lived in my memory ever since.

My last 4½ years of elementary education, from spring 1936 until autumn 1940, were spent at Broxbourne Church of England School; I gladly left then to start my first job – at the age of 14 years and 2 months. Although these were, on the whole, probably the best of my school years, I never liked school; it was something to be endured, like the bronchial asthma visited upon me since babyhood. I was appalled when seemingly intelligent adults insisted that school days were the happiest days of one's life – surely, I thought, the rest of life cannot possibly be worse than *this*!

The playing field of Broxbourne C. of E. School was a good vantage point to observe the antics of trainee aerobats up from the 'drome, much more interesting than the stupid ball games in which I was forced to participate. One day when Miss Rushton was conducting a game of rounders and I was supposed to be fielding – or whatever – I became fascinated in a particularly splendid display of aerobatics by a Club Moth: loops, rolls and spins. I was entranced! But I was brought back to earth violently when the schoolmarm's hand landed forcefully on my right ear; since that moment I have despised *all* ball games!

Later, when I was in the Seniors, Miss Rushton left to become Mrs Green, and Mr Green visited the school with her to collect a wedding present from the pupils. He seemed a nice sort of chap; whatever possessed him to want to marry *her*, I wondered!

For Christmas 1936, my brother Albert bought me a splendid Meccano set and put me on the path to a lifetime of engineering. This diverted my enthusiasm from aircraft toward cranes, bridges, trains and especially motor vehicles. I learned about multi-sheaved pullies, of the function of the differential in a motor vehicle back-axle, of pulley- and gear-wheel ratios, levers and steering mechanisms. Nevertheless, I still found time to experiment with a retractable undercarriage on a Meccano-built lash-up airframe, and discovered in the *Meccano Book of Standard Mechanisms* how a balanced aileron worked and how a dual control system linkage was devised. All this knowledge was of immense value when I eventually became involved in real-life aeronautical engineering.

It was a nasty shock to find at the beginning of the autumn term in 1938 that my favourite teacher, Mr Verrender, had left, and that his place had been taken by a Lancastrian woman whose tongue and features vied for sharpness. Under Mr Verrender's tuition, I had become reconciled, not actually to enjoying school, but to finding that there were interesting things to learn. He taught us how photography developed from the simple 'pinhole' to plate cameras and cinematography: explained how our intestines worked: and on one occasion brought a side-wheel lawnmower into class, dismantled it to explain its function and then reassembled it once more to trim the school's grass borders. To this day, I still recall his strictures on 'apostrophe-s' and the proper use of past, present and future tenses – some present-day TV news headline writers could well benefit from such tuition. He even managed to get me to accompany him on the field during a rugby lesson, to throw in the ball during scrums. I never liked ball games, and he seemed to appreciate my reluctance, doing his best to encourage me to participate, albeit in a minor role.

His successor, Mrs Clack (that is not her real name), was a thin-faced woman with a mean mouth and mousy hair drawn to the nape of her neck in a bun. The contrast from Mr Verrender was like waking from a warm comfortable bed to fall into a bath of icy water. She seemed to take a dislike to me at once, and I now realise that she probably thought my accent a bit too 'posh' for an elementary C. of E. council school, due no doubt to our Mother's insistance on proper use of English (as she in turn was influenced by her military forbears and years of domestic service). If Mrs Clack disliked *me*, in return I *loathed* her!

Because of illness, I had lost a lot of schooling, and in consequence it was an almost impossible task to catch up. One day during arithmetic she mentioned tens and units and was gleefully scornful on finding that I had no clue as to what she was talking about.

"Raaaeight then, *Mister* Smith! You can take your book along to the infants' class and ask Miss Swallow to get the infants to tell you what tens and units are."

To say I was appalled would be a gross understatement; humiliated and devastated, I presented myself to Miss Swallow, who asked the class to explain to me, but I was in a state of confusion upon my return and naturally got the answers the wrong way round. Another tirade descended upon me and I was summarily despatched once more along the seeming miles of smooth cement-floored corridors to the other side of the block where the infants' class rubbed shoulders with the other junior classes. To her credit and my slight relief, Miss Swallow behaved kindly, as if it were normal for senior school pupils to arrive in her class and ask basic questions of her charges.

There were many instances of Clack's nastiness toward me. Once, she waged a campaign for cleaner hands, and all those pupils she considered below standard were dispatched to the Headmaster's office for some sort of punishment. As an adjunct to my bronchial troubles I suffered nasty-looking eczema on my fingers which made my hands appear dirty, so just before class assembled I made the best effort I could on my hands with the resources available (cold water, hard green soap and grubby roller towel). Upon inspection and despite my pleas that indeed my hands were newly washed she pointed an imperious finger and said "Go!" Five or six of us boys had to present ourselves to Percy Bancroft, but none of the girls were singled out! I reiterated my excuse to Percy who, I think, was beginning to get a little tired of our unesteemed teacher's methods; he just sent us all back to class unpunished and told us not to worry. When I resumed my seat, I favoured the female hellion with a look of hateful contempt.

On another occasion, she ranted that no way were we to wear wellies in school. Some children in those days had no alternative footwear and in a country district they were normal attire; Percy Bancroft, being a fanatical gardener, wore them all the time, even when taking morning prayers! The extensive gardens were a feature of Broxbourne School, and we senior boys were expected to tend them as half-, or even full-day, lessons once or twice a week. As fate would have it, on that particular day my normal shoes were at the menders and I was wearing a pair of slim, hand-me-down wellingtons. Mrs Clack flew into a rage when she saw me and made me rake around in the cloakroom lockers until I found a pair of old once-white smelly plimsolls about four sizes too big in which I had to slop around for the rest of the day.

During the autumn term, a boy in another class obtained a lot of cigarettes and sold them to three or four boys in our class; I knew nothing of this until the whole of our form were obliged to stay behind after school hours, whilst Rush and Percy B. conducted an inquest. In those days, being in posession of cigarettes was akin to drug-running and liable to punishment, along with stiff notes to parents. But it was a bit of a storm in a teacup, as the boys concerned had got rid of them anyway. After we had been made to turn out all our pockets onto the desks with no incriminating evidence, it was realized that nothing could be done.

The Clack female of course, had to jibe at me in front of everybody. From her meagre income, Mother allotted me a penny a day to spend in the school tuck shop. By strict economy, I spent a ha'penny each morning and the other half in the afternoon, but my time thus spent in the T.S. queue twice a day had not gone unnoticed by the Rush Gestapo, who then enquired in her loud nasal whine: "You seem to have a lot of money to throw about, Mister Smith! Are you trying to tell us that you haven't bought cigarettes?"

I was an hour late getting home that evening, and Mum was very anxious as she had an outing planned. When I recounted the above remarks, she was livid.

"How dare she say such things! I'll come to the school tomorrow and give her a piece of my mind!"

It was with difficulty that I managed to persuade her not to; the subsequent repercussions would have been too much for me to bear.

One day at the beginning of autumn term Mrs Clack announced that there was to be a junior football match in nearby Wormley, and that if anyone wanted any tickets she had them for sale. Pressing further, she began to ask around the class to find out who wanted to attend and was obviously a bit miffed at the lukewarm response. Fixing me with a steely eye, she demanded: "And what about you, Mister Smith? You've always got a lot of money. How about you buying some tickets?"

Alas! Diplomacy was never my forte, so I replied in all honesty: "I'm not really interested, Miss."

Had we been in a Texas saloon, I am quite sure she would have gunned me down on the spot with a pair of smoking ·45s. As we were instead in the classroom of an English country school, she had to make do with a verbal barrage and proceeded to do so, using the whole arsenal of 15-inch shells. A lot of what she said went over my head but certain phrases still stick in my mind; she alluded to my asthma, implying that if I continued in the way I was then going I would get worse, not better, that my lungs would rot and I would be a burden to all about me, and that I ought to seize every opportunity to follow healthy pursuits. (What, I wondered, was healthy about standing in a damp field watching 22 half-dressed hooligans kicking and yelling on muddy turf?) Halfway through her tirade, when pausing for breath, a loathesome little sneak named Eric submitted the information that he had seen me with another boy returning from Broxbourne Woods with spades strapped to our bikes.

"They'd been digging, Miss!" he accused.

This merely increased the crescendo of her spite, and she heaped more venom about my seeming unhealthy lifestyle. Until that moment, I had never wished a bad asthma attack on anyone, but on that day I wished one on her with heartbreaking fervour.

Mrs Clack bestowed her disfavours in other directions and some of my classmates suffered cruelly under her lashing tongue. A girl named Joyce was another victim: a pleasant sort of girl, not very bright, the sort of character that producers of comedy drama British 'B' pictures cast as 'tweenies' or kitchen maids. She was also stoop-shouldered and easily upset. Once we all had to file into the Hall for simple eye tests. The oculist covered each of our eyes in turn with a card whilst his assistant pointed to a chart of diminishing-size letters and we had to sing out the appropriate letter. Joyce was unable to read them all and quickly dissolved into tears, but no one saw fit to hug her and say it did not matter! Mr Verrender had dubbed her 'granny' once but in a kindly, jovial way, but one day, however, when Joyce was subjected to a Clack tirade, sneaky little Eric piped up: "Mr Verrender called her 'granny,' Miss!", whereupon with an evil grin the shrew savoured the word and repeated it several times in a spiteful way.

But the worst episode I witnessed occurred toward the end of Rush's stint in Lower Form Seniors. Betty Brett was the youngest daughter of Mr Brett, farm manager at Spitalbrook Farm; she was a large girl of jolly and amiable disposition but not particularly academic, her worst subject being reading. This, in our curriculum, meant standing in turn in front of the class and reading aloud a paragraph from a specified book. Stumbling over the words she soon became confused and somewhat stupified, and halted over the next word which happened to be 'bite.' Maybe she had become word-blind; today, dyslexia would be considered. The more the Clack woman harangued her, the more confused she became.

"The word is 'bite,' you stupid girl! Now read it out loud!"

Betty was beyond rational thought and her eyes were staring into space; she was totally incapable of reading any more and seemed transfixed. At this point the virago exclaimed: "You'd soon know if somebody bit you!"

As the idea crystallized, she ordered one of the boys to go and bite her arm. Reluctantly, he mouthed the sleeve of her blouse.

"Go on! Bite her harder!" she raged. Peter mouthed her sleeve two or three times more without any response until the harridan left her desk, stood over him and made him bite the girl's arm really hard, bringing forth a yell of pain from the unfortunate victim. Confusion reigned until at last the class came to an end, but the matter did not stop there.

Mr Brett was a fair-minded and hard-working son of the soil who was seldom roused to ire, but when he was, a panzer division might be needed to halt him. Next morning he bearded Percy Bancroft in his den and frightened the wits out of him by demanding an explanation of the assault on his daughter. Our class became aware of trouble when Percy, red-faced and perspiring slightly, put his head round the classroom door and said: "Mrs Clack, will you come out here for a moment?"

Through the half-open door we glimpsed a rubicund, angry Mr Brett and mentally rubbed our hands at the prospect of ensuing altercation; Betty and Peter Clark were also called to join them in the corridor. An excited hubbub rose in the classroom so that I was unable to hear the argument, but Mr Brett's angry voice surmounted the riot of children's chatter despite the closed door. Although we were unable to distinguish actual words, the irate nuances left little to the imagination. Later a chastened and white-faced Mrs Clack reentered the room to try and restore order in her disrupted and unruly class.

We did not learn the outcome of this exchange of words – maybe the parties involved were sworn to secrecy – but after that the crone was never quite so evil in my experience.

In early January 1939 our Mum fell and broke her leg, and I was sent to stay with her sister in London until she had returned from hospital and convalesced for some weeks, so I was not present at the vixen's swansong. She had conveniently become pregnant and thus avoided the inevitable censure and sacking that was her due. A school friend recalled how Mrs Clack had taken music lessons toward the end of her last term, standing on the stage in the Hall, conducting and waving her distended abdomen in time to the music and the sniggering enjoyment of the class.

According to the same friend, she vented her spleen in one more spectacular gesture before she left. Jim Boltwood, the unfortunate who had incurred her wrath on this particular occasion, had the presence of mind to quickly raise his desk lid and duck behind it to avoid being struck by the heavy oak inkstand containing both red and black inkpots that she hurled at him in her temper. The artifact slammed against the vertical desk lid with a loud crash and red & black ink combined in a small cataract down its outer face.

The last I heard of Mrs Clack was the news that she had given birth. Our Mum was very broad-minded and quite used to me saying outrageous things, but she was more than a little startled at my response to that piece of intelligence.

"Poor little brat!" I exclaimed; "fancy having that horrible hellcat for a mother!"

Briefly summing-up my attitude to school, I found male teachers friendlier than females and I learnt more from the former than the latter. Two exceptions to this generalization were Miss Thornton at Rye Park Juniors and dear old Miss Pearce, in whose class I resided for the last summer term of 1939; she gave me a good grounding in English and generated in me the interest in my native language that survives to this day. It was no coincidence that in her class I received the best end-of-term report I ever had.

I never saw Mrs Clack again after 1939. I regretted not meeting her socially at some function in later years to make her squirm as I related the choicer events of the foregoing to the assembled company; she might, with any luck, have dwelt with some regrets upon her appalling past behaviour. I also regretted not having bashed seven kinds of you-know-what out of the loathsome Eric at the time for being such a smug toady, but in retrospect that would have lowered me to their own base levels. Mr.Verrender did much to help me gain self-confidence; the Clack woman then destroyed it in a way that affected my life for years. *I could never forgive her that!*

Family fortunes improved somewhat in early 1939; sister Hazel, having recovered from rheumatic feet contracted through a cold, damp and draughty room whilst in service with a local doctor, was now employed in a leather goods shop in Hoddesdon High Street; brothers Albert and Joe had married; Bob was still in the Army based at Gosport with the 1st Battalion, Rifle Brigade; and Mum had two lodgers, Mac, an ex-Tank Corps soldier and a Mr Lissenden, a boatbuilder.

In early May we moved to a bigger house in Ware Road, Hoddesdon. I had no need to change schools as the 2½ miles was easy on my Hercules juvenile 24-in wheel bicycle (and in the event of punctures, the bus service was available!). I think that those last 3½ months before the war started were the best of my childhood. Just before the summer holidays I managed to save and scrounge enough money to purchase a Frog (*Flies Right Off Ground*) Silver Arrow flying model aeroplane; beautifully boxed with instuctions and spare parts list, it cost half-a-crown (2/6d). It was something of a compromise, however, as what I really desired was a Frog Mk. IV Fighter, but at 5/- it was well beyond my means! I had first seen one at Rye Park Junior; it was owned by one of the masters and he flew it from the playground on occasions. I enjoyed my Silver Arrow though, even if its flights left much to be desired. On our way home from school we usually stopped to window-gaze at Allen's cycle shop in Hoddesdon High Street; they had Triang, Frog and Schuco agencies, and we spent hours debating the merits of Minic and Schuco cars and the wonderful range of aeroplanes produced by Frog.

In October 1939, a month after the outbreak of WWII, I began my last year at school. Broxbourne C. of E. was in a reception area for child evacuees from London and upon resumption of the autumn term – some weeks late due to the outbreak of hostilities – we were faced with a huge influx of strange children and even stranger teachers! However, we all soon blended in together and the schooldays passed uneventfully through to the next summer holidays. By then balsa wood kits of model aircraft were in vogue and I invested two weeks' pocket money in a 1/- kit of a 15 in-span Morane Fighter. (They had no Hurricanes left in stock – it was then the start of the Battle of Britain!) I made a reasonable job of constructing the machine, but it seemed not to want to fly; maybe it was a mistake to finish it with Woolworth's house paint!

My 14th birthday, on 11th September 1940, was the day that RAF Fighter Command suffered its greatest losses in its struggle with the Luftwaffe. We were used to seeing aerial dog-fights and the blitz had begun; nightly sojourns in the nearby public Air Raid Shelter became a pain, and on one night sister Hazel and I agreed that we could stand it no longer and went home to bed. Notwithstanding the discovery of broken bits of slate ridge cappings in our sideway (blown off our neighbour's roof), we slept soundly for once!

I did not attend a school leaving ceremony. Absence due to enemy action, coupled with a short interval when the school was closed because of an unexploded bomb in its grounds, caused me just never to go back to school after the end of the summer holiday. I confess, I could not have cared less.

CHAPTER 5

FIRST ADVENTURES ON TWO WHEELS

In the early spring of 1933 I was 6½ years old and, with our Dad out of work and family income restricted, my yearning for pedal-motor transport was very much on the back burner. Ever conscious of this deprivation, my hard-pressed parents obtained for me a used, umpteenth-hand fairy cycle and efforts by father, brothers and sister to teach me to ride it appeared doomed to failure. However, when left to paddle it around on my own, I soon discovered balance and managed short distances with both feet clear of *terra firma* until confident enough to pedal. This small bicycle, although endowed with generous pneumatic tyres, was starkly bereft of brakes, mudguards, chain guard and bell. Its 'freewheel' rear sprocket had been repaired by jamming in oversize pawls to make it 'fixed.' Braking, therefore, was mainly by reverse pressure applied to the pedals; alternative emergency stopping by means of foot pressure on the unguarded front tyre was an option, but which might cause its rider to leave the machine abruptly and stand on his head in front. Occasionally, fixed-wheel braking failed and not only was freewheeling restored but pedalling in either direction became a fruitless exercise.

By 1936, with family fortunes moderately on the mend, my 10th birthday present was a brand new 24 in Hercules juvenile bicycle – complete with pump and a moulded-rubber toolbag attached to the rear of the saddle containing a selection of flat spanners and a tin oilcan. The bicycle's catalogue price of £3-19s-6d was then equivalent to two weeks' average wages for a man. Later, the oilcan leaked and rotted the toolbag, which fell apart. I kept this machine until after my 14th birthday, when I took over a former lodger's Raleigh Sports machine with drop-handlebars and Sturmey-Archer 3-speed gear.

During WWII, my eldest brother Albert, in his spare time from teaching shop assistants and domestic servants how to operate complex machine tools for the war effort, renovated bicycles, which were both in demand and in short supply – as were cycle mechanics. Albert, however, had learnt the technology from our Dad, a former cycle engineer who once partnered his brothers in their cycle shop at Peckham. I helped Albert in the summer evenings after work and learned how to build and true wheels and overhaul 3-speed-gear hubs. Learning from this experience, I converted my sad-looking Raleigh Sports machine into a smart tourist model with upright handlebars and oil-bath chain case; it lasted for the next 20 years, after which I was persuaded by my wife to let it go to the tip.

When searching around for second-hand cycle parts to refurbish and use for his enterprise, Albert, a compulsive collector, spotted and obtained an early autocycle, a 1935 Cyc-Auto.

A minimum petrol ration for pleasure motoring was restored soon after VE Day (8th May 1945) and a friend became enthusiastic about an elderly 150 cc New Imperial motorbike, which he subsequently purchased. Also, a colleague had obtained a gleaming, new-looking 1940-registered 250 cc Velocette which I coveted. Having traversed many a mile on my faithful pushbike I yearned for the luxury of pedal-free locomotion and thought of Albert's Cyc-Auto. Mum, with good reason, was particularly anti-motorbike, so I won her over by pointing to its tiny engine and assuring her it was unlikely to be fast (how right I was!). Proceeds from the sale of my treasured Meccano set to a chap at work, plus other savings, enabled me to close the deal with Big Bro' to the tune of £6, or 1½ times my gross weekly wage in 1945. Thus, the machine – and all of its troubles and technical shortcomings – became mine.

1935 Cyc-Auto JD 5850 had a 98 cc two-stroke engine set low in the frame with its crankshaft fore-and-aft, driving a chain to the back wheel via a worm & crown wheel in the bottom bracket, opposite and concentric to the normal bicycle pedal cranks and chain wheel. Sprocket ratios of both chains were such that one or other was always a link too short or too long and either could jump off at inconvenient moments. A jockey-sprocket sprung-loaded onto the looser chain would have solved the problem but I did not know any jockeys – with or without sprockets. By sliding the pedal crank assembly to left or right, drive to the engine was engaged or not through a worn dog-clutch. A cylindrical half-gallon tank mounted athwartships behind the saddle was provided for the 'petroil' mixture; its filler had a tubular measure attached on the inside for proper ratio of oil per tankful of petrol. The cycle parts were all heavy 'trade bike' standard with 26 in x 1.5 in tyres and an open type 'ladies' frame.

I repainted the machine with cheap black enamel, unaware that it was petroleum soluble, but a leaking fuel tank stripped my optimistic rear mudguard paint-job back to bare metal, and the saga of trying to leak-proof the tank is too boring to record and was never properly resolved. Brakes were common roadster bicycle 'horseshoe' type at the front – pulling upwards onto the wheel rim – and a Perry 'Coaster' back-pedalling hub-brake at the rear. Ignition was by rotating magnet magneto fixed to the forward end of the crankshaft, with the field windings and contact breaker built into the flywheel casing; the whole assembly was positioned to face all that the front wheel could throw at it and beneath the carburetter to absorb drips of oily petrol that seeped through its static winding laminations, to the detriment of spark production.

I became adept at stripping the mag, wiping clean the innards and proceeding after reassembly until seepage gummed up the works once more, a problem later solved by degreasing the laminations with neat petrol and sealing their outside edges with two or three coats of black cellulose paint filched from my place of work. Having hoped for motorised freewheeling, I spent as much energy pedalling to get the damned thing started and helping it up hills as I ever did on my bicycle. Tooth marks on the upright handlebars indicated the number of times the badly worn dog-clutch disengaged whilst I was pedalling vigorously to start the engine. *'Light pedal assistance may be required on hills,'* as the marketing blurb put it in those days (joke!).

When cornering, saddle and handlebars seemed to rotate in different orbits – exacerbated to some extent by engine torque and the lack of stiffening effect a crossbar might provide.

Fuel pipe breakage, oiled plugs, cantankerous magneto, slipping dog-clutch & pedals and other parts vibrating loose when under way: these were all part of the rich pattern of my early powered two-wheel experience. For night riding, dry-cell cycle lamps were the only option; I thought about installing my cycle dynamo lighting but the trade-bike tyres were unsuitable for the little friction drive-wheel. Two things to be thankful for were the 250 cc petrol ration (smallest rationed quantity, but adequate for a 98 cc 'pop-pop') and an annual road tax of only 17s/6d.

To start from cold, one first slid the pedalling gear sideways to engage the engine with the back wheel, then lifted the decompressor and pedalled vigorously with the engine turning over and chuffing like an asthmatic locomotive. Absence of a proper choke meant that one had to reach down and insert the left index finger into the carburetter air-inlet orifice after dropping the decompressor valve lever and tweaking the throttle-lever, a circus performance that created fearsome wobbling until the motor had fired and begun to pull evenly; then one could restore both hands safely to the handlebars. To avoid an oiled-up carburetter – caused by petrol evaporation when standing idle – I developed the technique of reaching behind the saddle and turning off the fuel supply about half a mile from a journey's end, thus emptying the float-chamber to hopefully obviate starting problems. I learned the hard way early on that when refuelling it was wise to turn off the petrol tap to prevent neat oil gravitating into the carb, because one needed to put the measure of oil into the fuel tank first to allow inrushing petrol to thoroughly mix it.

All journeys undertaken were fraught with the possibility of engine failure. On even the shortest trip I carried spare plugs, tools and clean rag and often pedalled it home with a dead engine to the accompanying 'clickety-clack' of the dog-clutch as it chafed against its socket on the 'worn-beyond-acceptable-tolerances' spindle bearings. Hands and riding gear were constantly oily and dirty and I reeked of 'petroil' from each trip; I parodied Churchill's famous phrase and named the bike *"Mud, Oil, Tears and Sweat."*

One day when it was clean, repainted with oil-proof cellulose and as near mechanically sound as ever likely, I did the wise thing and sold it to a local bus conductor for £9 – but never saw him riding it.

Ever a glutton for punishment, I acquired another Cyc-Auto. DMP 337 was a 1936 model with crossbar and hence a stiffer frame. The dog-clutch had dovetail-form dogs – as yet unworn – and therefore did not suddenly pop out of engagement at embarrassing moments like its predecessor. Once though, I unwisely ear'oled it into a corner after rain on an adverse camber and, as the machine hit the road, the dog-clutch was banged out of engagement and the throttle-lever slammed wide open. The engine, thus having no work to do, screamed itself to hitherto undreamed-of high revs until choked to a stop by the flooding of its non-aerobatic carburetter; thus one learned to respect different road surfaces. Passing pedestrians were highly entertained.

Gleaning motorcycling folklore and all the tips and experiences from friends and workaday colleagues, I yearned for a fine machine of my own and drooled over an immaculate pale blue prewar Rudge Special each morning on my way to work as it passed in the opposite direction, and envied its rider his privileged situation. My Post Office Savings book remained depressingly low in funds; old copies of *Motorcycle* magazine were thumbed from cover to cover and dreams were dreamed. Ex-WD Ariels, BSAs, Matchlesses, Royal Enfields, Harley-Davidsons and Indians had been snapped up by all the leading motorcycle dealers, hastily repainted (often bright maroon with silver paint in lieu of chrome plate) and offered to the public at prices, which, although reasonable, were still beyond my means.

A glimmer of light hove in view at the end of the dark tunnel of impecuniosities at last with the prospect of a more powerful mode of transport. 1935 350 cc Calthorpe HV 4915 was another bargain (?) negotiated from Albert's collection and virtually a basket case. Originally black with a hand gear change, one of its previous 9 owners had replaced the hand-change cog-box with a later Burman foot-change unit. At Big Bro's home one evening, we slapped on the rusty exhaust pipes and other loose ancillaries and inflated the bald and perilously unsafe tyres for my friend to tow the machine and me home next day with his diminutive 'New Imp'. We secured one end of a stout rope to its rear carrier, passed the free end through the upper toggles of the Calthorpe's 'Druid' girder front forks with a turn around the stem of the steering damper and held it with the handlebar grip so that in an emergency one merely let go to release the tow. No tax or insurance, no crash helmet, horn or lights (it was daylight, so what?); imagine the furore if such were tried today. Apart from a dicey moment when Ken changed gear and the slackened tow-rope caught under the tip of my front mudguard, the 6-mile journey was completed without incident to a safe homecoming.

Help from Albert in its renovation then consisted of his lending me a stout leather bag of tools together with a laconic instruction to 'get on with it and learn as you go.'

With the machine in pieces all over our modest lean-to outbuilding, I became a regular customer of Stan Norris, our local cycle and nascent motorcycle dealer. His wartime National Service was spent at Broxbourne Aerodrome as a foreman ganger assembling Proctor and Magister aircraft after repair and overhaul; this was where I served my 'Unindentured Wartime

Apprenticeship,' so we were quite friendly. From him, I obtained a pair of 3.25 x 19 in Michelin retread tyres and some pale blue brushing cellulose, which I proceeded to daub on mudguards, tank, wheel-rims (I was still thinking of that Rudge!) and also many other minor bits and pieces. Funds were low and he kindly let me have fair amounts of credit.

Whilst in my possession, the Calthorpe had three rebuilds. In the first instance, I contented myself with cleaning, repainting and assembling what there was of the original machine in order to get riding.

The detachable segment of the rear mudguard had been lost, so I attached a temporary rear number-plate a bit higher up. There was a dearth of electrical equipment: there was a headlamp shell but no innards or glass; its battery plates had long since sulphated into useless lumps of gungy lead; and the dynamo would not produce a milliamp of juice. A panel mounted in the top of the petrol tank carried an interesting-looking switch, ammeter, fuel filler and gaping hole for an unknown ancillary, but unfortunately the handle of the switch was missing, as was the horn. All the electrics were Millar components and their spare parts were as rare as hen's teeth. Ken, my 'New Imp' friend, sold me an ex-WD electric horn, unused and painted in pristine War Department matt khaki. This unit refused utterly to give forth the slightest peep; it was probably a 12-volt item for a car or lorry, hence its refusal to perform on the meagre current from a 6-volt bike battery. I bolted it on anyway to make the machine appear legal. My cheap new battery required frequent re-charging due to the defunct dynamo and was rarely installed. Later, a near-neighbour flogged me an old BT-H headlamp of late 1920s vintage with a built-in switch, enabling me to wire into it a cheap rear light to operate with the headlamp.

Although unquestionably reliable, two or three months' riding showed up certain problems needing to be addressed: a rebored cylinder, new valves, guides and springs, a working dynamo and horn and the need to reset the valve timing manifested by clouting the exhaust valve with the piston when revving the engine one day. With these items attended to, I repainted the tank and mudguards a more modest black, added a substitute rear mudguard quarter, proper number plate and new exhaust silencers. Shortage of cash and the ambition to obtain a new machine then persuaded me to offer the bike for sale to a workmate (see later in Chapter 12).

Rob Capper, a temporary unpaid apprentice, joined us at Broxbourne Aerodrome thereabouts and he sometimes came to work on his elder brother's new Triumph Tiger 100. We became friendly and talked motorbikes in general and Triumphs in particular when we should have been working.

Ernie Lyons had just won the first postwar Manx Grand Prix on his race-prepared T.100 and I hung onto every word of Graham Walker's commentary of the broadcast event. Graham was an excellent radio commentator, concise, knowledgeable and with the ability to paint the scene in a way that made the listener feel he was there and almost smell the Castrol 'R.' Although enthusiastic, he never became hysterical and knew when to shut up and let us hear the glorious sound of highly-tuned bikes. (What a pity his son Murray never inherited the same skill!) I became a Triumph enthusiast after that.

Finances marginally improved but I was still a long way from target, suffering acute motor-biking withdrawal symptoms. My near-neighbour of the BT-H headlamp bought an early 1920s Royal Enfield motorcycle combination for its sidecar and, not wanting the bike, offered it to me for fifty-bob (£2-10s). Sucker that I was, and desperate for another motorbike, I jumped at the offer.

1921 976 cc V-Twin Royal Enfield MD 8503 was, unusually for the time, all chain-drive. Most motorcycles of that era had belt-and-pulley transmission. It retained the standard large pulleys on the road wheels, into which segments of friction material were wedged for braking. The rear brake was reasonably efficient, being operated by a longish pedal lever adjacent to one's heel at the rear of the long RH footboard. That for the front however – operated via Bowden cable and the right handlebar lever – I referred to as the booster-brake because, when applied, rather than retarding progress, the machine seemed to go faster.

It also possessed the luxury of a primitive hand-cranked engine starting system as befitted a staid family conveyance – preferable to the usual 'run-and-jump-and-hope-not-to-miss-the-seat-when-it-fires' engine-commencing routine of lesser models. Instead of a conventional gearbox, transmission was via two parallel primary chain-drives of different ratios engaged one or other by turning a tram-driver handle alongside the tank which operated internal expanding clutches alternately in each of the rear primary drive sprockets to take up drive to the rear chain. What one might expect to be the clutch lever located on the left-hand handlebar was, in fact, an exhaust-valve-lifter. Starting procedure therefore, was as follows: turn on petrol and oil taps, flood carburetter and administer one stroke of the oil plunger in the tank, set throttle lever a couple of degrees open and ignition lever to full retard; slide starting-handle in to engage dog and wind clockwise with right hand whilst holding exhaust valve lifter against handlebar with left; when sufficient kinetic energy has been introduced to the flywheels, release exhaust valve lifter and keep cranking until the engine bursts into life; lastly, fully advance ignition lever and adjust throttle for a steady tick over. Finally, apologise to neighbour for ruining her line of washing with oily smoke.

Access to the valves in the non-detachable-head side-valve cylinders was through large screw-in plugs above the valves. The engine had cast iron pistons with two compression rings on each. Engine lubrication was by total-loss system via a patented Vickers oil-pump fed by gravity from a compartment in the large slab-sided fuel tank set between a pair of vertically parallel crossbars and the aforementioned hand-operated pump also set in the tank for boosting oil distribution. In the cylinder heads and set centrally above the bores were little taps with cup orifices to pour neat petrol into the cylinders for cold-start priming. A well-sprung pan-shaped saddle and long cow-horn handlebars provided a quite comfortable driving position.

With the machine dismantled into its component parts, incentive to continue was dealt a severe blow in the autumn of 1947 when the Labour Government terminated all private motoring fuel ration and allowed only "essential" motoring. Private flying was also affected and I feared for my job at the aerodrome. However, fuel for flying training was grudgingly allowed and work continued with more emphasis on overhauls and preparation of the aircraft for the following spring, in the hope that a motoring fuel ration would then be restored, as the flying customers needed to get to the aerodrome in order to fly.

In the early spring of 1948 identical twins Stan and Les Kimm returned from National Service in the Royal Signals and joined us on the staff of Herts & Essex Aero Club (1946) Ltd. They had each ordered identical 500 cc Ariels (JLY 187 & JLY 188) and took delivery from Godfrey's of Great Portland Street soon after. Due to the fuel restrictions, they were obliged to bring them home by train and push them the last quarter mile from the station. I had also been to Godfrey's – to place an order for a Triumph Speed Twin (marginally cheaper than the T.100 but to me just as exciting) – but the sales manager declined to take my order due to the unpredictable delivery date of two years at least and, for Tiger 100s, some time into the next century. I had not at that stage worked out how I was to pay for it! He tried to assuage my disappointment by showering me with catalogues of available models (Ariel, BSA, Douglas, Matchless, Norton, Velocette etc.) and, although tempted, I had set my heart on the Triumph model and was not persuaded.

A petrol ration for non-essential motoring was promised for sometime in the summer, and meanwhile I asked Stan and Les to assist in refurbishment of the old Enfield. Les made an excellent and professional-looking job of repainting the tank and Stan achieved a similar quality result in recovering the saddle with soft grey leather which had once graced the cabin of a Percival Proctor. New beaded-edge Dunlop tyres were purchased and my brother Albert took the cylinders away for removal of the valve plugs, which refused to budge – even under force exerted by large spanners of the sort usually found in railway platelayer's toolkits. He had to drill out two of them and search around breakers' yards for replacements. We also prevailed upon his good nature to manufacture special frame bolts that had disappeared with the sidecar. Eventually it all came together and was submitted for an engineer's report for insurance to a local garage and to obtain road tax as, by then, a 'basic' petrol ration had been grudgingly allowed.

In view of the outlay and work put in by Stan and Les, we agreed a three-way arrangement to split the costs that gave us a machine we could all share. On our first test ride we quickly learned that a snappy gear-change from primary chain '1' to primary chain '2' was not a good idea; the somewhat staid family machine tried to perform a 'wheelie' and nearly threw Les backwards off the pillion as I spun the tram-handle a full 180 anti-clockwise. The proper technique, we learned, was to ease away from standing start in '1,' allow the engine revs to peak until everything blurred, then ease into neutral, shut the throttle until the heavy flywheels condescended to slow to a moderate tick-over, then ease the handle into '2' and slowly open the throttle to chunter along merrily at a good cruise. With such a good engine torque range, the designers obviously thought that more than two speeds was excessive over-engineering.

Our first journey of any length was from Broxbourne to Brands Hatch in company with a group of like-minded nutters from nearby Stansted Abbots with whom we were acquainted. (At that time Brands Hatch was still just a motorcycle grass-track raceway.) Stan rode his Ariel and Les and I took the Enfield; our proposed route passed through Blackwall Tunnel where lights were needed, so we rigged cycle-type lighting with a dry-cell battery box attached to the rear carrier. Lack of time precluded any switch, so connection was made by bare-ended wires onto terminals on the box lid. I thought we might stop before the tunnel entrance to allow lighting connection.

Les rode the machine on the journey out and I was on the pillion in charge of electrics. We entered the tunnel without stopping and Les yelled at me: "Lights!" I whipped off my gloves and held them in my mouth whilst fumbling behind to try and connect the wires. I gave up as a bad job any idea of clamping them to the terminals and tried holding them in place with my fingers whilst being bucketed about and sucking bad-tasting leather; it was a relief when we emerged once more into daylight.

Les had the best of the bargain that day. We had set out in bright sunshine but at the end of the meeting it started to rain and continued all the way home. Taking my turn at the front I was soaked whilst providing Les with a reasonable weather shield. I shouted for lights as we entered the tunnel on our return, but Les merely said: "Sod it!" and kept his gloves on. Nobody noticed!

After one or two forays taking turns to ride the machine, it was decided that a sidecar might be a good idea. Stan obtained a chassis and we looked about for a suitable body and found one in the back yard of a North London dealer, a homebuilt affair that was within our price bracket (£2). Mr Kimm, the twin's Dad, kindly collected it for us on his own sidecar chassis (he ran a '39 1000 cc Matchless V-Twin with Watsonian double-adult sidecar) and we were soon able to cruise merrily around as a trio.

One Saturday afternoon, Stan and I rode it to the aerodrome and practised Royal Signals type 'charioteering' on the airfield, by giving the 'bars a quick twist and lifting the 'chair' to ride on two wheels. Later we had a bit of fun by taking turns sitting in the sidecar and driving it around solo by steering it with the left handlebar. Unfortunately, I misjudged the speed in a right turn and had the frightening experience of the bike soaring over the top of me as I baled out of the chair. Stan said later that seeing me scramble out of the sidecar as the machine rolled over was as funny as any slapstick silent. Luckily no serious damage to the outfit ensued and only my pride was hurt.

It was Stan who was not so lucky later; he had to make an emergency left-turn avoidance which lifted the chair and, as he straightened to lower it, it hit a ditch, damaging his knee, after which he spent a short time in hospital. The frame was badly twisted and ended our vintage sidecar fun. Some years later an enthusiast purchased the machine with a view to restoration; I hope he succeeded.

TOP: Elder brother Robert (extreme L.) at Gosport barracks in 1934; 'C' Company 1st Battalion Rifle Brigade (Prince Consort's Own). Army photo.
BOTTOM: The author and his 'basic bike' at Walton Road, Hoddesdon.

Official 'stand down' photo of Hoddesdon & District National Fire Service, 1945. The author is sitting on the ground far R., at the feet of a ravishing blonde! Official NFS photo.

CHAPTER 6

A BRAND NEW BIKE AT LAST!

By the time of Stan's accident, I had realized my dream and owned a Triumph Speed Twin. 1948 Triumph Speed Twin KLD 708 came into my possession brand new and with zero mileage via a somewhat roundabout route. My brother Albert, now a senior machine shop instructor at the Government Training Centre near Brimsdowne, learned from one of his trainees that a Triumph Speed Twin he had ordered two years previously was awaiting collection, co-incidentally at Godfrey's Great Portland Street showrooms but, having since married, he could no longer afford it. So, did my brother know anyone who could take his place in the queue? (Not half he didn't! Or, as our friends in Oz would say: "Too right mate!")

Big Bro' contacted me via a neighbour's phone and next day I arrived at the Centre to get a note from said trainee to Godfrey's sales manager, authorizing me to purchase the machine on his behalf. A quick trip to Great Portland Street and it was arranged for me to collect the machine the following week ready taxed and subject to insurance and money-raising. The basic 5T Triumph Speed Twin was then catalogued at £180; I could raise the £100 and borrowed £80 from my brother-in-law, however upon my first visit to arrange the deal I was aghast to find that a specified 'extra' was the patented Triumph internally-sprung rear wheel. Although I was delighted with this added piece of luxury, it meant £20 added to the price, but by scrimping and further borrowing the money was available by the time Stan and I set out to collect it, me with a couple of envelopes stuffed with folding currency burning a hole in my cheap raincoat pocket and Stan as minder.

Not until 1935 was it a legal requirement for all motorcycles of 150 cc and over to be fitted with 'a speed recording instrument,' but in 1948, despite them being compulsorily factory-fitted, all speedos were still considered optional extras and were therefore added to the catalogue price. So, as well as my invoice carrying the cost of pillion seat and footrests, tax disc holder, a month's road tax and number plates (in those days all road tax terminated on 31st December of any year) it carried the item: 'Speedometer £4-10s plus Purchase Tax, total five guineas.' My bill thus grew to £215-17s-6d. Stan kindly took out his wallet and handed me a £10 note. The following year was penurious as I strove to pay all my debts; even so, it was quicker and cheaper than Hire Purchase (and a lot less hassle), although I failed to appreciate it at the time.

In between accepting the deal and actually collecting the bike, the twins and I, along with some of our Stansted Abbots friends, took a day off to visit the first postwar Cycle and Motorcycle Show in London at Earls Court, where all the latest models and their accessories for the following year (1949) had been brought together. What a fantastic experience it was for those of us who had been starved of new products and endured the dreary postwar Cripps-generated 'austerity.' General Montgomery (Lord Montgomery of Alamein) opened the Show and was presented with the latest mist-green Sunbeam S7. In his speech he mentioned at length how he had once relied upon his trusty BSA dispatch-rider's motorcycle when a young Subaltern (Sunbeam, coincidently, were part of the BSA Group).

Exports still took priority and long waiting lists remained for certain models, but there were wonderful new designs to savour such as the updated Ariel 'Square-Four,' the new 125 cc BSA Bantam, Sunbeams S7 and S8, the revolutionally new design silent 150 cc 'LE' Velocette, Vincent and the fantastic Wooler with its strange four-cylinder beam engine. At the war's end, all manufacturers had followed Matchless's wartime example and now fitted telescopic front forks; EMC and Scott ventured into using Dowty oleo-pneumatic ones. Triumph had restyled their models with nacelle headlamps enclosing speedo, ammeter, switch, horn and steering damper. In place of the oil pressure gauge, a small indicator button on the timing case popped out when the engine was running, which now left the top of the fuel tank free of instruments to allow a small parcel carrier to be fitted. However my bike, being pre-show standard, still had the separate headlamp with a panel of instruments set in the top of the fuel tank.

After all the vicissitudes suffered with previous mounts, it was a joyful experience to own and ride a pristine new and stylish machine. I savoured every inch of its gleaming amaranth red paintwork, picked out with faint gold lining, which complemented the chrome-plated and polished aluminium parts.

A trip to Portsmouth for the 1949 Easter holiday weekend, in company with the twins on their Ariels, afforded the bike its first journey of any length. We saw Arundel and Chichester and took the bikes on the passenger ferry for a circuit of the Isle of Wight. There we happened upon Bembridge Aerodrome where the twins (who had each attained their PPLs) indulged themselves in an hour's familiarising with an Instructor in an Auster. Continuing our clockwise Vectis peregrinations, 2½ hours later we truncated the tour to get the evening ferry back to Pompey. Later, sampling the Southsea funfair, we tried out the big dipper and Ferris wheel and, as all good motorcyclists should, watched the Wall of Death show. On our way home on Easter Monday, we took in the second-ever Goodwood motor-race meeting and saw Reg Parnell win just about everything in his 4CLT Maserati.

With our Stansted Abbots friends, the twins and I indulged in a number of café runs and motorcycle events. It was mooted at one stage that we form a Club and a title was suggested, "The East Herts Motorcycle Club." Brother Albert designed a badge for us, a hart's head in the centre of a spoked wheel with the Club title around its periphery, but after an abortive attempt to get some made we gave up the idea. Certain elements within the group disdained any association with other properly structured Clubs but seemed quite willing to attend events organized by them. I began to weary of riding around in a group merely to attend cafés and cinemas.

When Rob Capper returned from his RAF National Service, we renewed our friendship and began attending various motoring events. Just prior to his call-up he had built himself a bike mainly from Harley Davidson parts which he called the 'RAC Special' (nothing to do with the Royal Automobile Club but the initials of R.A. Capper). It looked very English with straight handlebars, light alloy mudguards, Lucas headlamp and dual seats, and it had a somewhat hit-or-miss homemade foot-operated gear change we had devised. With his girlfriend Pauline on the back (or sometimes driving at the front) we had many pleasant trips around the countryside. Petrol rationing was ended by then and we volunteered as marshals at motoring events and joined The Berkhamsted Motorcycle and Car Club, which organized the Tewin Water Speed Trials near Welwyn. Through them we were able to participate in other Clubs' fixtures and soon competed in various main road trials suitable for touring bikes; these mostly consisted of route-finding between checkpoints with penalties for early or late arrival, plus special tests such as slow hill climbs and stop-and-start between lines where the fastest competitor set the standard time.

Our first experience concerned one particular Club (Farnham Royal) who had organized a long distance night trial starting near Slough and ending at a south coast destination. Rob by then had sold his RAC Special and had a 1948 Triumph 3T de luxe 350 cc twin. With Pauline navigating for Rob and Stan for me, we met at Eddie's Café at Cippenham and were sent off at one-minute intervals according to our competition numbers. Stan and I were No. 11 so we set out at eleven minutes past midnight.

We were allowed one kick-start of the engine at send-off and a mark was deducted for each one thereafter. A chap in front of us failed to start the engine first kick and his navigator was obliged to push-start him: six marks gone before he left the venue. A one-mark penalty was imposed for each minute early or late at specified checkpoints within a tolerance of 30 seconds either side of corrected time and mileage between checkpoints, to be covered at an average speed of 24 mph. We were provided with a route card to follow that contained cryptic instructions such as 'BR, TL, SP' and so forth, which translated to Bear Right, Turn Left, Sign Post etc., followed by town and village names and stated mileages between checkpoints to allow estimated arrival times. We soon found that the printed mileages differed somewhat to those clocked up on my trip odometer. And although 24 mph may seem slow to some, a slight deviation from the route might find one knotting along at 60+ via winding country lanes in order to check in on time unless the mistake was rectified quickly.

That first night trial was straightforward enough: the route followed the A30 for a lot of the way and was posted to competitors prior to the event enabling them to plot it beforehand. Even so, it was a first experience for Stan and me and we lost points on the special tests as well as time. Rob and Pauline, however, were better prepared and gained a Second Class award. The trial finished by the Clock Tower on the front at Weymouth and we enjoyed an excellent breakfast arranged for all participants in a nearby restaurant. When heading home later, the weather changed and we rode a long way through drizzle and on wet roads; it was a damp end to a night of fun and new experience.

Working at the aerodrome, I often collected parts and materials for the aircraft at various places: de Havilland Aircraft Co. at Hatfield for Rapide parts, Rotax at Willesden for switches, Titanine at Colindale for paint and to other aerodromes such as Panshanger, Stansted and Croydon for materials. In this way the Speed Twin earned its keep and, although given no monetary mileage allowance, I always collected a tankful of aviation fuel, which was compensation enough in my book. No doubt a union agitator would think otherwise, but I was happy.

Maintenance-wise the machine needed an oil change every 1,500 miles and engine decarbonising about once a year. Engine oils in those days were devoid of detergent properties and the Triumph oil filters were no better than wire mesh tea-strainers so, for engine longevity, low mileages between oil changes were vital; added to which the engine carboned-up fairly easily. Exposed rear chains could quickly wear and obtaining new ones presented difficulties. Removing, cleaning and graphite lubrication was therefore a frequent, essential and messy chore. Once, when marshalling at a Sporting Trial, the internally-sprung rear wheel became immersed in a deep puddle that introduced muddy grit to the detriment of the cycle-type large-diameter bearings; replacing these caused headaches in more ways than one. A later design introduced Skefco heavy-duty ball races in the Mark 2 sprung hub.

With two other club members I entered the 1951 Farnham Royal Club main road night trial as part of the Berkhamsted MC&CC Team entry. Pauline and Rob did not compete that year due to other commitments. Lessons learned from the previous year ensured that route finding was made more challenging. Getting mixed up with the Clerk of the Course on Marlow Bridge caused us to shoot off in the wrong direction and lose too many points at the first time check to have any hope of an award, but at least I managed to set standard time at the final brake test in the shadow of Corfe Castle. For this, competitors had to stop by a line marked at the top of a hill and, with the engine switched off and the gear in neutral, and with only one push of one foot, coast down the hill to stop within a defined area; that competitor doing so in the shortest time set standard time with other entrants losing points for each second longer. I shoved off and crouched as low as possible over the tank like a TT rider to reduce wind resistance as much as possible and left braking to the last second by quickly sitting upright and applying both brakes hard. It paid off! Luckily, the road was dry rough tarmac. The trial finished on the front at Swanage with a very welcome English cooked breakfast laid on especially at a nearby café.

One tragic incident occurred during the night as competitors passed through the New Forest. One speeding rider, no doubt trying to make up time, omitted to heed the warning notices concerning stray animals and hit a cow meandering across the highway: both animal and rider died. On my way home I passed the spot again and saw the badly damaged machine standing on the gravel verge awaiting collection. During breakfast we overheard the Secretary of the Meeting and Clerk of the Course discussing whether to cancel the event, but in the end they let it run its course to avoid even more difficulties. I was relieved in a way not to get an award that time.

In the early postwar years, Dunlop produced tyres with a batch of below-quality canvas which gave rise to alarming numbers of tyres splitting at the walls. The standard fitted tyres and a couple of replacements on the Triumph had all failed in this way and for years after, few motorcyclists would fit Dunlops. (*"Got a 3·25 be 19 tyre, mate? Anything but Dunlop!"* was a typical query heard at motorcycle spares counters.) In about 1951 Dunlop brought out a new series of tyres with redesigned tread patterns, and they were superb.

Soon after obtaining my Speed Twin, brother Albert was offered a mid-1930s 250 cc New Imperial in bits ("partial restoration," it would be called today!) and asked what I thought; I realized that he expected to refurbish it, not to ride, but sell at (hopefully) a profit. Having been unwillingly involved with friend Ken's machine, I was cognisant with certain design faults and troubles of the marque: the 150 and 250 cc models were identical except for cylinder capacity. Both were unit construction with rearward rotating engines connected by direct helical gear drive to the large single-plate cork clutch. Also in mesh with the clutch gearwheel was a brass pinion which drove a Lucas 3-brush dynamo carrying a contact breaker on its opposite end for the coil ignition. This gear train gave out a distinctive hollow whine, enabling one to identify the model by sound alone from a fair distance. The dynamo's third brush was adjusted to balance the charge to the battery, thus obviating the need to fit a voltage control unit. Later models were fitted with a device known as a "Maglita," which was a magneto with a built-in coil for battery charging and generally a more satisfactory machine in many ways.

I warned Albert to look carefully at the eight rocker box attachment holes in the cylinder head and to walk away if there was the slightest sign of cracking. For some reason, the makers tapped these holes 5/16 in diameter cycle thread (which is very fine pitch and prone to stripping) instead of the more practicable coarser pitch Whitworth threads for cast iron. The wall thickness of each of the holes adjacent to the outside edge of the rocker box seatings were rather thin, hence the tendency to crack.

A few days later, he triumphantly showed me the partially dismantled machine; I was dismayed to note that not only were there cracks in the cylinder head, adjacent to the rocker box holes, but two of the threads had stripped. In addition, one pushrod had been crudely repaired by brazing and had a loose piece of metal rattling inside it.

After a few abortive attempts to rebuild the machine at his home, we transferred it to mine and eventually I got it all back together. One bright spot was the new Lucas three-brush dynamo, its only new part. Engine lubrication was 'total loss' and fed from the wet sump by a small Pilgrim oil pump attached to the outside of the timing case. When the engine was running, a small drop of oil was supposed to emerge from a little pipe visible through its sight glass, presumably to find its way into the works. A tendency to piston seizure indicated that lubrication was not working as well as hoped, but despite dismantling the unit and bleeding the system I was unable to solve the problem and returned the machine to Big Bro' to do with whatever he wished. Some innocent soul, no doubt, was lumbered eventually. Another of his 'bargains' was an early 1930s Francis Barnett Falcon with a 196 cc Villiers two-stroke engine which I set out to rebuild for him at the aerodrome during lunch hours and idle moments whilst attending for ground duties for any flying that might occur.

This particular model – referred to by the *cognoscente* as a 'Fanny B' and by my workmates as a 'Frantic Bastard' – had two unique features: its frame was made up of straight tubes with flattened, perforated ends bolted together like Meccano in an amalgam of triangles attached to a forged and machined steering head and also (unusually for two-stroke engines of the time) it had a separate oil system activated by crankcase pressure via piping to and from the oil tank under the saddle.

As well as dismantling, cleaning and repainting, major repairs consisted of welding thin sheet steel patches on the oil tank to make it pressure-tight, a similar patchwork job for the headlamp shell, and reaming out to fit oversize pivot studs for the front-fork links to remove appalling amounts of wear and side-play. With colleague Barney's help, these jobs were completed with a high-quality professional finish. When the machine was successfully re-assembled and run, we were unable to make the auxiliary lubrication system function despite having carefully pressure-tested the entire installation. We shipped it to Big Bro's domicile and some time later I saw a man wheeling it along the main road away from the house – I hope he had more success than we did.

TOP: 1935 Cyc-Auto autocycle (gents' model).
BOTTOM: Taking light refreshment at the end of a one-day m/c road trial (we won a Second Class award, an initialled tyre pressure gauge).

The author (R.), overall winner of the 1958 All-Britain Triumph Rally, with navigator Pete Longland holding the trophy. Photo: *The MotorCycle* (via *Aeroplane*).

"Humped-back bridge," WMA Pillion Trial 1952.
Cartoon by Ray Clapham.

"Foiled by a Post Office messenger boy," WMA Pillion Trial 1952.

"A close one!" Farnham Royal MCC night navigation Road Trial. Cartoon by Ray Clapham.

"Asking for trouble!" This actually occurred at Broxbourne in 1952.

CHAPTER 7

TRIALS AND TRIUMPHS

I continued to compete in various day and half-day events with the Speed Twin and in the August of 1951 accompanied Les Kimm with Eric Soulard as his pillion passenger on a tour through Belgium and Germany down to the Black Forest (Schwartzwald). We travelled during the day and stayed at small hotels and *pensions* each night until we reached Neustadt, where we remained for a while before returning home in easy stages to stay overnight in Ostend to catch the car ferry the next morning.

It was to be an enjoyable and interesting holiday and put another 1,600 miles on the clock of the Speed Twin, and I was grateful to Les for inviting me along. Our machines created a lot of interest throughout the tour, and several times local enthusiasts pointed with astonishment at my Speed Twin, exclaiming *"Treeoomph!"* and then questioningly: *"Ist der Deutsche Tree-oomph?"* because there was in fact a German-made small capacity Triumph which, when exported to the UK, was called a T.W.N. (short for 'Triumph Werke Nurnburg) to avoid confusion with the Meriden works product. NSU, BMW and Horex machines abounded; the Horex was very pretty with its chromium and red & black paintwork but a local told us that it had a depressing habit of breaking at the steering head. BMW at that time were producing quantities of single-cylinder shaft-drive 250 cc models; it appeared as if they had removed one cylinder from a standard 500 twin and then rotated the engine/transmission unit 90° to position the remaining cylinder vertically under the tank. I later heard that their shaft-drive transmissions disliked the pulsations of a single pot and failed with depressing frequency.

Whilst we were in Neustadt, it was amusing for us to see, one Sunday morning, local couples going to church in full national dress with the Tyrolean-suited man riding the motorbike with his wife sitting side-saddle on the pillion, her voluminous skirts and long trailing hat ribbons flapping in the slipstream.

Back in Ostend once more, loading the Belgian State Marine ferry was a protracted business as the vehicles were individually craned aboard and stowed one by one. The Belgian stevedores seemed to do a lot of dashing around and shouting at each other and took twice as long to load the ship than did the laconic and unhurried British Rail personnel on the journey out. When we put to sea the weather was somewhat less than clement, causing great distress among the less seaworthy passengers; I overheard one passenger remark to his companion, upon returning from the loo, that it was "awash with vomit." As we docked, Les and Eric decided to visit the facilities and asked if I was going to accompany them; I craftily declined and noted how pale they both looked when they returned – Les merely remarked: "Bloody Hell!"

I won my very first award in 1951. It was an afternoon road trial run by our parent club, the Berkhamsted Motorcycle & Car Club. By coming fourth in an event that had a mere handful of competitors I received a 'First Class Award' consisting of a modest engraved plaque.

In the late 1940s and early 1950s, motorcycle clubs proliferated all over the country; cars were hard to obtain and very expensive, so motorcycles offered economic motoring for the multitude and clubs became a focus for technical help, sporting activities and social gatherings. The annual road tax at that time for a motorcycle-sidecar combination was £5 so families were able to enjoy motorcycle outings together. Our club, like most, was affiliated to the Auto Cycle Union (ACU), the governing body for all motorcycling competition and sporting events in the UK. For administrative purposes, the ACU divided the UK into 'sections'. Berkhamsted came under the South Midlands Section, which in turn was sub-divided into three 'groups'; our group was known as 'Meteor Group.' Each group had its own newsletter which contained articles, reports of events and entry forms for any forthcoming rallies or sporting trials and such. Sporting trials, colloquially known as 'mud plugs,' were set off-road on rough terrain, required specially prepared lightweight trials bikes and were unsuitable for our normal touring machines. I would like to have attempted sporting trials but could not afford two motorbikes and, as I needed a touring bike more than a trials bike, contented myself with what I already had. Fortunately, there were a number of road events available with other clubs in our group that enabled us to compete. The Farnham Royal Club's annual long distance night trial was one we entered regularly.

In the spring of 1952, Rob and I entered the West Middlesex Amateur MCC's half-day 'Pillion Trial,' which was devised for touring machines but with certain off-road special sections suitable for fully-equipped road bikes. With Pauline as Rob's navigator/pillion passenger, I persuaded friend Ray Clapham to be my N/PP. The course was routed via winding country roads in Hertfordshire and South Bucks. One stretch of road between check points meandered via 4 or 5 sharp humpback bridges and, as we sped to make up time, Ray was intrigued at the way we left the road at each one to land with a short squeal of protest from the tyres, as he himself clung on grimly to avoid ejection into the pastoral beauty of Buckinghamshire. At one check he laughed as Rob walked over the section seeking any bits to trap the unwary as another competitor drummed his fingers waiting to start his special test on it. At another section we were amused at the antics of a teenage rider wearing a large helmet and bearing a passing resemblance to a Post Office messenger boy. It was a taped section and the object was to negotiate it feet up and without crossing the tapes. A dab with the foot incurred a 3-mark penalty, whilst stopping or fouling the tapes lost the rider 5 marks and he was deemed to have failed the section. This lad's machine was a low-powered two-stroke and so he charged the section at high revs in low gear, crossed the tapes and ran the bike a short way up the sloping trunk of a tree whence both he and his passenger fell off in a heap. Once things were sorted out it was our turn; telling Ray to keep his feet on the pillion footrests no matter what, I selected first gear and let my trusty Speed Twin trickle along over the dead-leaf-covered bumpy woodland at little more than tick-over. By judicious throttle control I just managed to stay within the confines of the 2 ft 6 in-wide zig-zag taped path around the aforementioned tree, and crossed the finishing line 'clean.' Ray was even more excited than I and bruised my shoulder with thumping. Thanks to his excellent route card reading, plus more good luck on the other special test sections, we won a First Class Award.

Flushed with that success, I recruited him as my navigator for the following Farnham Royal night trial in July. By this time Rob had sold the 350 Triumph Twin and had purchased a 500 cc single-cylinder 18s 'Springer' AJS. He also entered and asked another DH Tech School type, Peter 'Needle' Bone, to join us to make a Berkhamsted team entry. My entry form went in earlier than the others and I was entered as No. 33, while Rob and 'Needle' were in the 140s, so Ray and I set off from the start at 00.33 hrs, an hour or so before our team mates.

At this point I think it worthwhile to describe the route card: this was in two sections, the first sheet handed to the competitor at the start and the other sheet issued at the halfway break. There were paragraphs of route instructions, each paragraph detailing a coded route to a time check whereat there might be a special test. The mileage between each section was given in the left-hand margin adjacent to the paragraph along with the average speed and time of arrival, and the total mileage covered to that point in the right-hand margin – the importance of this will become clear later. The route instructions were typically as follows: "Leave start and head toward Slough. Then in 1·4 TR SP Little Widdel on the Green." Such baffling intelligence could be translated as: "In 1·4 miles turn right by signpost to Little Widdel on the Green."

Between us Ray and I developed a system whereby at the first checkpoint we took note of any discrepancy, to the nearest tenth of a mile, between the mileage quoted on the card and that shown on the bike's trip odometer, and to make an allowance so as to arrive at the next checkpoint as nearly as possible spot-on time. I therefore reset the trip to zero before leaving each checkpoint. We noticed, after leaving the second or third checkpoint, that halfway through the paragraph of route instructions was a sentence that said "... and in 10 miles turn right SP ..." We had already travelled about 7 miles and I was uneasy about that last instruction; I did not believe that the Clerk of the Course would devise a route with a 10-mile stretch between instructions. A couple of miles further on I stopped and asked to see the card. Ray was adamant: "It's plain enough," he said; "we have to carry on for 10 miles!" So I checked the estimated total mileage of the section and found that it only totalled some 12 or 13 miles. Ray was not happy about turning back to the last instruction point but my dander was up and so we did so, whereupon I laboriously reset the trip mileage to what it should be at that point. "Now!" I said, "when it shows 10 miles from the section start, we'll take the next turn." Unsurprisingly the signpost at 10 miles tallied. When we arrived breathless and slightly late at the checkpoint, the marshal was optimistic on our behalf about our late arrival. "Don't worry!" he said, "I've only seen half a dozen or so up to now."

At the halfway stop for rest, refreshment and to collect the second part of the route card, Ray remarked that we needed a boost; he produced a miniature bottle of rum and poured half its contents into my teacup. I do not particularly like rum and it ruined the taste of a rather nice cup of tea. During the second phase of the trial, rum fumes persisted in my nose and tended to make me feel dozy – the opposite of Ray's good intentions.

But the second half of the trial was interesting in more ways than one. At one point, passing through wooded countryside, a fox ran across our bows; this delighted Ray, who immediately yelled out "Tally-ho!" (a better cry than "There goes the little bastard!"). And for the second section we noted that the average speed for the route was only 14 mph (hitherto it had been 24). We soon found the reason: it was through open country on unmetalled roads. Luckily, we traversed it without problem but, halfway through the next, the heavens opened and drenched all and sundry with a spectacular thunderstorm. Dawn was breaking, and as we negotiated the sleeping streets of Chichester, lightning struck a metal milk crate in a shop doorway as we passed, which very nearly served us as a rapid purgative.

The last but one checkpoint included a timed brake test. We had already competed in earlier special tests such as slow riding, where one is required to ride the machine as slowly as possible feet up between a pair of narrow lines, slipping the clutch to reduce speed below that transmitted at tick-over in bottom gear, and a fiendish stop-start test where the rider has to stop the machine at a line, restart and ride it to stop bike and engine between two further lines, then restart and flash across a final one. The final brake test was down a winding road in forest country. I followed my now usual technique of decanting Ray to follow on foot whilst I pushed off in neutral with a dead engine and crouched low for more speed. This time, as I sat up and applied the stoppers with enthusiasm, the stop-line flashed under my locked wheels on the greasy road surface and bike and I slithered to a halt about 10 yards further on. The rules stated that the machine must be stopped across the line with the rider sitting astride before the stopwatch is stopped, so I perforce was obliged to leap off and run the machine backwards uphill, straddle the line and leap onto my seat and collapse in a gasping heap. The marshal remarked that although I was by no means the first to overshoot, I was in fact the first to get the bike back across the line to qualify for time. "And a pretty good time too – in spite of the extra footwork!" he grinned.

We arrived on time at the finishing line at East Wittering, had our machine checked to ensure everything was in working order with regard to the proper number of lights etc. and signed off. We were more than a little disconcerted to be greeted by Rob and Pauline who should have been an hour or so behind us; it appeared that they had fallen for the 'in 10 miles' instruction and got hopelessly lost. They eventually arrived at the halfway stop just as the officials were about to leave, and extracted from them the final destination. 'Needle' and his passenger arrived later, having not done too well on times and tests; they too were fooled by the "10 miles" instruction. After breakfast we sunbathed on the nice sandy beach and those who had thought ahead enough to bring a 'cossie' bathed in the sea. It had turned into a lovely sunny day as if to make up for the horrendous thunderstorms earlier on. After a light lunch, Ray and I left, pausing on the way home for a short sleep on Ham Common. When the results were posted to us, Ray and I were chuffed to find that we had won a First Class Award. With our Club Team's aggregate loss of marks though, we won no Team Award.

We next entered a one-day semi-sporting road trial starting at a pub in Goffs Oak, organized by a North London Club. One of the special tests listed in the regulations was a slalom event whereby solo machines were to be ridden in and out of a line of poles 7 ft 6 in apart and slightly staggered. Sidecar combinations were to traverse a larger version. Having tried something similar in a small club event and making an almighty hash of it, I set up my own line of poles in an unused corner of Broxbourne Aerodrome and practised every lunch hour for a couple of weeks prior to the event. By the end I had developed a technique to ride in and out of the poles non-stop and feet up. Apart from the slalom, there were the usual special tests including a slow hill climb (slowest rider to complete the run without 'footing' set the standard time. One penalty mark was lost for each second less than 'standard').

As we all gathered for the start, I was disconcerted to note that the organizers had allowed trial bikes to enter. This gave them an unfair advantage in special tests over fully-equipped road bikes. Also competing were a couple of lorry-loads of army dispatch riders on well-worn WD BSAs and Ariels. The course was a winding one back and forth across Herts & Bucks, and we kept running across Army DRs riding in all different directions. Would-be helpful locals and school children kept waving frantically at various points and yelling things like "They went that way!" Heavy rain seemed to follow us and sometimes we couldn't find the checkpoints. We came upon the slalom test eventually and the marshal wearily requested that, in the event of failure, please would I not ride over the side tapes? When I negotiated the course successfully, the marshal jumped up and down and called across to his colleague: "Didja see that? He 'cleaned' the section!" I must have been the first to do so. We didn't get the team prize that time either, but Ray and I managed a Second Class Award – a Dunlop tyre pressure gauge engraved with my initials.

Pauline and Rob invited me to join them for a camping tour of Scotland in the last two weeks of August that year. I had never tried camping before, so with panniers stuffed with borrowed tent and other vital equipment we set out from their home in Walkern and made our way north. Rob, Pauline and I had devised a set of plywood panniers and top case for his AJS, made when I was on weekend duty at Broxbourne. They took with them their pet West Highland terrier, which stood or sat in a holdall on Pauline's lap with the bag zipped up to allow just the pooch's head to protrude. This was a source of great interest and amusement to all we met during the holiday. Pitching camp each evening and moving on the following morning, we covered a circular tour up the western side, across Sutherland and down the eastern side. In so doing, we visited Lochs Ness, Fyne and Lomond, Fort William, Ben Nevis, Mallaig, Skye, John o'Groats, Stirling, Edinburgh, Yorkshire and the Lake District. Camping I found to be somewhat less comfortable than 'three star with *en suite* facilities' but I could never have afforded the trip otherwise.

Halfway through the holiday, one day was so wet that we put up for a night at a small hotel at Kinlochewe – it being tricky to erect the tents in such moist conditions. (That was the weekend Lynmouth suffered the disastrous floods.) By the time we arrived back at Walkern, we had covered over 2,000 miles.

In the autumn I traded in my trusty Speed Twin KLD 708 for KVE 741, a new 1952 650 cc Triumph Thunderbird, painted light metallic blue and fitted with an SU carburetter. Ray came with me to Hallam's of Cambridge to collect it and leave the Speed Twin. In 1952 the Government placed restrictions upon the use of nickel plating, which is the essential base for chromium; only those products for export were allowed such aesthetic finishes, so certain parts hitherto chromed were painted instead. For instance, the handlebars on my T/bird were metallic blue. By the time of the deal, next year's models were already appearing in the showrooms, and this no doubt helped me secure a good price for the Speed Twin. I looked forward to doing great things with my new bike in 1953.

On Twelfth Night (6/1/53) Ray and I attended Rob and Pauline's party at Walkern, along with a number of Rob's de Havilland Tech. School colleagues, including Bill Bowker, 'Needle' Bone, Forbes Leishman, Pete Longland, John Maynard and Tony Heath, among others, and a great party ensued. Ray and I gingerly made our way home on the Thunderbird in the small hours on slippery snow-packed roads. Ray, at any rate, was in a well-oiled, convivial mood and laughed most of the way home. That was the last time for a while Ray and I partied, as he emigrated to Australia shortly after.

Easter 1953 provided the opportunity for a long run on my new treasure when the Berkhamsted Club arranged a jaunt to Woolacoombe Bay for members to stay at a small hotel there, to allow those who wished to spectate on Saturday at the Motor Cycling Club's Land's End Trial. There was also the Wood Green Motor Club's "Beggar's Roost Trial" on Easter Sunday.

Beggar's Roost was a winding uphill Devon track of greasy loose shale used as a severe test section for many years in the classic Land's End Trial. Few solo riders managed to ascend without 'footing' (3 marks – penalty) or stopping (5 marks – failure). On the first morning after our arrival, I was awakened at 4 am by Rob coming into my room and calling "Wakey-wakey!" He, Pauline and I then piled into fellow club member Bill Alderton's new Austin A40 and headed for the venue to see the early arrivals attempt to ascend the section. There we met and conversed with Arthur B. Bourne, Editor of *The Motorcycle* magazine and who wrote a column in it under the pseudonym "Torrens." I was a regular reader of "Torrens" and gleaned much wisdom from him. (Another regular contributor was "Ixion," a pen-name for Canon B.H. Davis.) After breakfasting back at the hotel, we set out on our bikes and revisited Beggar's Roost to see the cars' and three-wheelers' attempts. Later we went to Lynmouth and saw the devastation caused by the previous August flood.

Porlock Hill, between Lynton and Lynmouth, was itself an interesting experience, but no problem for our modern machines, either in ascending or descending. Next day we rode over a lot of Devon countryside, visiting the sections for competitors of the Wood Green Beggar's Roost Trial. I saw Jim Alves, the official Triumph factory trials rider, on his works-prepared Trophy model, negotiate a particularly tricky section of sticky deep mud, riding the section 'feet up' with no penalties.

Next day came the long trek home, mostly in pouring rain. Bill and his family took pity on Pauline and offered her a seat in their car for part of the way. By now the Thunderbird's engine was freeing up nicely in its running-in period.

Without Ray as my navigator, DH Tech School apprentice Pete Longland volunteered for the task and we participated in one or two half-day road trials. In one event, a special test comprised four white lines across the road about 6 or 7 feet apart marked 'A,' 'B,' 'C' and 'D.' With navigator dismounted, the rider had to stop at line 'A,' start up and accelerate to then stop between lines 'B' & 'C,' stop engine, put the gear in neutral, restart the engine, engage first gear and accelerate across line 'D.' The competitor in front of us managed it in 22 seconds, so then I started up, stamped in first gear, revved like mad, dropped the clutch and braked to a stop 'twixt 'B' & 'C' whilst leaving the clutch in – which stopped the engine with a shudder. Quickly selecting neutral, I heaved on the kickstart and, as she fired, crunched into first gear, revved and dropped the clutch and spun across the line – 16 seconds! Pete said that the marshal was so astonished he thought his stopwatch had failed. "Brutal but effective!" he added.

We entered our Club team of Rob, 'Needle' and me for the next WMA Pillion Trial. Pete was unavailable so Jock Ogilvie's son Roy came as my passenger/navigator. In spite of Roy putting his foot down unnecessarily in one section, we achieved another First Class Award and this time managed to get the team prize. Rob & Pauline gained the best marks of our trio. Pete and I gained another First Class Award in the next Farnham Royal night trial, which Rob won. By the time of that 1953 Farnham Royal Night Trial I had already accepted a job with de Havilland SDCR at Leavesden and was due to start the following week. We all entered the Night Trial once more as a 'Berko' team and Pete was my passenger/navigator again. For the third time in the Farnham Royal event, I was running number 33. The trial was much as the previous year with a slightly less ambiguous route card. There were varied time schedules due to more cross-country routing, but thanks to Pete's impeccable navigation we seemed to arrive at each time-check within the 30 second tolerance and qualified for a First Class Award once more. This state of affairs was becoming a habit – three times riding number 33, two FCAs! Another DH-er, Bruce Bosher, was a team member who was well experienced in these events. We all had a great time on the south coast beach afterwards and Pete and I trekked wearily home in the afternoon.

Due to my new job, I had little time for other events; 50 miles a day, 7 days a week sometimes, began to build up the mileometer figures and what with any spare time devoted to oil changes, de-cokes and other vital maintenance, fun and games on the competition scene took a back seat for a while. I did, however, enter once more for the 1954 FR night trial with Pete, my worthy navigator. Rob and the others were not involved due to pressures in other directions, so Pete and I would uphold the honour of the Club. As an early entrant, I drew No. 13. Shrugging off superstitious doubts, we set off full of hope and enthusiasm. They still started the event from Eddie's Café at Cippenham and we rolled away from there at 00.13 hours with nary a hiccup. One of the final sections before the halfway stop was routed via a winding uphill minor road with some tight hairpin bends, through a forest. Behind us, riding No. 14, was a bespectacled character astride an ageing BSA, snapping at our heels. He had no passenger, so maybe found it easier to tail us rather than trying to read a route card on the move. Anyway, whilst attempting a tight left-hander at 30+ mph, we drifted off the road – leaving on it a line of rubber filed from the left-hand footrest – and came to rest too few inches from a rather large and very solid tree. We both had visions of matey behind us doing likewise and piling in on top of us, so we panicked a little to get back on the road and under way. Our trailing friend did not immediately appear, however, so perhaps he had made a similar excursion further downhill.

It was our practice, after each time-check stop, to crack on at a reasonable rate for the first two or three miles to allow time for any navigational errors or wrong turnings before the next point. A mile or two beyond the first time check after the halfway break at a steady 35 mph, I eased the throttle and then powered on for a gentle right-hander and we came an almighty purler. "We're No. 13" was my thought as bike, Pete and I slithered along on our collective starboard sides. When all came to a stop, Pete was about 30 feet astern and the bike and I were lying cuddled together on a damp greasy road. As I began to disentangle myself Pete, white-faced and full of concern, rushed up and asked if I was all right. I, however, was more concerned about any damage to my inadvertently jettisoned passenger. We established that both passenger and rider were still fully functional, but Pete noticed that his leggings were in a greasy state – indicative of an unseen oil spill. I was wearing my recently acquired black thornproof twill Barbour suit, originally designed for – and worn by – all the British entrants in the International Six Days Trial. As we slid along the road at about 25 mph, the road surface abraded through the double thickness of the Barbour sleeve and the sleeve of my Harris Tweed jacket and flannel shirt and slightly grazed my arm. When I nowadays see motorcycle and scooter riders in summer riding about with bare arms and legs, I recoil in horror at the thought of what a similar spill would do to them.

We inspected the bike and were dismayed to note that the right footrest and gear pedal appeared to have been knotted together, but we were relieved to find that a well-directed shove with a stout wellie pushed the footrest back to roughly where it should be; it was still bent, as was the gear pedal, but we were able to continue and reached the finishing line with no further loss of marks. The finish-line marshal greeted us with the words: "Welcome home, you unlucky b******!" – referring to our No. 13. I pointed to the damage and asked "How did you guess?", which made him purse his lips. He then checked all the lights for functioning and found that the rear light was unlit, but it came on when tapped and remained on with further tapping.

"I'll have to allow that mark; it didn't go out again," he conceded.

We thus won the "Farnham Royal Main Road Night Trial Premier Award" by only one mark from the runner-up; had the rear light failed to come on, we would have been runners-up instead. I later found that the bulb had a broken filament that welded itself when tapped and broke again when switched off.

By now I had joined the Triumph Owners' Motorcycle Club (TOMCC), and for 1955 they arranged the first big nationwide road trial and rally to terminate at the Triumph factory at Allesley, near Coventry, from five different starting points around Britain. As it also included a 'Concours d'Elegance,' I spent a lot of spare time preparing the machine mechanically and aesthetically. Pete had by now finished his apprenticeship and in consequence had been called up into the RAF. Ray had returned to the UK but was on duty with Scottish Airlines on the date of the event. My soon-to-be-fiancée Connie gamely agreed to navigate when no one else could be found and enjoyed the excitement.

At the Bedford Start Point we met a number of fellow TOMCC members for the first time; they seemed to differ somewhat from the usual 'dyed-in-the-'Stormgard"-and-waders' trials type and had a tendency to embellish their hardware with what I considered useless cosmetic accessories. However, they were a good crowd and the magazine editor, Ron Quennel, was among them and most welcoming to us. The route card, printed in seeming shorthand gibberish, soon became logical and thus we wound our way around the counties of England, stopping at appropriate check points for tests and questions on the Highway Code. We finally rolled into the hallowed precincts of the Meriden Works of Triumph Motorcycles Ltd, to be put in line with hordes of their products for checking by knowledgeable scrutineers from the factory staff, whilst we competitors freshened up and enjoyed a packed lunch in the works canteen provided by the management. Among the ranks of other Thunderbirds was one particular machine so immaculately pristine that several other nearby riders ceased their final polishing with such comments as: "No point in bothering; can't compete agin' that!" I noticed from its number that it had only been entered for the *concours* part of the event. Later, entertainment, fun and games were laid on in the sports field where the Royal Signals motorcycle display team gave a wonderful show of trick riding.

Back in the work-a-day routine a couple of weeks later I had a nice surprise, receiving through the post a First Class Award shield for combined trial and concours. With it was a list of competitors' marks and I was amazed to note that the pristine T/bird was marked too low – due to mechanical faults and non-standard presentation – to qualify for any award.

The 25 miles to and from work during the winter of 1954/1955 had been vile. On snow-packed roads, the safest place to ride was close to the kerb due to frozen ruts created by cars and lorries. Fresh fallen snow required very careful riding, but idiot motorists persisted in the nasty habit of trailing two yards behind – ready to drive over machine and rider should one slide off. They never took the hint when I eased into the roadside and frantically waved them past. Another bind was the would-be good citizen who could not wait for it to stop snowing in order to relive his childhood by shovelling it all into the gutter where it solidified to prevent drainage when thawing. I drew great satisfaction when such a twit was doing just that as I was passing through Hertford. Hemmed-in by a commercial vehicle, I had to keep close to the kerb and the bike got into a sort of speedway slide, so that the rear wheel churned all the slush back onto his feet. I grinned to myself as his cries of "Oi! Oi!" faded behind – trials practice had its uses.

Apart from a holiday trip to Swanage in the summer of 1956, my motorcycling was now mostly mundane to-and-from work with the odd social visit thrown in, interspersed with necessary overhaul work (in common with most bikers of that era, I never entrusted any work on my machine to dealers or other hands). It was to be 1958 before I competed seriously once more.

TOMCC organized the second All Britain Triumph Rally in 1958 – one year late due to the Suez crisis. The original idea was to hold it on alternate years to allow for the enormous amount of organizing involved with mostly volunteer workers. By now Connie and I were married and living in a new small 'semi' which was set on a plot of ground that was doing its utmost to defy my unskilled efforts of turning a builders' site into a garden. Preparing KVE 741 for the event required a lot of spare-time effort, which was none too popular with the other half of the partnership. Pete was back in civvy street and volunteered to be my navigator again. Learning from experience of the first rally, I spent a lot of time studying the Highway Code.

Starting once more from Bedford, Pete soon got me traversing the route in the right direction and on time. At one checkpoint, in reply to a marshal's question on stopping distance, I replied: "185 feet."

"You know your Highway Code!" he said. I failed to let on that I had been mugging it up that very morning at breakfast.

We arrived at the Triumph factory gates, signed off and parked the T/bird at its allotted spot on the grass in front of the main building. Serried ranks of short wooden boards – to accommodate rear or centre stands – were provided in case the bikes sunk into the soft grass and keeled over. We queued for our free packed lunch and strolled to the nearby sports field to enjoy the entertainment provided: tug-o'-war contests, the Royal Signals team etc. Later, all the Officials gathered on a platform at one end of the arena to announce the various winners. Edward Turner (Chief Designer and Managing Director) and Alan Jeffries (Team Captain for the winning British team in the 1948 International Six Days Trial in Europe) accompanied the TOMCC secretary and president on the platform. The overall winner of both road trial and concours was announced: "Number 29, H.A. Smith!"

The rest of the day passed in a whirl. Presented with the Trophy by Edward Turner himself and handed some useful dealer-donated accessories by Alan Jeffries, there followed a session of posed photographs for the motorcycle press and company publicity. Pete rode the Thunderbird home with me on pillion, my mind too full to concentrate properly on driving. The next Thursday my copy of the 'Blue'un' carried a full report of the TOMCC Rally, with a picture of Pete and me standing beside the bike and the large silver trophy balanced on its twin seat. At work, I became something of a celebrity in the Manor Road DO.

Deciding to quit whilst ahead, I sold the Thunderbird to Ray Bradbury (a friend of Pete) a year later when we bought our first car. But wedded bliss was once more put under severe strain in early 1960 when I read in the TOMCC magazine that another All Britain Triumph Rally was scheduled for 1961. I cast around for a cheap second-hand Speed Twin to rebuild, in order to defend my title, as it were. In the end, for budgetary reasons, I settled for a rather sad-looking 1948 Triumph 3T, 350 cc twin, KKT 648, with a logbook full to overflowing with previous owners' names and addresses. As always with restorations, whether aeroplanes, cars, steam engines or bikes, the job takes three or four times more effort and time than anticipated. Due to workspace shortage, I stripped the machine down to components and sent all the frame parts away for stripping and stove enamelling, and the tank for repainting, to Jack Nice in Walthamstow. Having re-assembled the frame I then overhauled each major component one by one to be refitted to it in sequence. I became a regular mail-order customer of H & L Motors of Stroud in Gloucester, the main Triumph spares supplier. I practically wept at the way previous owners had mechanically maltreated many of the components. Low funds meant devising crafty schemes and dodges to overcome minor disasters perpetrated by cretinous mechanics.

A year later, and in time for the Rally, the machine was ready for its foray into the great world of motorcycling road trials. As Pete had also married and moved up north to work for English Electric at Bradford, his friend Ray Bradbury asked if he could be my passenger. For the third time we started at Bedford and were interested to see that a group of German Triumph enthusiasts, who had ridden their machines from Germany, were there to attend the Rally, to be escorted from Bedford by a TOMCC official. They seemed very interested in the 3T, as only the bigger bikes were sold in Germany at that time. Ray was a good navigator, and we finished the trial feeling reasonably confident but kept our fingers crossed with regard to the concours judging. Once again the Royal Signals Motorcycle Display Team – this time on new special Triumph Trophy models – put on a really splendid show, and at the end attained a 5-tier pyramid with 16 men on 5 bikes in line, whilst on the move.

The winner this time was a sidecar man. I came second and won the Club Cup for highest-placed TOMCC member. The Club publicity officer notified my local paper and I was interviewed about the event in general and my success in particular. Inevitably the reporter mentioned racing and I delivered a lecture to the effect that it was a timed road trial, at modest speed, with emphasis on road safety. Of course his editor had to use the emotive word 'race' somehow, and the report finished with the words: " . . . Mr Smith confirmed that the event was not a race." (Never mind the facts, we want a good story!) That was the last competition I entered and, apart from a trip to Seaford in Sussex and appearing in a local hospital money-raising vintage vehicle event, I only used the bike thereafter for short journeys and travelling to work. In 1979, when I took the 3T for its annual MOT, the total mileage had increased barely 100 miles in a year. I sold it soon after to vintage car and bike enthusiast Mike Beach from Barnet.

I enjoyed my 34 years of motorcycling; it improved my health and engineering knowledge to a satisfying degree, as well as giving me valuable experience of road conditions in all weathers. In 1946, I had seriously considered learning to fly. Then, with my gross weekly wage at £4-10s, even buying lessons at 'trade,' so to speak, would have cost about 65% of that figure. Also, there was no certainty of continued employment at the flying club in those days of petrol shortage. Furthermore, I needed transport and there were limits to the distance one could cycle. I had thought about selling my old Calthorpe to pay for flying lessons but the most optimistic amount it would fetch would have been swallowed up in the first two or three lessons, so motorcycling won. Motorcycling has an affinity with flying, solo bikes and light aircraft respond to lightness of touch, balance and C. of G. And motorbikes, like aircraft, make banking turns. Also, as in open-cockpit flying, special protective clothing is a good idea and weather conditions need to be considered.

Once, I gave a fellow draughtsman a lift to work in my Ford Popular on a frosty morning following a wet night. We were in plenty of time, but he was agitated at my modest speed. "Can't you go a bit faster?" he moaned.

"Slippery roads," I tersely replied.

"Looks just wet to me," he grumbled.

I waited till we were on a curving quiet bit of road and gave a twitch to the wheel and trod the throttle. The car took the curve in a controlled slide, at 45° to the road centre line (Richard Burns would have been impressed!).

Smoothing his risen hair and pushing his spectacles back with a forefinger, he remarked: "Yes, it is a bit dicey!"

There were no more complaints.

At 75, I still occasionally yearn to ride a powerful two-wheeler – but don't tell the wife!

CHAPTER 8

STARTING ON THE BOTTOM RUNG

My working life started on the 18th November 1940 when I joined Herts & Essex Aviation Ltd as a shop boy at Broxbourne Aerodrome.

The Herts & Essex Aeroplane Club had ceased operating from 11 am on 3rd September 1939 and all their flyable aircraft that could be useful to the RAF were dispersed to training establishments, unwanted ones being dismantled and stored in the various lock-up wooden sheds adjacent to the large steel main hangar.

During the summer of 1940, a number of old cars were towed onto the field and strategically placed to deny the enemy a convenient landing ground. When the threat of invasion receded, the aerodrome was brought back into use and the company Herts & Essex Aviation Ltd was formed as a contractor within the CRO (Civilian Repair Organization), a wartime official body set up to co-ordinate repair and overhaul of Service aircraft by civilian companies. Assembly and modification of recently stored new Percival Proctors was undertaken and they were test-flown and delivered from the newly cleared aerodrome. A nucleus of pre-war employees formed the backbone of the staff including the former Chief Engineer, Mr B.D. Whittaker, now installed as Works Manager. Other peacetime engineering staff filled posts as inspectors and foremen. As the pace quickened and the work force expanded, damage repair and overhaul of time-expired aircraft was put in hand and, due to success with Proctors, other types were also brought in for similar treatment, as well as the preparation of various civilian machines impressed into Service use.

That was the situation when, at the tender age of 14 years and 2 months, I joined the firm and increased the 'detail fitting' staff by 33% at a wage of 10/- per week (which would equate in spending power to about £30 nowadays).

A family acquaintence working at the "drome' (as we always referred to it) had offered to show me around the previous day (Sunday), and I had bolted my Sunday lunch and pedalled off with alacrity to keep the appointment; I had not realised that my mother, sister and eldest brother had plotted with him to get me a job there! First, he showed me round a Proctor that was nearing completion after repair and was displaying large areas of red-doped fabric. I was slightly disconcerted at this; my model aircraft were coated with clear dope and in my innocence I thought that all fabric-covered real aircraft were similarly treated. To me, it looked as if someone had splodged red lead all over it!

I was quite starry-eyed when I beheld all the exciting things in the hangar. A twin-engined machine with its mainplanes removed outboard of the engines seemed to dominate the building (I later learned that it was a Percival Q.6). There were several other smaller aircraft in various stages of dismantling or re-assembly, engines in crates and wings stacked on their leading edges in racks, other components were on trestles, with white-overalled woodworkers rebuilding quite complicated structures with slender pieces of spruce and thin birch plywood, which they formed into the fine aerodynamic shapes that were the trademark of Percival Aircraft. And the glue they were using was quite unlike any we had in the woodwork class at school.

Along one wall of the hangar were benches full of tools, parts, and sundry *bric-a-brac*, and adjacent to the opposite wall an oxy-acetylene welder was spraying sparks as if it was bonfire night. Next to his bench a milling machine and lathe were in use, both driven via shafting and flapping belts from a single large electric motor mounted high up on the hangar wall; it reminded me of the way our woodwork lathe at school was powered, but this was much bigger.

We had made our way toward the rear of the hangar, where the stores were located in a wooden structure across the end of the building. Above the stores were the offices, reached via wooden stairways each side of the hangar running parallel to the stores & offices and linked by a verandah in front of the offices. The Chief Engineer's office was at the top of the left-hand stairway with windows overlooking both the hangar interior and the aerodrome. We went in and I was introduced to a stocky Yorkshireman with dark crinkly hair and wearing a dark blue pinstripe suit; he was sitting, hands in pockets, on the table that was attached to the wall adjoining the other offices.

"This is Mr Whittaker," my guide said in introduction.

Being fresh from school, I addressed him as "Sir" and unwittingly made a good first impression.

"So, lad! You want a job, do you?"

Up to that point I had not even considered the possibility, but on reflection thought it highly desirable! My companion vouchsafed the view that a lad would be useful in the fitting shop and the interview terminated with the offer of a job as shop boy at the aforementioned 10/- a week. We then went to the general office, where my details were recorded and a letter typed for me to take to the Labour Exchange the next morning; I was given instructions to obtain from them a green card and, from the Post Office, a Juvenile Stamp Card and to report for work at 1:30 pm. After that, I was taken downstairs to the stores, where the chief storeman stamped '55' on the back of a 'CAG' badge which was to be my gate pass. (CAG stood for 'Civil Air Guard,' the organization that gave the Royal Air Force access to a number of trained pilots when the balloon went up, but as the organisation had become defunct with the cessation of civil flying at the start of the war, Herts & Essex were making temporary use of the badges for Works Passes.) I felt very important sporting my own identity badge!

On Monday morning at the Labour Exchange, I seemed to have to wait interminably for the clerks to action my letter. Three times I repeated the instructions from Mr Joy (unofficially Acting Personnel Manager at H & E, although I doubt if such a post had been invented in those days), and to a different clerk each time. Finally they passed me the appropriate documents and pointed out that the green card was actually a grey one.

It was then a rush to grab some lunch and cycle three miles to the aerodrome to arrive at 1.30 pm, which I managed with just a couple of minutes to spare. I operated the 'Stafsyne' clock that displayed a paper with the time stamped on it when one raised the handle – upon which one signed one's name through a little window – and handed my sheaf of cards to Mr Joy.

I heard someone behind me say: "Aha, he works!" They were the first words addressed me as a working boy.

I was introduced to the white-overalled fitter I had noticed the day before having a fitting welded at the welder's bench. "This is Denis Green. You'll be working for him; he'll tell you what to do."

Our fitting bench was located inside the front end of the hangar near to the personnel door and adjacent to the table upon which rested the 'Stafsyne' clock. Despite the blackout 'airlock' built onto the outside of the door, it was the coldest corner of the building! I now realize that, considering the work we were doing, the hangar was very poorly equipped; for instance, our only drilling machine was a large electric breast-drill mounted on a stand with a spring-loaded handle to pull it down onto the work-piece. Unfortunately, the trigger button was broken so the operator had to hold the switch 'on' with one hand and operate the drill with the other. In order to drill holes in small fittings which needed to be hand-held, three hands were needed! So it was one of my tasks to operate the drill switch for Denis when he wished to use the drill.

It was an abrupt transition from school to working life. The 26-hour school week gave way to a working week of 57 hours; we worked from 7.30 am till 5.30 pm Monday to Friday and to 12.30 pm on Saturday: and then from 9.00 am to 5.00 pm on Sunday, with an hour for lunch each day. In the early part of 1941 finishing times were changed to 7.30 pm on weekdays and 2.00 pm on Saturdays with Sundays off (61½ hours per week – big deal!) No one told me not to work the same hours as the men, and it was not until late summer 1941 that the Ministry of Labour cracked down and insisted that junior staff (i.e. those under 16) should not exceed a maximum 50½ hours per week.

Another trauma was the three to four-mile cycle ride to and from work in the blackout during winter. Failing lights, icy roads and punctured tyres ensured a fair amount of walking and certain admonition for lateness; it was bearable of course, by virtue of my being involved with real aeroplanes. One of my tasks was making steel washer plates and discs to reinforce welded transverse bracings for Q.6 undercarriages. The firm had received a contract shortly before I started work to manufacture 10 complete spare Q.6

undercarriage sets including tailwheels. However, as the most junior employee, my primary function was tea boy to the rest of the staff. Twice a day I visited the local café to bring back tea, coffee, cocoa, sandwiches and cakes (and also cigarettes and tobacco) for distribution among my fellow workers. Collecting money and orders, waiting for them to be made up and then delivering them to the rightful recipients from the odd selection of tins, jugs and bags took up most of the day. Time on the bench, therefore, became a precious interlude in the everyday toil of a tea boy-*cum*-messenger-*cum*-floor sweeper.

When in the café one day awaiting collection of my afternoon orders, I saw a Supermarine Walrus land on the aerodrome. Whilst doling out the usual tea and buns to the men, I had a chance to look over the old 'Shagbat' (as it was known in the Navy) where it had been parked outside the main hangar doors. Two repairs to the underside fabric of the top mainplanes had been made with doped-on patches and the red dope had trickled toward the trailing edges prior to drying. I was intrigued to note that the 4-bladed pusher airscrew was in fact made up of two 2-bladed ones mounted at 90° to one another on a common shaft. The aircraft left next day at lunchtime after an hilarious performance when Alec Ellis and Dave Osborne (Works Foreman) had cranked the heavy inertia starter and wound the starter magneto respectively, plus pulling the engagement handle when the pilot had shouted from the cockpit that the inertia flywheel revolutions were sufficient. It looked rather quaint as it waddled across the field to take off – the first non-trainer Service aircraft that I had seen at Broxbourne.

Just before Christmas 1940, after only two or three weeks with the fitting section, I was temporarily transferred to the Stores and began to learn about such things as requisitions, Release Notes and the difference between Quarantine and Bonded Stores. I was not happy with the change of position, being anxious to help build aeroplanes, but it was better than tea boy duties and enabled me to explore some of the large wooden sheds to the rear and side of the main large steel hangar, in which were stored some exciting pre-war aircraft: a couple of Leopard Moths, a Taylorcraft (G-AFVA), a selection of Avros (504, Avian, Cadet & Tutor) and three BA Swallows. One of these, yellow-painted, was rumoured to be owned by the Weston Brothers – at that time popular radio entertainers. Mainplanes for the three Swallows were stored in the roof trusses of the main hangar, as were those for a mysterious small aircraft, G-AEXT, and a delightful little Carden Ford-powered blue & silver Chilton DW.1 (G-AFGI). During the spring of 1941, much excitement ensued when the Chilton was brought out and refurbished – retaining its bright civil paintwork and registration – for the use of Prince Bernhardt of the Netherlands, who came to Broxbourne with his *entourage* and flew it away himself.

The Leopards were the first to go, though, being readied for Service impressment early in 1941. On the way to their new base one of them suffered engine failure and crashed. I remember that, about ten years later during conversation with 'Buster' Frogley, I asked if he knew why this had happened. "There was nothing wrong with the engine," he told me. "The pilot refused to believe the fuel gauges when they showed 'empty,' but their accuracy was emphasised when the engine stopped!"

The Taylorcraft was later overhauled and painted in camouflage and yellow, also to join the RAF; I believe it survived the war and returned to civil use.

Soon after starting work in the Stores, I was told to help in labelling loose parts from a number of strange-looking French aircraft which had arrived on RAF Queen Mary trailers. These were the first of two batches of Caudron Simouns brought out of France (prior to German occupation) and which we were to restore for duties with the Free French Air Force. These aircraft were similar to the Proctor with four seats in two staggered rows either side of the rather long cabin, giving them a quaint hump-backed appearance, and they were powered by heavy-looking Renault Bengali Six engines with Ratier electrically operated, variable-pitch airscrews.

I found the Stores work very tiring, having to spend most of the day running to and fro and standing behind the counter serving quantities of nuts, bolts, tools etc.; woe betide anyone who let so much as one screw or washer be issued beyond what was specified on the authorized Requisition Note!

At that time of National Emergency, our brightly-coloured windsock was only displayed when an aircraft was in the circuit, verified friendly and obviously needing to land; when not in use, it was kept safely in the stores. One day Tim Tribble and Bert Nichols came rushing to the counter and demanded the sock in a hurry.

"There's a Wellington in the circuit and we think it wants to land!" one of them yelled in some excitement.

I let them in, and after grabbing the item they rushed straight through to the back door of the Stores which opened onto the field and proceeded to haul it up its flag-pole. Not wishing to miss seeing an operational aircraft at close quarters, I hurried after them to the door just in time to see its bulky silhouette circling the field and getting lower, much as the Valentia did back in 1935. A couple more circuits later it lined up on the longest run and came in over the greenhouses to touch down a few yards inside the boundary. After the first touch it bounced up to 20 feet but recovered to land safely near the corner of the 'drome opposite Monty's Café. After shutting the door I ran through the hangar in time to see it come to a halt between hangar and Clubhouse; as the crew descended from its belly down the little ladder, I thought how huge it looked at rest in our small flying field.

Next day another Wellington landed and taxied to a stop beside the first one, then shortly afterwards they both took off to return to base. Rumour was that the first one had lost its way and touched down at Broxbourne before running out of daylight and that the other one flew in to show it the way back to base – a likely story, I remember thinking!

During the time I was with the fitters and, afterwards, my spell in the stores, priority was given to completing the overhaul of the only retractable undercarriage Q.6 in the UK. This was originally registered G-AFIX, but we knew it by its Service serial X9406. The Q.6 was really meant to have retractable gear and looked superb flying past 'gear up.' The underside received its yellow paint one weekend and on the Monday we found everything in the hangar covered with fine yellow dust! During the time '406 was under repair another Q.6, the prototype G-AEYE (X9328) came in on a RAF Queen Mary; this had only had its outer mainplanes removed and straddled the QM with one trousered undercarriage protruding 3 ft each side of the vehicle. Thus I found out how the undercarriage fairings were assembled, having previously seen them lying around the tinbashers shop; I thought they were overlarge spats which went the other way up!

In the early part of 1941 I was moved again, this time to be shop boy at Bridgeworks; in order to gain more room and shorten aircraft repair time, H & E had taken over one half of a small wallpaper factory near the River Lee and close to Nazeing Glass Works, this space being used for the repair of flying surfaces and components; its proximity to the road bridge over the Lee in Nazeing New Road gave rise to the obvious connotation. The pleasant heated workshop was ideal for glue- and dope-drying and was big enough to accommodate Proctor and Q.6 mainplanes and centre sections, with spare room for flaps, ailerons and empennage components. My allotted tasks seemed retrograde to an aspiring fitter – each morning ridding the work area of about six loads of shavings and old fabric, making tea with a huge kettle and teapot twice a day, and in my spare time cleaning rust and old paint from dismantled fittings prior to repainting them with grey primer. Much as I hated it, I think – in roseate retrospect – that it was, nevertheless, excellent training. Among the components under repair at Bridgeworks were the port and starboard mainplanes and centre section of Q.6 P5638; this aircraft had been bombed and strafed during the recent Battle of Britain, and its fuselage aft of the cockpit had sustained most of the damage while the nose section, bereft of fabric and with obvious shrapnel wounds, was on trestles in the main hangar at the 'drome with a new part-built rear fuselage behind it. Its centre section at that time was in component form with the newly-repaired spars still separated, the whole project being of long-term low priority.

When sweeping some old newspapers from the floor one day, I noticed a picture of a Frenchman who had escaped from occupied France in a twin-engined aircraft which looked similar to a Q.6 except that the windscreen frame looked uncannily like those on the Caudron Simouns. Later that week, I overheard an inspector, Ernie Shepherd, saying on the telephone that among other things we were contracted to overhaul a French Caudron

Goeland which was, as he put it: "A bloody great thing like a Q.6!" It was in fact, the same one as pictured in the newspaper.

Soon after this, word went round that we were to move back to the aerodrome and be located in DeeKay hangar, as Bridgeworks was needed for conversion into an engine overhaul shop to rebuild the Renault engines for the Caudrons. In fact, two Renault engines, still with their bearers attached, had already been brought to Bridgeworks and I was given the job of blanking all the sparking plug holes and taping up the ends of pipe joints to keep out dust and dirt.

In pre-war days, a small purpose-built workshop was erected for the manufacture of an experimental low-wing light cabin monoplane known as the DeeKay Knight which had been built to prove a new wing form. One day, its engineers had been running the engine with the machine facing the hangar and, with the engine at full chat, it had ridden the chocks and slammed into the hangar wall, breaking the arm of the attendant ground engineer, smashing one mainplane and gashing the corrugated steel cladding of the hangar with its propeller. At this time, its somewhat stalky undercarriage and Cirrus Minor engine still reposed in DeeKay's adjacent store room, and that particular small hangar was ever after known as 'DeeKay,' right up to the final demise of Broxbourne Aerodrome in the mid-fifties. As to the gash in the hangar, I once heard someone say that it was caused by shrapnel from a German bomb!

DeeKay had now been readied for us as a small component woodwork shop wherein we were all duly installed. Instead of hot steam pipes, a medium-sized 'Tortoise' stove was provided, and in view of fire risk it was my job to look after the wretched beast, lighting it each morning, stoking it during the day and drawing and dousing it before we went home. Such an exercise is not conducive to the continued good health of asthmatics and soon I was laid low with a massive and protracted illness. An elderly sage had warned me about the effects of "this dratted red dope" but in fact I found that cellulose fumes if anything eased the problem slightly – it was rotten old-fashioned dusty coke fumes that nearly killed me. But it is an ill wind . . . and when I returned to work some weeks later, I was back with the detail fitters.

It was very enjoyable to be back; the staff had increased to ten and there were many interesting projects under way. As well as Q.6 spares, a fair number of fittings was needed for the Goeland which was being rebuilt outside. Its length and span were too great for the hangar and all hands were needed to lower the fuselage onto its one-piece wing to assemble with the big 'halving-joint.' When ground tests began, I noticed that the engines were designed for left- and right-hand rotation respectively – to counter each other's torque, I guessed. Every check short of actually test-flying the beast was carried out. Thanks to continuing fine spring weather, it had even been resprayed, in the open air, in British Service camouflage and 'trainer yellow.' But no test-flight and landing was attempted at Broxbourne.

Then, one day, three intrepid French types in dark blue uniforms appeared, climbed aboard, ran the engines and took off; everyone turned out to watch and there was one heart-stopping moment when we all wondered if it would unstick, but it finally clawed its way skyward, circled, gave a low pass and disappeared into the wide blue yonder with its undercart still down.

That spring, quite a lot of work was carried out on the Simouns. The woodworkers repaired the airframes and a proper clean engine overhaul workshop had been established at Bridgeworks. At the fitting benches a number of Renault induction manifolds were repaired with welded sheet steel and then pressure-tested. This was another new experience for me; blanking-plates, Hermetite, pressure gauge, foot pump and bucket of water were the tools used, and trying to achieve 100 psi with a grotty foot pump was a mite energy-sapping. Simoun cast-aluminium tailwheel fairings were modified to accept British pneumatic-tyred tailwheels.

A Percival Aircraft Co. draughtsman was busy crawling around one of the Simoun airframes with a notebook and 6-inch rule. Percivals had taken on Design Authority for the Caudrons and were busily engaged in a conversion design to install de Havilland Gipsy Six engines and constant-speed propellers, plus modified Proctor undercarriages, to make up for the shortfall in those areas that could not be served by cannibalizing. Our one and only pattern maker constructed mock-ups for the proposed new engine bearers and, after trial fit-ups, Percivals provided drawings for us to make the first formed steel sheet ones. These complex double-cranked tapering square-section beams were developed from flat sheet steel and bent to shape for welding and riveting by Johnny Marlow, employed as a toolmaker. His parents owned a brush factory in Broxbourne High Road; he was a great leg-puller and, despite making my life a misery at times, I enjoyed working with him and learned a lot in the process. He had a 24-inch straight steel rule and sometimes walked around the place with it in his breast pocket swaying about in a dangerous ear-slicing sort of way.

H & E had obtained a contract for certain parts for the new Beaufighter, and Johnny made a press tool for banging out the slots in small plates required for the project. To put it into practice, he mounted it in the fly-press and we worked together; he swung the handle of the press whilst I had to place the plates in the jig and replace each one as it was stamped. We got into a terrific rhythm and after about ten minutes he suddenly exclaimed: "Jesus Christ! The bloody boy's working like a machine!"

Detail fitters and sheet-metal workers shared the same corner of the main hangar, and one of the features I enjoyed was the singing that both groups joined in, quite often in very good harmony. Mostly they were old favourites like *I'll Be Your Sweetheart, Wedding Bells,* and one hilarious number that ended up: ' . . . *Did you ever see a cow with a green eyebrow? Down by the eee-eye-ohh!*'

One would never hear a group of working men singing like that today; 'pop' songs that seem to have their lyrics written by illiterate cretins do not lend themselves to sweet harmony and seem to require vocalists to bellow out in a way that varies only between agonized squawking and amplified vomiting! Drug-sodden disc jockeys and money-mad marketing men have a lot to answer for.

During that time, prototype Q.6 X9328 was completed and test-flown. Unfortunately, due no doubt to differences between prototype and production, there was a technical hitch that caused a mix-up with the fuel cocks and gauges, and on the second test flight the pilot (on loan from Percival for the occasion) selected 'full' tanks which were in fact quite empty. When we reached the aircraft, the pilot had pancaked it neatly just short of the river in a field of holiday huts; it looked nearly as second-hand as the huts. One of the Essex Regiment soldiers who guarded our establishment at that time opined that it was bound to crash because he had noticed that the tail came up as soon as it moved forward!

The need for an overhaul shop for the Renaults ceased during the summer and the small component woodworkers were reinstated at Bridgeworks. This left DeeKay vacant and it was decided that the fitters and tinbashers should move in; as the salt bath and small electric furnace were still installed there, it was only common sense so to do.

Works Manager Whittaker arrived on the scene just as all the lads were installing their benches, guillotine, pillar-drill, welding equipment and large Edwards hand-roller. Calling them all together he delivered his homily: "Now listen to me you f***ers! There've been a lot of f***ers in here, and they've all been chooked out through piss-ballin' about. Now I'm warnin' you! If there's any piss-ballin' about, you'll all be oop f***in' road!"

With that he turned on his heel and strode away to a stunned silence. Johnny Marlow, appalled and being used to handling working and business people through his father's business, forcefully opined that that was no way to address any group of men.

Those members of staff employed on the Renault engine overhauls were absorbed into other jobs and I suddenly had a couple of companions of my own age. Stan and Les Kimm (see previous chapters) were identical twins, four months younger than me, and had started at Bridgeworks whilst I was in the throes of the asthma attack. We had much in common, including a passion for model aircraft. They were both superb modellers and their rubber-powered flying models were always beautifully finished. Mine were somewhat shabby by comparison through me being too impatient to get them into the air! I soon got to know which twin was which but others were not so lucky. The foreman once bawled one out for not being where he thought he should be, only to discover that it was his brother on an errand for someone else. I suspect they took mischievous delight in creating confusion. As the general foreman once asked: "Are you *you* or your bloody bruvver?" at which an unknown wit called out: "That's his next of Kimm!" With two other lads as well, Dick Milton and Colin Stout, at least the onerous task of getting tea, buns and fags could be shared five ways.

That summer of 1941 was hot and fine. I was getting more experience in making small fittings and was beginning to assemble a modest tool kit. I helped one of the men to rebuild a Proctor undercarriage and he showed me the proper way to split-pin the bolts by bending the tails of the pins round the nuts and tucking them into their slots on each side. We lads were sometimes sent out to fetch things from the town; I was sent on one occasion to cycle the six miles each way to Wickham's of Ware to fetch a gallon of soluble cutting oil for the machine shop. It was one of the hottest days of the year and felt like it! Try cycling uphill with a full gallon can balanced on the handlebars on a hot afternoon – those *Tour de France* riders don't know they're born! We were never paid anything extra for using our bicycles, only chastised if the foreman thought we had taken too long.

One morning we came to work to find that a Hurricane Mk. 1 had arrived the prevous evening and was picketed at the back of the main hangar; it was the mount of Battle of Britain pilot Jack Belton, whose parents owned the Beltona liniment factory at Hoddesdon. He returned from his parents' house later that morning and after take-off proceeded to give us a beat-up and aerobatic display as a 'thank you' for looking after his aircraft. As he swept past DeeKay at seemingly nil feet the wooden doors rattled fit to shake them from their tracks and he zoomed up over the telephone wires into a victory roll, a manoeuvre that he repeated two or three times. To see a real combat aeroplane was thrill enough, to have a free air pageant was a real bonus!

Johnny Marlow was appointed View Room Inspector at the end of summer 1941 and two or three weeks later he asked me to be his junior assistant. I had to stamp inspected parts with part number and inspection stamps, enter them in records and be general dogsbody – clean equipment, sweep up and fetch tea.

As autumn began to merge into winter, the wire-cage View Room set between the staircases and abutting the front wall of the stores in the unheated main hangar became extremely cold and draughty. Johnny Marlow asked the Chief Inspector, Duggie Henderson, if it could be boarded in; Duggie was reluctant to give permission for extra expense on maintenance, but finally agreed that the lower half could be shuttered with beaverboard to divert the worst draughts. JM only needed to be given an inch to take several miles, and soon persuaded Harry Mercer, the maintenance carpenter, to fully line the entire inside and supervised the operation to ensure that it was neatly done so that a smooth grey interior – including ceiling – resulted. He had even cadged a small sliding hatchway for the customers to use so that we could be snug when they were not about.

Soon after, other inspectors discovered how convenient it was to gather within for tea and lunch breaks. At times, a sort of social club atmosphere prevailed and, when the women inspectors arrived, some men inspectors found it an ideal place to lecture them on the technical and legal mysteries of aeronautics. I got a bit piqued with certain males falling over themselves to teach the females all there was to know about aircraft and inspection procedures when they had previously passed off *my* queries with a curt rebuff!

Once Ron Kitchener, the senior assistant, had just dropped off into a deep repose in a chair out of sight from the hatchway when Percy Palmer, one of the older inspectors, came in with one of the girls to collect a megger for a bonding test. He playfully touched its wires on Ron's hand, unaware that behind his back the girl (Nora) was vigorously cranking the handle in an experimental sort of way. The result was shocking in more than one sense. Ron achieved a Mach 1 lift-off that was immediately terminated by the underside of a stout shelf above his head. His yells were accompanied by the clatter of books and instruments that fell about him like hail as he frantically massaged his hand and head in rapid alternation. He swore volubly without repeating himself for nearly ten minutes; I had never before witnessed such virtuosity in blasphemy.

Another inspector – strongly addicted to alcohol and women in equal proportions – found a variety of ways to assuage his desire for somnolence. He would insert head and shoulders through the 12 inch-square inspection hole at floor level in a Q.6 cabin rear bulkhead and while away an hour or so head-on-arms whilst who, outside, could tell that he wasn't inspecting the inner rear fuselage? He also developed a way of holding fittings and 6 inch rule whilst resting his elbows on the desk and sleeping in a sitting posture; to the casual observer he could have been carefully checking dimensions. One day he fell into a deep slumber by the surface table that was placed like a desk for convenient dimension checking; Johnny Marlow passed a couple of turns of string around his lap and the chair seat, tied the ends and crept out, persuading Ernie Shepherd to tell him that Duggie wanted him. The slam of the hatch awoke him with a start and Ernie's urgent "Quick! Duggie wants you!" galvanized him into action; he was halfway through the door before realizing that the chair was still attached.

I liked to watch inspectors checking airspeed indicators, altimeters and oil pressure gauges, using water-tube manometers, bell-jars and screw pressure-balances which were based in the View Room. Later on a fuel tank pressure-test bay was installed. In the early days, when the chippies brought their pots of casein glue for inspection and labelling, Johnnie's response was often: "Let it stand for four hours, then chuck it away and make a new lot!" One day a chippy brought a pot of glue for inspection and was told that Johnnie was upstairs in the inspection office, so he took his glue pot up there to him. As it happened, Mr Frankland, the designer from Percival's, was in the office, and after Johnnie had stirred the mixture and declared it fit, Mr Frankland turned to him with an amused grin and said: "What do you know about glue anyway?"

Johnny left the Inspection Department soon after to take charge of the fitting and sheet metal section in DeeKay. Ernie Shepherd was his replacement in the View Room and my job was expanded slightly to collect serial numbers of all the main components of aircraft as they arrived and before they disappeared into various departments for stripping and repair etc. Every major component had a unique serial number and could, through its record cards, be traced right back to the origin of its raw material. For example, if a serial number read 'HX/SB/R/HC/PAC 456,' we could tell at a glance that it was built by Hills & Company of Manchester sub-contracting to Percivals, had been rebuilt by Shrager Bros and overhauled by Herts & Essex.

We had, in the past, kept a book in the View Room for listing any components that were transferred from one machine to another. From time to time a fitter would visit the View Room and ask for a particular unit to be transferred from one aircraft to another. Whoever was on duty at the time would record the details in the book and the fitter would sign the page, which went to the Chief Inspector while we retained the carbon copy. This system was quickly altered when it was found that according to records, a particular Proctor returned to base after rebuild with two propellers, three mainplanes, four undercarriage legs and two instrument panels!

Once, I helped one of the inspectors when he surveyed Q.6 X9406, which had returned for repair after stalling in at 20 feet, to the detriment of its undercart; it was decreed that it would henceforth have a fixed and trousered set of wheels. At about that time Q.6 X9454 was placed aboard a QM at Duxford to be transported to us for routine overhaul. In common with every Q.6 after the prototype, its wing centre-section protruded some 12 inches outboard of the engine nacelles (X9328's centre-section outer ends finished level with them). When the lorry crew found that the vehicle could not negotiate certain gaps and turns with its 2 ft extra width, and were faced with strongly objecting local law men, they hacked through the centre section inboard of the engines and threw the nacelles in on top of the mainplanes, which had been carefully laid along the bottom of the trailer beneath the fuselage. Just for good measure, they also hacked a couple of feet off the nose. Faced with so much scrap woodwork, it was decided that the wing and nose sections of P5638 should be married to salvageable parts of X9454 to make one servicable aircraft; thus X9454 ceased to exist and P5638 lived to fly again. Such are the fortunes of war.

As many Simouns as practicable had been rebuilt from available parts, and the residue had been consigned to the bonfire. Only two were converted with de Havilland engines & propellers and Proctor undercarriages at Broxbourne, and all had been sent to Luton for test flight and delivery because the longest run at Broxbourne of 680 yards was too marginal for their high landing speeds. All the Simouns were fitted with 'back-to-front' throttles in the French manner of those days – back for 'open,' fully forward for 'closed'; even those converted to DH engines had a special lever arrangement to attain this. It was no surprise, therefore, to hear via the grapevine that Simoun No. 81, on test at Luton, had nosed over and bent its prop when the engineer inadvertently snapped the throttle back to shut down the engine!

We had had many fittings of Percival design for the Simouns pass through the View Room, their drawings carrying the prefix 'AC.' Later we had some which were similar to Proctor parts but had the prefix 'AE'; these, we learnt, were for the new 'AE Trainer.' Some of the drawings, I noted, had the name Preceptor in the title box but when the aircraft entered service it was designated Proctor Mk. IV.

After the new hangar was completed, the View Room was expanded into the space vacated by the relocation of aircraft assembly, and this gave us more room for fuel tank pressure-testing and control cable proof-loading. This latter consisted of a winch on the floor at one end of a long bench. At the other end a stout bracket was let into the concrete floor. The cable to be tested was then hooked to the bracket, passed along under the bench and attached to the winch with a large brass-faced spring balance between; on its dial were marked in red 5, 10, or 15 cwt at the loads appropriate to 75% of the breaking strain of each size of cable. I was fascinated to see how the control cables were spliced at the ends and then whipped or served with fine cord after testing; after that they were protected with translucent blue 'Sozol.' Previously, proof-loading had been carried out by hauling on it with a block and tackle cornerwise across the hangar doorway.

Our splendid new hangar had been built parallel to the existing main one and was joined to it by a purpose-built stores of large capacity, accessed from both buildings. The new hangar was twice the size of the old one with full-width sliding doors each end, fan heating in the roof and with a row of offices built on to its outside along its length. Also a super new dope and paint-spraying shop was erected nearby.

With the View Room reverted to its uncomfortable wire cage status and now five times its original size in a cold unheated steel hangar, I agitated to be transferred to the woodwork section on the strength of my efforts at evening classes. I was not entirely motivated by desire for creature comfort; prompted by questions of what I hoped to do after the war, as there might not be too many vacancies for aircraft inspection assistants, I thought there might be more chance of employment for woodworkers, my idea being that houses and furniture would be required in greater numbers than aeroplanes. Also, Ron Kitchener had moved to the hangar floor in order to be more involved so I thought it time for me to branch out as well.

A lot of the dogsbody work in the View Room had been taken over by a marvellous ex-Sergeant Major who looked a score or so less than his 70-plus years; Bill Ablett was his name and when I told him that my maternal grandfather had been a Regimental Sergeant Major in the Royal Artillery, he smiled warmly, patted me on the shoulder and said: "Good boy, good boy!" Asked why he still wanted to work at his time of life, he favoured his questioner with a shy grin and said: "Have to do me bit, I s'pose." I brought into the View Room my large woodworker's toolbox I had made at evening classes and, in answer to his unspoken question, told him about the proposed move. On the day I started in the woodwork section, he insisted on carrying it for me to my place of work; we walked together to the new hangar, he with my heavy box on his shoulder and me with a pair of overalls under my arm – it was a proud moment.

CHAPTER 9

MRS LUCAS – A COCKNEY CHARACTER

Mrs Lucas worked in the dope shop and was our best fabric worker. Her youngest son, Jimmy, was my own age and was one of the shop boys; he had been evacuated with the rest of his school to unite with my own school (Broxbourne C. of E.) at the start of hostilities when autumn term belatedly began in October 1939. Their London home was bombed during the 1940 autumn blitz, obliterating all their worldly possessions; the rest of the family then came to Hoddesdon and obtained local employment. After Mrs L. started in the dope shop, the Lucas family moved to a house in Lower Nazeing – a short walk from the aerodrome – and Jimmy's elder brother obtained a job in one of the local nurseries. At that time the Lee Valley was a major growing area for tomatoes and cucumbers and many visiting pilots were hard put to find our small aerodrome in among all the greenhouses.

Mrs Lucas was the epitome of an East End Londoner and, in spite of many tribulations, was irrepressible in spirit and a stickler for her own standards of conduct; woe betide anyone on the shop floor who let loose a four-letter word within her hearing – especially when she was accompanied by any teenage female workers. A certain rough-tongued 'toughie' was reduced to red-faced jelly when, not realising he was within her earshot, he told someone to: " . . . look wotcha f***in' doin'!" At once Mrs L. berated him with some heat and told him to clear off and wash his filthy mouth out with carbolic and not let her hear him using foul language again in front of "'er young gel" or she would "'ave him up before the boss!"

One day Jimmy was running his finger along the blade at one end of the foot-operated sheet metal guillotine when another lad at the further end experimentally sliced a piece of aluminium sheet, also neatly taking the tip off Jimmy's finger. After first aid and a trip to hospital he was on sick leave for a week or two.

Not long after this episode, another more tragic event heaped itself upon Mrs L.'s shoulders. It was normal practice in the nurseries for employees to start work at about 6 am and depart for breakfast at 8. During that hot summer of 1941, Jimmy's older brother left work at breakfast-time and went for a swim in the nearby River Lee; apparently, he dived from the bank at a deep part of the river and failed to surface. Two days later his body was found wedged in a hollow under the riverbank. The Lee was notoriously dangerous with deep sections where long reeds hid below the surface and only a certain area near to the Yacht Club was normally used for bathing. It was also speculated whether perhaps he had dived in too soon after his breakfast and had contracted sudden cramp. Another wrinkle was added to Mrs L.'s stoic brow.

Sometime later, when my co-worker Les Miller was collecting for the widow of our late mentor, Bert Johnson, Mrs Lucas was among the first to eagerly contribute. "I've 'ad to attend too many funerals love, an' know wot it's like to grieve!" she told him.

Soon after the D-Day landings in France, southern England began to be attacked by V-1 flying bombs and these were followed later by the even more sinister V-2 rocket projectiles that achieved a speed of 3,000 mph in the upper stratosphere before finally contacting the earth at about 2,000 mph. Consequently, one never heard them approaching and a sudden almighty bang was the first inkling of their presence, to be followed seconds later by the roar of their flight passage. At first, the authorities denied knowledge of such weapons, but eventually admitted their existence.

One autumn Sunday the news was released and the tabloids filled their pages with guesstimated diagrams as to their function. I was visiting my eldest brother's house in Cheshunt that day and, pointing to the crude 'artist's impression' on the back page of the *Sunday Pictorial*, I said to him: "I see they've come out into the open about the rockets."

At that precise moment there was an almighty heart-stopping stomach-churning bang that shook the ground; we looked white-faced at one another and Albert remarked: "That was bloody close!" In fact it was about four miles away, as the crow flies, in St. Leonards Road, Nazeing, and had plunged into the middle of the road – where four small boys were playing – leaving an enormous crater and blowing away the houses and bungalows either side.

Now the Lucas bungalow was on a raised bank by the road near the point of impact, and at that moment Mrs Lucas was cooking Sunday lunch in the kitchen while Mr L. was reading in front of the living-room fire. The blast completely wrecked the dwelling, causing Mr Lucas to be badly burned by the fire and Mrs Lucas to disappear completely; I think it was nearly a week later that her body was found in a tree over a mile away.

The four boys playing in the road where the V-2 struck were virtually vaporized and I heard later that the father of two of them became an atheist from that moment.

CHAPTER 10

JOHNNY L.

Raffles were a way of life at Broxbourne in the war years: tools, Savings Certificates, little luxuries, black market sweets, booze, anything in fact that might raise interest in the punters and revenue for the particular instigator. Soon after I joined, someone raffled a motorbike at 5/- a ticket – and to me, as a special concession out of consideration for my lack of years and modest salary, half a crown (2/6d); needless to say I did not win it!

Sometimes an item might be raffled as the only way to get rid of it with some small profit. One character had a venerable Austin Seven of questionable reliability that he could barely afford to run and, despairing of takers at the modest sale price of £5, raffled it at 2/6d per ticket throughout the firm and raised about double that amount. With no petrol available except for essential journeys, cars could seldom even be given away! The winner of that particular raffle could not drive and did not want the car, so the raffler bought it back for a fiver, pocketed the rest and continued to use it!

One day, a particularly notorious leg-puller put it about that he had raffled a donkey, and pinned up a notice saying that it had been won by John Marlow, who was at that time View Room Inspector. We were astonished, soon after, when Johnny L. came to the View Room hatch and asked JM if he would be prepared to sell him his prize.

"What for?"

"Well, I want to use it to ride to and from work."

At that point, JM went red in the face and was seized with a sudden bout of coughing.

Johnny L. lived in North London about 20 miles away. In a somewhat quavery voice, JM then asked if he had considered feed and keep for the animal.

"It can sleep in my bike shed. And I will ask Mr Frogley to let me graze it on the field whilst I am at work."

The question and answer dialogue continued for a time and in the end I think JM said he would let Johnny L. know but thought that the beast might not be strong enough for workaday transport.

When he had departed, we all gave way to our various bouts of hysterics. John Marlow was convinced that he was serious although Ron Kitchener wondered if he was indulging in a subtle counter leg-pull. The whole thing became a popular topic among the younger element with imaginations running riot at the prospect of Johnny L. riding into the sunset astride a long-eared quadruped, his thin legs scraping the ground as they went.

I had not thought of Johnny L. as particularly gullible; he had been one of the pre-war staff and we had become acquainted during my stint in the stores when he and I were tasked with the job of labelling parts and components of a number of aircraft brought in on RAF Queen Marys. He was in charge and I deferred to his instructions. Later on, he was told to assist me when I had protested that with the increased number of staff I had difficulty coping with all the teas, buns, sandwiches and fags demanded and expected to be delivered quicker than I could cope. But as he cycled to and from North London each day and in consequence left early, by the time I most wanted help he was ready to leave for home.

Soon after the donkey episode John Marlow took over the fitting shop and was replaced by Reg Turner. Reg had partnered his brother in a motorcycle retail business in Edmonton and had been directed into war work by the Ministry of Labour, and thence to us. A pre-war flying member, he once owned an Avro Avian that previously belonged to Miss Winifred Browne. His most famous adventure occurred during his early pupil days when, flying solo in a Club DH.60 Moth, the throttle jammed open at 90 mph; after no less than 18 attempts to land the machine, his predicament became apparent to the management and Roger Frogley took off in another Moth to guide him over to North Weald, where the long runway gave him confidence to switch off the engine for a dead stick landing.

Reg entertained us with another chapter regarding Johnny L., this time concerning the Desoutter Mk. 1; this particular machine, G-ABMW, had been sent to us for refurbishment for service impressment and, having passed through the woodwork, fabric & paint shop, was being put together by yet another Johnny, Johnny Osborne (brother of Dave who was shop foreman when I first joined). Johnny Osborne had been made up to foreman ganger and was given Johnny L. to assist him in the task of reassembly and making 'BMW airworthy. Soon after, Johnny L. began to worry Denis Green – now promoted to Assistant Works Manager – to upgrade him to chargehand. Denis had plenty to concern him apart from Johnny L.'s particular whim, and one day when he was discussing a thorny problem with Reg, Johnny L. came into view and approached Denis with about his tenth request for charge-handship. Reg recalled that Denis's shoulders sagged, he clapped his hands to his forehead and exhaled forcefully through his cigarette, spraying ash and smoke all over his office. In exasperation, he conceded to Johnny L. that he could consider himself chargehand, but only on the Desoutter project under Mr Osborne and with no increase in salary. Johnny L. went away in triumph, grinning from ear to ear.

Denis turned to Reg and, shrugging his shoulders, said: "Well! What is there in a name anyway? And no one else is involved."

Reg chuckled when he told us, and said that from then on Johnny L. took his teabreaks in that part of the canteen reserved for chargehands and Inspectors.

I do not remember Johnny L. leaving but, during the summer of 1943 or maybe 1944, I – with a cousin and friend – went to see the Army Exhibition in Oxford Street on the bombed site that had once been the main John Lewis store. On the way home afterwards, when about to board the Hertford train, I noticed two RAF LACs smartly turned out in their 'best blues' chatting with their female companions at the station buffet. At that moment, one of the LACs went to the counter, returning with beverages and buns; his familiar moonface was smiling: not the grin of a simpleton but of a competent airman in full control and enjoying himself with his companions – he was of course, Johnny L.! He did not see me and, with our train due to leave, I had no time to greet him. As the train pulled away from the platform, I wondered who had been pulling who's leg a couple of years before!

After the war, Jock reminisced to us about his pre-war doings at Broxbourne and mentioned how he thought that Johnny L. was slow-witted and incompetent; he admitted to calling him names and making his life a misery and, at one time, being taken to task by L. 'senior,' a well dressed 'city gent' type of man, who came down from London especially to investigate his son's complaints. I prefer to think that Johnny L. at that time was probably confused with such leg-pulling which, as I know from personal experience, can be particularly debilitating to self-esteem and confidence. Maybe in the end, he fought back at his tormentors by playing up to their jibes and, in the final analysis, showing that it was *they* who were the idiots.

CHAPTER 11

ENGINEERING IN WOOD

I found aircraft woodwork immensely satisfying and, as assistant to two of the best joiners in the firm, was able to make a modest contribution. Bert Johnson was a craftsman of the old school with an up-to-date outlook and totally undismayed by aviation technology then prevailing. Basically a joiner, he had experience in many aspects of woodwork and woe betide any who dared refer to him as a carpenter! His experience in tennis racquet manufacture was put to good use for making laminated formers and wingtips, and cricket bat-making added expertise for longeron splicing (or 'scarfing' if you insist!). I had been proved wrong: ball games did have some use after all.

Actually, up until the war, Hoddesdon and district had been a centre for the manufacture of sports goods and gymnasium & playground equipment; such firms as T.M. Gardner and Burts & Sams were renowned for such products. This fact put Broxbourne Aerodrome into an ideal position with a ready-made work force of ideally skilled woodworkers within the district. If the foreman had a tricky job or needed a special jig, he usually called on Bert. His time spent pattern-making paid off when working from engineering drawings to close limits. Jack Odell, the other joiner, was younger but equally skilled, and between them they guided me in the proper way to do things and the right tools to buy.

They were working on a Proctor port mainplane when I joined them and it was near completion; they had spliced new tip-ends on both main spars and were engaged in replacing the wing ribs on them. My first job was to plane 4 ft strips of spruce to ¼ in square. Bert wisely discouraged me from using my Marples wooden jack-plane and offered the use of his splendid Stanley '4½' iron smoothing plane; it gave the strips an almost mirror finish. I was later given the job of attaching some of these strips to form around the wing nose-ribs to be assembled to the wing.

After a spell on some empennage units, we were given a Proctor fuselage/wing centre-section as our next joint venture. By that time, and encouraged by Bert and Jack, I was told to make a new centre-section landing flap on my own. In the words of my late mother, I was "thrilled to bits." Working from one of Percival's superb production drawings made me think that I was helping to build real aeroplanes at last; I followed the drawing print assiduously and was delighted that it passed inspection first time. Until 1943, various teams of woodworkers repaired, rebuilt and modified complete fuselage/centre-section assemblies. There might be six or seven units at a time under repair, each with a group of thee or four chaps in attendance, but usually two men and two boys. As well as rebuilding big chunks of fuselage and centre-section, we had to carry out the 'floor mod'; this involved removing the ply-balsa-ply cabin rear floor sandwich and replacing it with a complex hollow structure of members and intercostals carefully designed to allow for adequate moisture drainage. (It appeared to us as if some aircraft flew with incontinent crew members.) To install this mod the aircraft had to be inverted, and it was a splendid sight to see all hands heaving, straining, grunting and swearing as the machine described a 180° slow roll from hand to hand until it rested on trestles with its cabin brow 6 inches from the floor. Later, each aircraft, as it arrived for overhaul or repair, was stripped to its component parts in more easily handleable production line methods.

Splicing in new sections of ply skin on the fuselages and wings demanded some skill; the minimum splice width was 1 in 9, so that a section of 1/16 inch-thick ply had to be feather-edged from thickness to nothing in a 9/16 inch width. There were no disc sanders, so it had to be done with a razor-sharp smoothing plane finely set. Placing a new piece into the top-decking, usually between formers, was in effect a frustum of a cone, so that accuracy was at a premium in order to attain a flush repair. To secure the new patch in place whilst the glue dried we used narrow strips of thin ply with ½ in x 20 swg brass gimp pins set at 1 in intervals; these were placed onto the ply over the joins and members and hammered home as quickly as possible, four men hammering away like the rattle of machine-guns. When the glue had dried, the strips and pins were removed and the joint sanded flush.

I sometimes had to make the new stern-posts, which were 5/8 in-thick spruce sandwiched between 1/16 in-thick birch ply glued on to give a finished thickness of ¾ inch precisely. Accuracy of planing was important for thickness, truth and parallelism. Once the glue had dried the piece was finished to size, bevelled and notched to accommodate the longeron ends. Rebuilding the fuselage stern was a another task that had to be accurately set up using plumb lines and levels and inspected before & after glueing and during ply covering. Tailplane and fin attachments were all-important to ensure proper aerodynamic balance.

As well as the Percival products, H & E overhauled a number of types and makes of aircraft. Once, we rebuilt a couple of de Havilland Puss Moths, another time an Avro Commodore registered G-ACZB (until it left us with serial number HH979 and the usual camouflage and yellow paint job). Between 1941 and 1943 we had a run of Miles Magisters interspersed with two or three impressed civilian Hawks and Whitney Straights.

But in the main Proctors were our speciality – Mk. Is, IIs and IIIs – and toward the end of the war some Mk. IVs came for overhaul and modification. Comparing the Proctor and Magister was like comparing a Bentley with a Ford Eight, I thought. Proctors were really a service development of the luxurious civilian Vega Gull, which was a 4-seat cabin low-wing monoplane with 6-cylinder engine, constant-speed propeller, nicely appointed cabin and tasteful grey leather upholstery and trim. The Miles Magister, also a low-wing cantilever monoplane, was a Service trainer based on the Hawk Major: simple structure, two tandem open cockpits, 4-cylinder engine and fixed-pitch wooden propeller. For some strange reason, Miles Aircraft always applied the plywood skin of their machines with the grain direction of the outer plies running at right-angles to the lengths and spans, whereas Percivals fitted the ply to give maximum cantilever beam strength to fuselage and wings – outer grains lengthwise and spanwise. Some years later this became the subject of an amusing encounter!

After 1943, a steady stream of Proctors enabled the firm to organize rebuild on a production line basis. They were first dismantled and the main components were then stripped and inspected in the old hangar while engines and propellers were dispatched to the makers for refurbishment and the main components passed to the woodworkers who carried out repairs and mods; after this they were sent to the dope shop for the fabric to be made good or renewed. Meanwhile, undercarriages, cowlings, fairings and bits & pieces went through the detail and sheet metal shops and, after painting, were stored in mobile wire cages ready for reassembly onto the appropriate aircraft. Several gangs of fitters, each headed by a chargehand, would take over the repaired components & parts and rebuild the aeroplane. Usually, each gang had two or three aircraft at a time: one on ground tests, one half-built and one just started.

Each aircraft was completed and test-flown prior to final repaint to ensure a pristine paint job for delivery flight. Its serial number was temporarily sprayed graffiti-style with a suitable colour to contrast with the assemblage of old paintwork, red dope and cockpit green. Mr Mills, the caretaker of the school where I attended woodwork classes, once asked why those aeroplanes flew around painted all those pretty colours!

As well as those previously mentioned, many different Service aircraft visited Broxbourne for a variety of reasons; some were lost, some were on official business and some, I suspected, contained pre-war Club members calling in for a nostalgic drink at the Club, which still operated a licensed bar. Until late 1940, sheep were grazed on the field: the Frogley family, who owned the aerodrome, were farming folk. Jed Frogley 'senior' was the father of 'Buster' and Roger, who were H & E directors. The sheep belonged to Jed and, when the Air Transport Auxiliary Anson appeared in the circuit, a mad panic ensued to round up the sheep and dangle the windsock.

Albacores, 'Stringbags,' Fulmars, Skuas, Battles, Gladiators, Oxfords, as well as the usual retinue of ATA taxicabs, all found their way into Broxbourne, nestling among the lakes of Nazeing tomato and cucumber nurseries. Only highly-skilled pilots ever tried to bring in Spits and Oxfords due to their high landing speeds; it was with great interest therefore, one evening in late summer as we left work, that we saw a Mk. Vb 'Spitter' in the circuit. The pilot obviously knew his aircraft: perfect approach, gentle touchdown, then braking to a stop with plenty of field to spare. As it taxied toward us, Len Mills (another teenage woodworker and son of Mr Mills the caretaker) and I were curious to see this veteran paragon of a pilot who had brought such a hot machine into our small field so skilfully. After the engine had stopped, a slim figure of some 23 summers, clad in the navy blue uniform of the ATA, emerged from the cockpit. Hatless, her nicely waved brunette tresses shone in the evening sunlight as she smiled at us and asked if we would be so kind as to chock the wheels. Mesmerised by this shapely goddess and delighted by the sound of her Roedean accent, we rushed to oblige and knocked into one another in our haste.

Later, as we cycled home, Len kept repeating: "What a spot-on girl! Wasn't she though?"

Dreamily, I could only concur. Many years later, I learned that our glamorous ferry pilot was Mrs Diana Barnato-Walker.

To my knowledge, there were no fatal crashes upon Broxbourne aerodrome itself until 1953, which for such a small field is remarkable, although three minor incidents during the war years, all involving ATA pilots, are worth recording. A lady ATA member misjudged a landing with a Fairchild Argus and endeavoured to bury the evidence in a Home Guard gun pit at the extreme end of the longest runway; it transpired that she had been a pupil of our incumbent Harvard test pilot, who sadly admonished her as she climbed out.

"As I told you many times, 'When in doubt, f*** – er – go round again,'" he ended lamely.

"Why, Mr Hall! Fancy you being here!" was her astonished answer.

When Proctor wheel bearings got a bit worn and the brakes were slack, the wheels tended to rotate in flight due to the airstream catching the portion protruding below the spat; this created a rumble in the cabin that could only be stopped by applying the handbrake. The Proctor handbrake was designed to lock on only when the button was pressed, although if grabbed and then let go it would fly off again. However it was a dangerous practice to lock the wheels in flight; when flying a Proctor from its base to Broxbourne for overhaul, one pilot must have suffered wheel rumble because as it touched down, the aircraft bounced once, touched again and then flipped over onto its back and in so doing converted a routine overhaul into a major rebuild.

The third event was an Anson bringing in some ATA pilots to fly away a batch of Proctors. Coming in on the short run, it was down and running toward the Nazeing New Road with still too much speed when the pilot did the only thing possible: he turned it sharply at the last minute and came to rest at right angles to its path of progress. The aeroplane stood still momentarily, then flopped sideways as its overstrained undercart collapsed.

Alec Ellis, one of the gangers and an old hand from pre-war days, had a brother, Harry, who was an ATA pilot; we caught a glimpse of him in a Crown Film Unit film about the ATA at our local fleapit. Word got around one day that he had to deliver one of the still secret DH Mosquitos and hoped to give us a buzz to show it to us on the way from Hatfield; it was a bright sunny day when the sound of twin Merlins stampeded us through the hangar doors to view this beautiful machine as it skimmed the field a few feet from the grass. It may be difficult for anyone today to realize how fast, sleek, powerful and modern it appeared to us all in those far off pre-jet days; the thrill of it lived with me for days after. Our Proctors – by no means ancient-looking at that time – seemed dated and angular by comparison.

I had first seen a Mosquito unknowingly one Saturday in late autumn 1941 whilst cycling near Waltham Cross; it appeared all-black in the late afternoon sky and, not having seen its like before, I thought it might be a German raider and, as it circled, took note of its unusual features from the safety of the shelter of Theobalds Bridge.

I described it as follows to my Inspector colleagues later at work: "It had a tail unit like a Blackburn Skua with the fin & rudder forward of the tailplane; the nose was level with the engines and similarly shaped to a DH Dragon Rapide – and it went like hell!"

One of them said it might be a Westland Whirlwind, but another correctly guessed at a Mosquito, which he had heard of but no one had yet seen.

More excitement stirred the work force when a visit from HM (in exile) King Peter of Yugoslavia was announced. Everyone rushed around like houseproud Mums surprised by unexpected guests, tidying and sweeping. We were told to remain at our posts during the Royal Visit and not to go rubbernecking but, as we stood at our benches awaiting HM's arrival in the hangar, Jack Wynne, our woodwork foreman, passed by and called out to Bert: "If the King wants me, tell him I'm in the 'bog'!" In the event, the King never left the field, so we in the workshops never saw him.

During the war years H & E staff numbers grew from 30 or so to nearly 500 at the peak, and inevitably some unforgettable characters emerged. Tom Green, Denis's brother, was another woodworker-turned-ganger and was renowned for his caustic wit. Once, one of his gang was crooning to himself "*I'll never smile again, until I smile at you . . . ,*" a popular dance tune of the time; Tom stood it for a while and then bawled out: "You won't bleedin' *breeve* agin if you don't shut up!"

Works foreman "Chic" Huckle was another unique character; his rough-hewn features and baleful glare belied a surprisingly kindly nature, but nonetheless he did not suffer fools gladly. Often criticised for his attitude and lack of sartorial elegance (misshapen blue serge suit, jacket distorted by carrying innumerable heavy objects, and stained tan cloth cap, its peak permanently unbuttoned), he was, nevertheless, totally devoted to his allotted task of ensuring that the machines were completed on time. Once, Den Green, by then Assistant Works Manager, was tearing his hair out to find two special switches needed to complete an aircraft for flight when Chic arrived on the scene, calmly produced the items from his bulging pockets and asked what all the fuss was about; Denny just smote his own forehead with closed fists in exasperation.

One day the Kimm twins approached him to report that they had completed a given task and needed another; Chic scratched his head for a second or so and then confessed: "I don't know what to give you; you're two such ugly buggers!" Another 'character,' young "Jumbo" Radley nearby, overheard this remark and, in a devil-may-care mood due to imminent call-up, called out: "You're no bleedin' oil-paintin' yourself mate!"

A hopeless ex-farmhand, his gangly gait and bowed legs earning him the nickname "Texas," had been invalided out of the Army, directed to us and put to work with the stripping gang, where it was considered he would do the least damage; he was egged on by his leading hand (a notoriously plausible leg-puller) that he might have the makings of a first-class fitter and persuaded him to approach Chic on the subject; when so confronted, Chic looked at him in disbelief and asked him to repeat the question.

"I want to be a fitter. 'Sailor' says he thinks I'd be a good one!"

For fully five minutes Chic stood, hands on hips, baleful deep-set eyes regarding the, by now, squirming questioner from head to toe as if he was something disgusting brought in by the cat. Finally he made his pronouncement: "You? A fitter? You couldn't fit my arse to a lavatory seat!"

When going away for his well-earned statutory one week's holiday, Chic set out from his home near Ware on the same train to Liverpool Street on which he normally travelled to work; his family had preceded him on an earlier one. Leaving the train at Broxbourne Station, he was halfway along Nazeing New Road when someone remarked upon his natty attire. He got as far as saying: "Yes, I'm off on my hol . . . !" before spinning round and dashing back to the station.

Ted Horseman was a joiner from the East End of London with all the traditional cockney wit and humour. One of his attributes was the ability to blow thunderous raspberries; by compressing his lips with finger and thumb, he blew a blast that resonated throughout the hangar. At about five minutes to seven each evening he would call out "Tools away!", then, shortly after, "Boxes Shut!" followed by "On the Clock!" This usually resulted in a cheer from the gang at which he would encore with his famous 'Bronx cheer,' to the delight of us younger ones.

By mid-1943 Herts & Essex had its own well-established Home Guard platoon, and those who were not otherwise engaged in other Civil Defence duties were obliged to join the 'ESX 10' unit. Ted Horseman was one such reluctant recruit and one evening, when the platoon were gathered in the billiard room of the club for a lecture, Sergeant Harry Mercer (the maintenance carpenter) was holding forth when the double doors behind him were flung open and Ted burst in, tunic undone, hat askew and equipment slung over his shoulders any old how. He raised his hand to his lips and delivered a real block-buster of a raspberry behind the Sergeant's back.

"Was that intended for me, Private Horseman?" demanded the indignant Harry Mercer.

"Nah, that was just among the boys!" he replied. "*This* one's for you!" and he blew an even louder one right in the Sergeant's ear! Soon after, he was given a fatigue punishment and told to polish up a section of the defence barbed wire!

Syd Simpson was a fitting ganger who had been drafted to us from the North; he had a pleasant Yorkshire accent and was quite knowledgeable about woodwork. Once, when I was sawing a fuselage panel he, in passing, indicated my panel saw and asked "Is that 'Enry Disston?" Pleased that he had recognized my prized quality tool, I answered in the affirmative and proceeded to have an enlightening conflab with him. In his gang was a large but very capable girl from London, another Ministry of Labour draftee; her squeaky little voice hardly fitted her robust frame and Stan Kimm was adept at imitating it. Syd had the misfortune to have a slightly weak bladder and was obliged to relieve it somewhat suddenly at times; on one occasion he was sitting in a Harvard and took the opportunity to make use of the urinal tube.

Suddenly, from beneath the aeroplane, Eileen squeaked: "Syd! There's all water coming out under 'ere!"

Quick as a flash Syd called out: "Aye, loov. Ah've joost cleared a drain eyelet!"

Another time he was down the field away from the hangars attending to an aircraft and decided to relieve himself by the tailplane. Stan crept up behind him quietly and called out in a fair imitation of Eileen: "Wotcher doin', Syd?" Syd hurriedly 'adjusted his dress' – as they put it in Gents' lavs at that time – and tried to appear as unconcerned as if he wasn't standing there wetting himself.

In January 1943, 14-year-old Les Miller, nephew of Jack Odell, joined the team and was put to work much as I had been. Being young and not having any tools, he was allowed the use of some of his uncle's. Planing some spruce strips with a small block-plane, Bert remarked: "Every time you put that plane to work, it starts crying!" Les favoured him with an old-fashioned look and then got the message that it needed sharpening! As he was my junior, I was often rotten to him and bullied him sometimes; nevertheless we got on well together and during lunch breaks on fine days we liked to explore the newly-arrived aircraft awaiting attention from the stripping gang; Jean Batten's Gull Six AX866 (G-ADPR) was one in particular, and Les confided to me recently that he still has a portion of fabric from it showing its original colour scheme.

One day we were exploring the dump where some of the old pre-war machines had met their doom. There was, at that time, the skeletal remains of a Hawker Audax donated by the RAF for Air Training Corps instructional purposes; Mr Whittaker was CO of a local squadron and he had arranged it but, due to the lack of premises and Whittaker leaving for pastures new, the machine had been left to rot on our dump. Not far away stood a chemical fire extinguisher and this evoked the interest of one of the other new young lads, who wanted to know how it worked.

"You have to turn it upside down," I explained, "and bash that brass knob hard on the ground."

Well, I wasn't to know that the idiot would actually do it! Les and I suddenly realised that our lunchtime was over; as we hurried back to our work we last saw the lad trying to force the nozzle into the earth so as to bury the evidence.

Mention of fire extinguishers reminds me of another incident. To test the fuel flow of the Proctor engine-driven fuel pumps, a large wheeled rig with an old fuel tank fixed to the top was set in front of the starboard wing, clear of the propeller, a pipe leading from it to gravity-feed the aircraft carburetters. The pipe from the engine pumps was disconnected at the carburetter end and fed into a quart measure when the engine was run at certain specified revs. The pumps had to deliver sufficient fuel to fill the jug in a given time, and an inspector with a stopwatch was in attendance to ensure satisfactory function. It was also a requirement that fire extinguishers were readily available, and the wisdom of the latter rule was soon proved!

On the day in question, the particular aircraft was facing the front of the main hangar with its tail pointing toward the distant Clubhouse. Les Barber, the ganger in charge, was at the controls, while I was strolling back from the Clubhouse after delivering a message. I don't know if a spark from the exhaust ignited spilled fuel, but I saw Les suddenly fling open the door and jump to the ground with more haste than elegance as the starboard mainplane fabric burst into flames. Passing at that moment was a rather unpopular Inspector, who grabbed a handy extinguisher and turned it onto the conflagration – with great success. On the other side happened to be someone who had reason to dislike the said Inspector, and he in turn snatched another extinguisher and, spraying it over the wing, managed to empty most of its contents over him!

Jack Odell left our group to become a rate-fixer as the firm had conceded to pressure to generate a bonus scheme; in his place came a joiner who had previously worked for Belling Lee at Enfield. His name was Fred Curtis and he had a repertoire of naughty jokes that went on for about three weeks, after which he began repeating himself. I don't know who gave Bert more pain: me, Les or Fred. Once Fred came up to me and said: "Doesn't that old chap get into a rage sometimes!" Fred later formed a duo with another new joiner and Les and I stayed with a more tranquil Bert. Alas the trio split up early in 1944 when Bert sadly died at the relatively early age of 54; he had been gassed in the first World War and suffered from a serious illness when employed as Clerk of Works during the construction of Hunsden RAF Aerodrome. I was devastated when Bert died; he had spent so much time showing me the way to be a proper woodworker and lecturing me on the use of tools. Even today, when I'm working with wood, I fancy I can feel his presence over my shoulder, approving – or otherwise – how I am tackling the job.

Les teamed up with a young boat-builder, Cyril Blanks, to refurbish the fuselage of a captured Gotha glider for use by trainee paratroops. I had one or two small solo jobs on empennage components and then for a time became itinerant snag repairer, which was interesting as I had to make odd repairs when damage occurred during assembly and ground tests, such as patching the cabin roof skin after shrapnel had punctured a Proctor at dispersal during an air raid. The first time I rode in a taxying aircraft was when repairing a battery box at a time when the aeroplane was on pre-test-flight final checks. It was nice to move around the different aircraft. After this I was teamed up with a former Shoreditch cabinet-maker, Bob Wilkinson (Wilkie), rebuilding fuselages.

In the spring of 1944, a dozen or so brand new Harvards flew into Broxbourne as vanguard of a contract to modify these Canadian-built aircraft to RAF standards. Beautifully made by the Noorduyn Company, they wore a transatlantic air of peacetime flying, being all yellow and showroom-shiny; were it not for the RAF roundels one might have expected to see a white-helmeted Clarke Gable swinging out of the cockpit, or Errol Flynn lounging nonchalantly against the fuselage. On the day of arrival they were parked in two serried ranks between Clubhouse and hangars and that night stood out in stark brilliance in the light of Luftwaffe flares during an air raid; luckily, no bombs were dropped within the vicinity. Next day, all movable aircraft were dispersed around the aerodrome perimeter and draped in camouflage netting. After modification and a requisite coat of matt 'dark earth & dark green,' each aeroplane had two or more test flights and volunteers to act as rear cockpit ballast were called for. Such was the enthusiastic response to this request that a strict rota was drawn up, but I never did get my turn! Mr Ewers, our PADO (Personnel Air Defence Officer) did, though, on an aerobatic test, and became rather ill. Perhaps Mr Hall was disgruntled about his fire-watching times; all employees not engaged in other Civil Defence or Home Guard duties were obliged to serve a fire-watching stint overnight at suitable intervals in case of incendiary air raids. Local residents disliked the supersonic crackle that issued from the tips of the paddle-blade Hamiltons when Harvards were climbing at full chat in fine pitch: this probably bred the germ of their antipathy toward the 'drome in later years.

By late summer 1944, all woodworkers were moved to Bridgeworks, leaving only Fred Curtis and his mate to act as itinerant snag repairers. Both halves of the wallpaper factory had earlier been taken over and the staff and directors conscripted into the Company; this gave us an extra workshop big enough to accommodate Proctor fuselages, though the air turned blue when the lads were nudging the 6 in-taller Mk. IV fuselages through the doors!

For those of us in the 16-19 age group, this period at Bridgeworks was a happy time, with plenty of interesting work and a nice atmosphere due in no small part to the youngish foreman and under-foreman, Don Saunders and Len Binks respectively. Les and Cyril soon joined us after their ex-Luftwaffe glider job had been completed. Ron Kitchiner had wangled a transfer to the woodworkers and was happily employed repairing tailplanes. Another kindred spirit in our age group was Ted Green, youngest brother of Denis and Tom, whose parents ran a pub in Ware; Ted must share the blame for getting me interested in motorbikes. At about that time he bought a 1939 250 cc Velocette that had been stored throughout the war years and was virtually new. Ted was allowed petrol for work because public transport from his home to Broxbourne was at that time difficult in the extreme. A lot of US Army Air Corps flight crews patronized his folks' pub and through them Ted had managed to wangle aircrew leather coat and trousers; he looked quite smart in these with his white helmet and goggles, astride his pristine 'Velo.' One day in the canteen (the former Clubhouse), Bill Carpenter the welder called across to him: "'Ere, Ted! A bloke asked me the other day: 'Wot's that bike your test pilot rides?'"

At about this time I had been split from Wilkie and was going it alone by concentrating on rebuilding Proctor fuselage front portions from forward of the rear-spar location. We had a new manager, Mr Bob Barnett, and he had completely reorganized the repairs on a production line basis so that by breaking down the rebuilds into small sections he was able to get things moving by familiarity through repetition. We no longer referred to the aircraft number but to 'Works Order' numbers; in this way better bonus payments resulted. There was a lot of agitation regarding bonus times, and union representatives were forever having meetings with the management. I had now been persuaded to join the Amalgamated Society of Woodworkers (Section 3, Juniors, 3d per week). At one stage, disagreement led to rumours of a strike, but I pointed out that I, for one, would not strike. Fred Curtis – with all the enthusiasm of the converted – said that there could be pickets on the gate and they might persuade me to keep out. At that I grew very red in the face and stated that with one brother in Burma with the Chindits and another in the RAF, I certainly would not dream of striking, and if any of those yellow-bellied 'non-coms' said I should, I would tell them to stuff their bloody union! In the event all was settled amicably so it was only academic.

Because of animosity toward bonus schemes by the ASW, there was a lot of reluctance by the members to join the scheme, but one day someone showed me an endorsement to the rule book stating in effect that, due to wartime control of engagement, any member who was employed in an establishment where such a scheme existed may cooperate to work on bonus: so I joined the scheme. At the next meeting of the branch at the Labour Hall, I was reported for a serious infringement of the rules. Brother Smith has joined the bonus scheme! Shock! Horror! "I'm not your bleedin' brother!" I thought secretly. After much debate among Branch Officers – who were, to a man, conscientious objectors, and totally unfamiliar with our work at Broxbourne –

it was reluctantly agreed that *'in view of the aforementioned rule amendment, no further action be taken against these brothers.'* Stupid sods! Later, I tackled the branch representative who had reported me, after finding out that he, despite the rules, had joined the bonus scheme. "I left the ASW," he informed me, "and joined NAFTO (National Association of Furniture Trade Operatives) – a better union than the ASW – and there is no objection to bonuses and piece-work." In later years, I was to learn that such hypocrisy is meat and drink to the 'Luddite' Mafia.

Some time between VE-Day and VJ-Day we began restoring Bridgeworks to its rightful owners. All the fuselages had gone and we helped to re-install some of the strange wallpaper equipment and storage racks. One by one, as we finished our allotted tasks, we were posted back to the aerodrome. Ted Green, Les Miller and I found ourselves reunited in a small Robin hangar next to the dope shop, where we were employed repairing and modifying Kirby Cadet training gliders for the Air Training Corps, an interesting change from Proctors; we hoped that a winch would be installed to test-fly them but were disappointed. Les and Ted were anticipating call-up. I had already been to St. Albans for my medical and been informed that I would not be called up due to being catagorized 'Grade 3.' That damned coke stove and a spate of yellow jaundice, no doubt! So, with the end of hostilities as well, we were all in a frivolous frame of mind. Les found some large and very mutilated wood-screws in an old packing-case; we graunched the slots a bit more, cut the heads off and laid them in a neat row along the upper boom of a Cadet wing-spar that Ted had just repaired; when he returned from lunch and perceived what he thought was blatant vandalism of his splendid handiwork, his lower jaw dropped about twelve inches. Luckily, before rushing to authority and screaming "sabotage!", he set about removing the offending objects with his largest screwdriver. Les and I remained to watch until the first screwhead tiddlywinked from under the blade and rolled along the floor, before dashing off to a suddenly-remembered previous appointment to avoid getting a London-pattern screwdriver blade through our black hearts.

It became evident about then that Herts & Essex Aviation as we knew it would soon cease to exist. All employees in turn had to sit before panels of self-important petty bureaucrats set to determine what we could do and where to direct us to best serve the new Socialist Utopia. I was only slightly mollified by the attitude of a girl in front of me.

"I don't give a damn what you lot want!" she retorted; "I'm getting married in a couple of weeks and leaving work anyway!"

Red-faced embarrassment all round among the four-eyed, fat, grey-suited consortium! I was incensed, though, by the attitude of a mere clerk at the Labour Exchange who assumed that, because I was a woodworker, I should be pleased to go to a firm of pre-cast concrete manufacturers repairing grotty old concrete moulds. At the start of the war he was a second-rate counter hand at the local branch of Williams Brothers grocery store and had wheedled himself into a safe Civil Service job throughout hostilities; now he had the gall to dictate what I should do. However, in view of my unlikely call-up, I stayed on with the commercial section that H & E had started in order to diversify into manufacture of table lamps, chandeliers and folding steel tubular babychairs.

Not all wartime staff went at once, although a good portion of them left early in 1946. A lingering memory is of seeing "Slosh" Saunders, cousin of my former foreman Don, with his arm around a colleague's shoulders – after a convivial lunch – harmonizing a sentimental song as they weaved through the hangar door for the last time.

Three dismantled Proctor Mk. Is had arrived on lorries earlier; it transpired they were to be the first post-war civil aircraft. One (P6251) was quickly converted and repainted silver with dark blue letters proclaiming its new civil registration G-AGZL. A new pilot wearing a smart white flying suit arrived; this was Denis Cather, a former instructor from pre-war days, now demobbed from the RAF. He spent a lot of time taking people for joyflights at 10/- for a 10-minute trip until the new Herts & Essex Aero Club (1946) Ltd. really got going. A brand new Auster Autocrat in shiny cream paint with green letters (G-AGXI) was obtained by the Club, as was a dismantled Tiger Moth, which a colleague on the table lamp group insisted on referring to as a "Gipsy"; he had had a number of flying lessons at Broxbourne pre-war, so could be excused the error, I suppose. All these goings-on were a great morale booster to me. A select few of the wartime staff were retained to maintain them but, alas, I was not numbered among them. Some of us who had never flown were keen to try a joyflight but found the prospect of shelling out a ninth of a week's wages at one go somewhat daunting, so we formed a 'Joyflight Club' by paying 1/- a week into a kitty and taking our flights in rotation; my turn came up after I'd paid in 6/- and I had my first aerial view of my home town.

A week later I was out of a job. I heard years later that some joiners were kept on in the commercial section in anticipation of a contract to rebuild a fair number of Proctors for civilian use. Foreman and previous ganger Syd Simpson – a man of considerable aircraft experience – had been flown in 'ZL to the contractor's headquarters to try to sell our services and assess the task for the firm; he had apparently done a great job because Bob Barnett the manager heard through a crony that we were in with a good chance. The management, however, decided that holding onto woodworkers for an indeterminate period was not worth the risk and so it all came to naught because suddenly we all received our cards and that was that!

It was a devastating experience for me; for 5½ years, from 14-year-old schoolboy to 19-year-old man I'd known no other employer, and now I had to find some other way to earn a crust. It did not cheer me at all to be told that there was plenty of building work about for skilled woodworkers.

TOP: October 1947, in front of Vic Ercolani's Gemini G-AJKV. From L. to R., standing: Pete Jackson, Bill Tate, 'Slosh' Saunders, Jim O'Donnel and Eric Soulard. Sitting: Ted Collins and Johnny Farrow.
BOTTOM: The author's flight of fancy.

TOP: The ex-Charles Lindbergh Miles Mohawk G-AEKW.
BOTTOM: Our unpredictable 'chief,' W.S. 'Jock' Ogilvie (autumn 1947).

TOP: L. to R. Robin, Dick, Denis, Barnie & Bill with Dragon Rapide, possibly G-AKTY (summer 1949).
BOTTOM: L. to R. Dennis French, Dave Parkhouse, 'Mitt' and Roy Ogilvie in front of Rapide G-AGZU, ogling the office girls, summer 1950.

TOP: G-ADHE, the Moth Major we rebuilt for Desmond Norman.
BOTTOM: VH-ASP, an ex-Service Taylorcraft Auster V we rebuilt for an Australian customer.

CHAPTER 12

PEACETIME PROSPECTS

I presented myself to the mercy of the local Labour Exchange a week after being made redundant from H & E. I had spent that week making a chicken house with built-in nesting boxes – to a design given me by Wilkie – as a special favour for my mother. She had started to keep chickens during the war years to supplement our one-egg-per-week ration; rationing remained in force until 1953.

She was in ill in bed at the time and, whilst at her bedside receiving instructions re domestic requirements, we heard the sound of a fighter plane beginning a dive. The noise increased to a screaming crescendo as the propeller tips oversped and went supersonic, then it stopped suddenly with a thump that we felt through the floor. As I cycled to the shops a few minutes later a Fordson 3-tonner Auxiliary Fire Appliance was making its way toward Broxbourne. My spare-time National Service had been as a messenger in the National Fire Service. We later learned that a RAF Mustang had power-dived itself deep into the middle of Broxbournbury Park; there was little that the Fire Service could do, hence the lack of haste of the Auxiliary I had seen. We were then living in Ware Road on the northern fringe of Hoddesdon. Broxbournebury Park was south of the town about three miles from our house.

When attending the Labour Exchange, I made it quite clear to the clerk that I was not in the business of patching up grotty concrete moulds. I had been briefed by joiner workmates to state that I was a 'joiner/improver.' This I did and so was annoyed when he gave me a card to attend for interview at Chaston's in Essex Road, the pre-cast concrete people. After protest he mollified me somewhat by saying that they were building houses and needed 'second-fixing' joiners. Second-fixing joinery is putting in doors, staircases, cupboards and window casements etc. after the brickies, carpenters and plasterers have done their worst. For the uninitiated, carpenters do all the heavy rough woodwork such as rafters, flooring, framing, concrete shuttering, etc. and joiners do all the finer work like hanging doors, fitting skirtings and assembling built-in wardrobes, kitchen cupboards and window fittings.

I was, at the time, running my 1935 350 cc Calthorpe motorcycle. As you will recall I had previously been introduced to powered two-wheelers by ownership of a 1935 98 cc two-stroke Cyc-Auto autocycle; this machine hardly won any prizes for reliability, I spent more energy pedalling the damned thing than driving it, so it was hardly a powerful mode of transport. The engine tended to stall if I tried towing off any rice pudding skins with it and it oiled up its plug about every 20 miles. Once, when travelling from Hoddesdon to Woodford (Essex) and back, I took four spare clean plugs with me, and had to change all of them *and* then clean two of them again before reaching home.

Arriving for the interview a trifle windblown and with my cheap goggles hanging around my neck in what I fondly imagined was a debonair fashion, I was quickly passed to the young foreman in the joinery shop, a cramped corrugated iron shed with no power, lighting or heating services. He regarded this unknown quantity with a certain justified suspicion, but when I recounted my experience he reluctantly agreed to take me on as an 'improver' at 1/11d an hour. I duly reported for work on the following Monday, with my suitcase-style tool box resting on one pillion footrest and roped by its handle to the rear mudguard, and clutching a batch of cards and Ministry of Labour forms for the office.

There were three joiners, including the foreman, and a young lad; they didn't look too favourably on my cabinet-maker's-style tool box, being used to the traditional heavy canvas bag with two handles into which tools were slung with careless abandon. However, when given the task of making drawers for a kitchen dresser, I set about it in the way that Wilkie had instructed and they realised that I wasn't just a pretty face. They were less impressed a week later when we were sent to the new houses in Wormley for 'floor-bumping'; I had to confess that I did not then possess a claw-hammer, and was obliged to stop off at the local tool shop to repair the omission whilst on the way to the building site.

Alf was the eldest of the quartet and really a carpenter; he took charge of the floor-laying and the young lad Pat and I worked on his instruction. First, the floor joists were lain at right-angles onto 'plates' which were 4 in x 3 in timbers cemented to 18 in-high openwork brick walls set on the foundation raft; the joists were set at standard 16 in centres and nailed to the plates. After the first couple of floorboards were nailed athwart them against one wall, the next six were laid alongside and pushed against them with powerful screw-clamps whilst someone stood on on top to prevent them bowing upwards and bursting out; they were then nailed in place with large iron 'cut-nails' about 2 in long and 1/8 in thick, tapered and with a little 'L'-shaped head.

At the end of that day, I went home with a splitting headache and bruised & blistered hands. Not only were the nails hammered home, they had to be set below the surface with a nail punch. Later, the foreman gave me an earful for carelessly making several 'half-crown' hammer marks on the boards; I had not but it was pointless to protest.

It was disconcerting to work by tradition rather than from drawings, especially in view of my ignorance of the necessary tradition. Only the site foreman was allowed to handle the plans, which in any case were merely a sketchy sort of GA (General Arrangement) drawing. I could not understand how a kitchen-dresser unit was supposed to be built in, and the foreman grew cross when I had not installed the damned thing quickly enough for his liking. Plaster and cement dust irritated my bronchial tubes and I hated working with warped, unseasoned and knotty 'builders' tree-wood'; my precious cutting tools suffered from hidden nails, grit and cement. Once, when chatting in the tea hut about our previous jobs, the others plainly thought me a lineshooter because I mentioned that certain aircraft jobs needing tolerances of plus or minus 1/64th of an inch.

"Don't be daft!" objected one. "A pencil line is near a sixteenf fick!"

"That depends, of course, on how you sharpen it!" I said, at which he sulkily reappraised his *Daily Mirror* sports page.

Once, Alf asked me to measure a door rebate.

"Eleven sixteenths wide by nine sixteenths deep," I told him.

"What the bloody 'ell's that in plain English?" he demanded.

"Sorry!" I remembered, "it's what you'd call 'a bare freequarters be a full 'ahhfinch."

"Well, why dincha say so first?" he grumbled.

I dare say he would have been really baffled had I said: "Point six eight seven five by point five six two five inches."

Soon after, there occurred one of those events which create what novelists refer to as a 'watershed' in one's destiny. (I am not quite sure, but it sounds rather like a melting igloo!) Anyway, one day I had gone for a cycle ride in the late afternoon along the towpath from Dobbs Weir towards Broxbourne, with a view to returning via the main road. About halfway along I met Wilkie cycling home from the other direction.

"It's fate!" he cried, grinning from ear to ear, "meeting you like this."

Taken aback at first by the emotion of his greeting, I too became excited when he revealed the reason. He was still in charge of the table lamp/chandelier production at the aerodrome and said that 'Jock' Ogilvie, the new Chief Engineer of the aviation section, had asked him if he knew of a competent woodworker who would be prepared to carry out other jobs on the engineering side of things between woodwork repairs.

Was I interested? As my eldest brother might have put it in his own peculiar perverse idiom: "can a swim duck?"

Next day found me in earnest conflab with W.S. Ogilvie Esq. in the new hangar, standing by a Tiger Moth being given a 30-hour service by Jim Lane, Eric Soulard and Howard Barnes (Barnie), all wartime stalwarts. Jock was impressing upon me the fact that in a small team we were all expected to take on a variety of tasks. I was trying to convey to him that that was exactly what I wanted and would be delighted to do so, when the Managing Director himself, 'Buster' Frogley, joined us and Jock explained the reason for the interview. I think he was unsure if I understood the difference from wartime to the working conditions now prevailing.

Mr Frogley had fewer doubts. "He should be all right; after all, he had a good all round apprenticeship with us in the war."

This generous contribution to the proceedings swung things in my favour so, having agreed upon a salary that Jock thought a bit high and I thought a bit low (£4-10s per 47 hr week), I next had to seek permission from the Labour Exchange. In those days of 'Control of Engagement' one could not change jobs willy-nilly without their say-so; luckily, the ex-grocery-counterhand clerk was absent and I poured out my well-rehearsed tale of woe to the more sympathetic ears of a kindly middle-aged clerk. In the end, all that was necessary was amiable mutual termination of employment with the builder, provided that all the paperwork passed through the Labour Exchange.

The joinery foreman obligingly wrote a note of termination which I submitted to the office manager at Chaston's; I think we were both relieved to part company. Indignant concern at my dismissal was expressed by the office manager, a charming Irishman with whom I got on very well; when I explained to him that it was at my request and also the reason for so doing, he was pleased for me and did all he could to speed the parting; he liked the said foreman even less than I did. So, on the following Monday morning, I transported my tools once again on my faithful Calthorpe into the main hangar.

It was grand to be back. Someone had taxied Proctor I G-AGZL into an obstruction and graunched the front wingspar during the weekend and the lad who up till then had coped with minor repairs felt a bit out of his depth with a spar job.

"You've arrived just in time, Smuthie," was Jock's gratifying greeting. "This machine has to fly to Rome at the end of next week!" Despite his impeccable Edinburgh English, Jock always pronounced his pet name for me as though spelt with a short 'u' rather than a short 'i'; if he addressed me as "Mr Smith" I knew at once that I was in dead trouble; on the other hand, when he called me "Harry," he obviously needed a special favour. It was very strange how everyone at home suddenly seemed better tempered!

Herts & Essex Aero Club (1946) Ltd. was expanding its fleet and getting into the swing of post-war activities. As well as the civilianized Proctors G-AGZL & G-AHLW and Tiger Moth G-AHMF, another Tiger, G-AHLS, and Hornet Moth G-ADOT had been bought already operational. Auster G-AGXI had gone to make way for more Tigers, and Ted Darlow had returned from the Royal Navy to be Club Secretary. Two flying instructors, 'Ace' Gilbert and George Parker had joined Dennis Cather. Component parts of another Tiger, G-AHRS, were in the process of assembly and Certificate of Airworthiness (C of A) overhaul for the Club.

At that time, Herts & Essex Aviation Ltd. still remained as a separate company and was under contract for engineering maintainance and repair of Club aircraft. Some other interesting aircraft inhabited the main hangar; Miles Hawk G-ACYX (placed third in the 1938 King's Cup Air Race at Hatfield behind Alex Henshaw, who won it in his Mew Gull G-AEXF), fitted with trousered wire-wheeled undercarriage, was slightly modified and re-registered F-BCEX to the requirements of its new owner, a Monsier Pougnet of Paris. Comper Swift G-ABPR, which had arrived dismantled, was soon rebuilt and stored pending engine replacement. Another Proctor, G-AGZM, had been robbed of some parts for the other two and was awaiting restoration on a low priority.

A single-seat Tipsy arrived, fully rigged but standing on its nose with wingtips fore and aft on the trailer; it had a camouflage paint scheme and red, white and blue stripes underlining black civil registration letters. Its owner, Neville Browning, had apparently flown it during the war. Jock said that mahogany was used in its spars and some good straight-grained stuff had been obtained from Wrighton's furniture factory who were about to take over all our new buildings for the manufacture of bedroom furniture. So I looked forward to rebuilding the Tipsy in an anticipatory, mouth-watering sort of way.

During the late summer and into early autumn we were still doing most of our work in the new main hangar. 'RS's mainplanes were refabriced and the aircraft was readied for re-assembly. Three new members had joined: Bill Tate, an ex-RAF rigger, Alan Slade, an engine fitter who, like me, had been employed only in a civil establishment, and Johnny Farrow, a young school-leaver, to help around and learn the business. Also, just before I had re-joined, a tall ex-WAAF had arrived to work on engine and airframe maintainance, swinging props, refuelling & so on; I think she became bored with sewing when we were recovering the wings of 'RS because she left soon after.

Eric and Barnie went with Jock and Syd to arrange for the collection of 10 ex-RAF Tiger Moths the Club had bought; five were readied to be flown to Broxbourne on a limited permit, the others were dismantled and arrived by road on lorries. Leaving Jim in charge whilst he was away, Jock instructed the rest of us to look to him for instruction, and that began my introduction to general aircraft servicing. I really enjoyed the routine of wheeling the machines out each morning, the refuelling and oil-checking and general daily inspections. Standing on the top cowl of a Tiger and filling its tank was far superior to standing on a builders scaffolding sawing away at rafters and such! I revelled in the delicious aromas of aviation fuel, doped fabric, engine oil and the tang of exhaust when an engine started up. What a thrilling sound to me it was to hear the deep-throated bark of a Proctor's 4 inch-diameter exhaust pipe as its Gipsy Queen's six cylinders burst into life – rather like a vintage green Bentley, only more so.

I began to find my way around Tiger Moths as we completed 'RS for its C of A inspection. One day, Jim was soldering the front brake cable of his M20 BSA motorbike when Jock happened by and asked what he was doing.

"Oh! Er, just fixing the nipple on 'RS's port brake cable," was Jim's quick-thinking reply.

Jock nodded and said "fair enough," and was almost out of the hangar when he realized; he turned back, red in the face, and stormed at Jim. "Ya dizzy b*****!" he roared, "Tigers don't have brakes!"

By the time 'RS was finalized for test-flight, we had retreated from the new main hangar in the face of the invasive hordes of Wrighton's men who began ripping channels in the concrete floor to insert power cables for the heavy machinery of furniture production. The old hangar was little changed from pre-war days and we set about clearing the offices for general use. We still used the new stores between the old and new hangars, so the engine shop in the old one remained in use for top overhauls and the like.

Jock was earnestly thinking of trying for his 'B' licence which would allow him to sign out airframes after overhaul. He already had unrestricted 'A' and 'C' for signing out aircraft prior to flight but 'B' & 'D' were needed for airframe and engine overhaul. Wartime works manager Bob Barnett possessed a 'B' so he signed out our overhauled airframes as a consultant, but he had left soon after termination of the Ministry Contract and was in business for himself.

Young Jack Davey and myself had our benches set against the wall adjacent to the lathe and milling machines and near to the large sliding main doors where we began to be involved fitting the Tiger Moth aileron differential box modification which was devised to prevent foreign bodies jamming up the mechanism. (37 years later I was able to advise Cathy O'Brien of SkySport Engineering at Benington when she was fitting the same mod!) To carry out this mod it was necessary to make large cuts in the wing fabric to gain access; this introduced me to fabric work and by accident I found that successful tautening can be achieved when the temperature and humidity is not all it should be; having sewn up the fabric with our best herring-bone stitching, Jack and I proceeded to dope 1 in-wide Egyptian tape over the sewed join and when dry, doped 2 in serrated tape over that and sloshed some coats of red dope all over the repair to tauten the existing fabric. A short while later, we were both alarmed to notice that it was 'sweating' with minute water drops all over and the dope was going a pale washed-out matt pinkish hue. We had not realized that the temperature had dropped in the October late afternoon and humidity had risen. Jock arrived at that moment and started to berate young Jack; I had to confess that I was responsible and that Jack had merely followed my lead, so to speak.

"Well, you should know better, Smuthie, being a technical bloke!"

Knocking-off time hove nigh, so Jock told us to leave it overnight but to turn the mainplane over so that the patch was protected somewhat. With trepidation next morning we turned the mainplane topside-up and were amazed to find that the patch was beautifully tight and smooth; by the time Jock arrived, we had brushed another coat of dope on to hide the pinkish 'blushing' which dried nicely in the warmer temperature and presented him with a nice smooth and glossy doped finish.

"That's better Smuthie!" he rejoiced; "why didn't you do it properly first time?"

Jack and I exchanged glances behind his back; I winked and he grinned back.

At about that time the Club sent away four Tigers for rebuild, two to Marshall's of Cambridge and the other two to a firm in Kinross, where our former manager, Mr Whittaker, was in charge. 'Slosh' Saunders was also working there and came to Broxbourne with Whittaker and another engineer from Scotland to finalize details. It was good to see Slosh again and they approached me to learn about the aileron diff. mod.

I think it was just before Christmas that the Tigers returned resplendent in the Club livery of silver nitro-varnish with glossy mid-green letters and struts and with a scimitar-shaped flash on the fin and rudder. Syd Simpson left at about that time and Slosh returned with the Tigers from Kinross to take over his post as chargehand. I was sorry that Syd had left, but pleased to have Slosh in his place. Meanwhile, Barnie and Jack Davey had received their call-up papers and went into the RAF, and we carried on rebuilding other Tigers ready for all the flying anticipated in 1947.

About then, the commercial side of H & E had been wound up and the aviation engineering had been absorbed to become part of Herts & Essex Aero Club (1946) Ltd. With DeeKay workshop no longer used for commercial activities, my woodwork benches were moved in and it became a general workshop for various tasks carried out away from aircraft and hangars. A welding bench, pillar drill and small grinder were already installed, left over from the war years and used for the commercial stuff afterwards. The small furnace and salt-bath had been taken away some time before and in their place a rough office for the use of the then chargehand had been erected.

It was whilst working on a Tiger Moth mainplane in there one afternoon that I heard a loud bang and looked through the window toward the new dope shop (now Wrighton's polishing shop) in time to behold Tiger 'RS momentarily poised on its nose on the apex of the roof before sliding down to smash itself between the buildings. Jim Lane and I dropped our tools and bruised our arms as we passed through the workshop doorway side by side. Luckily for the recently soloed lady pilot, only her pride was hurt, although the aeroplane appeared not to have any useful parts left. She had taken off, climbed a couple of hundred feet and then turned 180° back across the aerodrome. A sudden fierce gust had overtaken her airspeed and poor old 'RS, deprived of lift, just fell out of the sky.

Jock commented – belying the relief he felt at her lucky escape: "Why do it to our new aeroplane? You should have taken 'MF, it comes up for C of A next month!"

That awful winter of 1946-47 created the most uncomfortable working conditions I have ever experienced, which were made worse by the fuel crisis. With so little flying possible, we concentrated upon C of A overhauls and repairs. Encasing ourselves in extra coats and a welter of woollies and wellies helped a bit, but restricted movement horribly; to say that conditions were unconducive to glueing and doping is akin to observing that Labrador in December is not recommended for sunbathing, yet we managed, by concentrating large inspection lamps, to generate enough local heat to effect the usual run of repairs to leading edge riblets, patches, and so on. When I left my casein glue pot filled with water to soak overnight it became solid ice by morning. Wrighton's closed down for three weeks and paid off all their staff in line with government orders to conserve fuel. We kept going by only working during daylight and hand-cranking the petrol pumps. Our routine for starting the Gipsy Majors in the extreme cold was to flood the carb, pull the propeller over four compressions, flood it again, another four pulls and then try "contact." At that stage the magneto impulse usually stuck and when it had been freed with light oil, surreptitious tapping and a lot of foul language the whole process began again.

A rapid thaw following the weeks of intense and protracted cold created more problems, not least for the owner of Puss Moth G-ABLY, who arrived with a hired pantechnicon to collect his stripped-down aeroplane on the day when the River Lee overflowed and began invading the aerodrome. We had dismantled the machine for C of A quotation the previous autumn and, due perhaps to the owner's dismay at the quoted price for rebuild, it had been stored in a wooden shed in an unused part of the field. Noting the rising tide halfway between us and the Lee, Slosh advised leaving the van on comparatively high and hard ground by the hangar and instructed us to manhandle the fuselage and components to it from the shed. A temporary unpaid apprentice, Rob Capper and I wheeled the wingless fuselage assembly whilst the others carried the naked wing frames and components. Meanwhile, the van driver, growing impatient, decided to bring his van to meet us. Halfway between hangar and shed it bogged down axle-deep in the soggy ground; there was no time to tow it out, by then Tennyson's Brook began babbling around and rose to the Puss's wheel rims. We finally got it to the hangar and comparative safety, but the van remained stuck for a week. The flood reached its zenith by the hangar doors in late afternoon, by which time the Clubhouse was awash to a depth of an inch or two above its floor. It subsided from the field by next morning. Wrighton's were unlucky insofar as the new hangar was about 10 inches lower than the old one. A local ancient reminisced by saying that in his lifetime only once had the field flooded, about 35 years before; it has not recurred since.

As if to make up for winter's ill-humour, spring and early summer were ideal and business was brisk, keeping the Tigers airborne and enabling us to overhaul Proctor I 'ZL in record time for C of A renewal. It was whilst doping its port aileron, which I had just re-covered, that I saw an elderly joiner (remembered from my wartime days in the inspection department when he took three weeks to make an oak case for our new Vernier) talking to Jock. As the conversation ended, he came over to introduce himself and said that he would be working with me. By way of small talk he nodded at my pot of red dope and brush and asked in rather shocked tones: "Do your own paintin', then?" I could see he would be a wow if ever asked to do a DI (daily inspection) on the Tigers. He started work restoring the fuselage of our spare Proctor, G-AGZM (formerly P6259) in DeeKay. As he would not use machinery, I had to knock off from any job I was engaged in to cut up his materials on the circular saw; this was not too onerous a chore, as he worked so slowly. He was a nice old boy, with an unending fund of hilarious anecdotes about characters and events of times past in the local joinery and building trades. His grasp of the aircraft industry, though, was confined to having watched RE.8s and BE.2Cs flying over the trenches in WW1.

(The main structural timber for wooden aircraft is Canadian sitka spruce. For highly stressed structures such as spars and longerons it must be quarter- or rift-sawn, which means that the annular rings or grain should be at 90° to the widest surface to minimise the effects of warping and shrinkage. It must be properly seasoned with a certain moisture content, the grains a minimum number to the inch, a 'run-off' of not less than 20 to 1 and free from knots and whorls. It must also be properly tested for strength and fully documented for its source and verity.)

He knew about quarter-sawn timber but failed to understand why we needed to be so fussy about it on aircraft, and once I had to prevent him using a bit of commercial deal to make a longeron! With our second Proctor 'LW on C of A, a fair amount of structural woodwork needed repair and Slosh (a chippie before becoming a ganger and, later, inspector in the war years) worked with me. We were a good team, which made the work enjoyable and satisfying, despite having to dash round to DeeKay occasionally to see the oldtimer and try to instil the art of longeron splicing. ("Look! It's dead simple, just like half of a cricket bat handle splice, 1 in 9, but it must be accurate to 1/64 in and dead square!") A situation had developed where I, a 20-year-old, was instructing a higher-paid skilled joiner in his early sixties, who had to be guided step-by-step through the sort of jobs I had taken in my stride when a teenager.

I was awakened early on Monday morning, 23rd June; Mother was shaking me and asking if we had ten Tiger Moths. I thought I was dreaming; why should she be interested in our fleet strength? Wakefulness followed when she added: "It was on the wireless. There's been a big fire at Broxbourne and they said ten Tiger Moths have been destroyed."

I was dressed and out of the house in record time. I hoped that the fire had been confined to the Robin hangar, where the Tigers were mainly kept. Cycling down the Nazeing New Road I saw three Tigers and a Danish KZ Laerke dispersed some distance from the hangar and one another. Arriving earlier than usual at the hangar, it became obvious that the time clock would no longer record such a rarity. I was stunned by the devastation. Robin hangar, main hangar and the wooden sheds between were gutted and their contents – seven Tiger Moths, three Proctors ('ZL, 'LW and a new Mk. 5), Comper Swift, Tipsy and all our stores and tools were reduced to ash. So fierce had been the heat that electron-magnesium crankcases had ignited like incendiary bombs and every combustible part had been consumed. Tiger Moth fuel tanks, split and stark on steel struts, surmounted fuselage skeletons, which in turn rested on bare undercarriage struts. On the ground below the engine-bearer frames, fire-blackened and rusty crankshafts, camshafts, gears and cylinder barrels stuck out obscenely from solidified mounds of molten aluminium and electron ash. Bracing wires drooped shroudlike over bleak remains. Danish visitor Morien Hansen had rushed out in his nightwear to save his new KZ Laerke aeroplane and blistered his bare feet on hot concrete. Two of the rescued Tigers had slight damage where wingtips had fouled door frames in hasty evacuation. Three of the sliding doors had been opened from inside, the fourth was still chained and padlocked. The rescuers were unaware that the keys were on the Clubhouse kitchen table; consequently, whilst they were still manoeuvring 'ZL around the door, fire took hold of the wingtip and it had to be surrendered to the flames. The static water tank was drained and a chain of hoses brought more water from the Lea across the field half a mile away. Ex-Army Major Peter Ayles, then resident trainee flying instructor, was overcome by smoke and had to be revived by firemen's breathing apparatus.

By the time we staff members arrived, the fire was out and the appliances had departed. Only the steel main hangar survived as a more-or-less whole structure, windowless and bowed in at the far end where the internal wooden offices and stores had blazed with white-hot intensity. The Robin hangar, just beyond the black wooden sheds attached at the rear of the main hangar, looked as though it had been strafed with 30 mm cannon fire; most of its corrugated asbestos sheets had burst in the intense heat from its store of blazing Tiger Moths.

We were still standing around in a state of shocked inactivity when Jock arrived. Not having heard the news, he had to sit down on the running-board of his car until his knees stopped shaking. The cause of the fire was unexplained.

Safely underground, the fuel storage tanks were intact. The pumps had sustained no worse than scorched paintwork, being on the edge of the conflagration. However, destruction of the main switchboard had robbed them of power and they had to be hand-cranked, a debilitating exercise on a busy Sunday. Jock obtained needle and thread from one of the Club ladies and scrounged suitable linen and a 1 in paintbrush. We found an unsullied drum of clear dope in the paint store, which was brick-built, half under-ground, fire-proof and a safe distance from the hangar, but it still contained four inches of odorous stagnant water, residue from the floods that had defied the suction of our wartime trailer-pump. With these materials, Slosh and I worked on the damaged fabric of the rescued Tigers to get them airworthy.

Wrightons put a spare office at our disposal to enable our girls to start organizing important things like clock cards and wages, and to distribute forms for extra clothing coupons for overalls and such lost in the fire. A disused partition office in DeeKay was expanded to serve as the new stores. Hand tools were obtained and issued to the staff. The firm was not liable for our personal tool kit loss: it was our responsibility to ensure their safety. All my splendid woodwork tools, carefully and lovingly collected at no small sacrifice in pocket money, were lost. My union, the ASW, reimbursed me £4 and the firm made a percentage-of-value *ex gratia* payment to us as a goodwill gesture with no legal requirement to do so. In 1947, Lease-Lend tools had disappeared from the shops and quality British ones were all being exported; it was a long time before I could raise any enthusiasm to rebuild my tool kit.

Another incident occurred during that first post-fire week which could have imperilled our remaining aircraft. Our Tigers and a visiting Avro Tutor were parked 'twixt Clubhouse and hangar when a warning came through that a line squall was heading our way, so Club members, pilots and staff rushed to trundle them into the usable end of the hangar; I helped Jock and two others to push the Tutor in behind the Tigers. The squall hit us when we were about 30 feet from the doors and the aeroplane tried its best to get airborne. We yelled at the others for help; they appeared as blurred shapes seen through a cataract. We got the Tutor tail-first halfway into the hangar and hung on until the storm abated. Rain hit the blackened corrugated iron like a sand-blast and, though it didn't penetrate, it shook down quantities of soot and smuts from the underside onto our damp bodies. Slosh remarked: "We've been through frost, flood and fire for this firm, and now we've got black spot!"

We were all worried about our jobs, but in the event only three people were asked to leave, Alan Slade, one of the office girls (Little Audrey) and the ancient joiner; *two* woodworkers could no longer be justified. Jock apologized to the old guy and thanked him profusely for all he had done (?) and offered him re-employment when things improved. He seemed quite philosophical and unsurprised.

I was sorry to see Little Audrey depart. Earlier, one bright sunny hot afternoon, we were having our teabreak in the Clubhouse Billiard Room – as was our wont – and the double doors which opened onto the field were propped open to circulate a bit of fresh air. Audrey happened along looking for Pam, her cohort; momentarily framed in the doorway, brilliant sunlight shone through her thin summer dress outlining her frilly French Knickers in sharp silhouette. I regarded her with more interest after that.

The rebuild of surviving Proctor 'ZM now had priority and I was told to carry on where the old guy had left off. Despite my efforts to instil into his mind aircraft woodwork requirements, he had made a veritable cods-up of the longeron splicing; it was 1/8 in undersize in the middle of the splice and its thickness had been made up with a gash bit of packing-case wood glued to the underside and roughly levelled with coarse glasspaper. Slosh came along whilst I was contemplating the best way to tackle the problem and, when Jock appeared, remarked: "So much for your fine old craftsman! Young "Smig" here will have to pull it all apart and start again!"

On my 21st.birthday later in the year, my wages rose by five shillings a week.

Three Auster Autocrats (G-AJEG, G-AJEI & G-AIZV) and a red Miles Magister (G-AJGM) were obtained and put to work at once. After clearance of the debris, plans were made to rebuild the collapsed end of the main hangar, re-skin the Robin hangar (once the shattered asbestos sheets which had allowed sparks to spread the fire to the Tiger Moths from the adjacent blaze had been removed), and erect an ex-RAF blister hangar between the two. My somewhat singed woodwork machine was found to be repairable and, in its refurbished state, it was installed in DeeKay. Bob Collins, our welder (retained with his young brother Ted from the commercial section) and I formed an unofficial maintenance gang and ran a heavy cable from DeeKay's switchboard on an overhead wire to the main hangar to operate lights, petrol pumps etc. Hornet Moth G-ADOT returned from Marshall's of Cambridge wearing its Herts & Essex livery. Slowly things began to get back to normal. Whilst waiting for the stores to be re-established, we ran a shuttle service of employees' bikes and motorbikes between the 'drome and Broxbourne Motors, who kept us supplied with split pins and vulcanized the inner tube of the Magister's tailwheel which had deflated with depressing regularity.

Our first DH Dragon Rapide (G-AGZU) arrived in late summer and I had my second-ever aeroplane flight. Some of us had stayed behind after work one evening to act as human ballast to see how the machine would perform with passengers from our small airfield. It was quite a short flight and the landing was reasonable, but he bounced it a bit on touchdown. Taxying back, we mistakenly thought he would go up again but, as Peter Ayles explained to the onlookers unlucky enough to be left off the flight, he went back to inspect the non-existent bump much as a cricketer inspects the bump on a smooth pitch when caught out on a bouncer.

Toward the end of summer, the Westland team visited Broxbourne with the first Sikorsky helicopter in this country (G-AJHW) of the type they were about to produce under licence as the Dragonfly. They were on an extended sales tour and called at the 'drome after arranging to try their sales pitch on a tycoon due to arrive the next day. Bob Collins and I stayed behind that evening to chat with the attending ground engineers, who obligingly explained all about such things as tail rotor steering and cyclic rotor control, and we nodded sagely as though we understood what he was talking about.

Next day we had a grandstand view as the Dragonfly was put through its paces within the aerodrome boundary. One of the tricks they performed was to lift a surviving fire-damaged Gipsy Queen – crated and boxed – and fly around with it dangling some 10 ft underneath, before gently lowering it onto our 4-wheeled flat-bed hand truck. The team stayed a second night and before departure gave rides to the management, pilots and select members of staff, including Reg Randall, the Club barman & general factotum, and Chief Engineer Jock Ogilvie; we lowly ground staff erks were only allowed near enough to refuel it.

An exciting new arrival in the form of a brand new Miles Gemini (G-AJKV) came on the scene about then, privately owned by Vic Ercolani, a long-standing pre-war member and head of London Cabinet Industries. Vic was a charming man and very generous and thoughtful toward us ground crew. For a week or two the machine was kept in the back of the hangar when not in use with a terse 'KEEP OFF' notice in front of it, but due to the fact that we had to refuel and service it, it was not long before we handled and taxied it much the same as the other aircraft.

Bill Tate came to my workplace one day and asked if I could make him a couple of small hardwood blocks for Tiger jacking pads.

"Sure!" I replied, "just give me the measurements, and I'll make them."

He started gesticulating with his fingers.

"It needs to be about so long, and wide as this . . . "

I cut him short rather rudely.

"Look! Just go and measure up what you want and come back and give me the dimensions."

He was away for a time, and returned with a battered piece of pencil roughly sharpened both ends. With a sinking heart I listened to his requirements.

"It needs to be as long as this pencil, as wide as this mark is from this end of it and as thick one end the same; the other end to be as thick as the second mark from the same end and it needs a slot on top just wide enough to take the width of a penny and no deeper than the thickness of a penny."

I gave up arguing and began to make the blocks from a scrap length of walnut 2½ in long by ¾ in wide; the rear ends were ¾ in deep, the fronts 7/8 in. Slots were 1¼ in long across their full widths and 1/16 in deep; they fitted between the tops of our wartime screw jacks that were Percival Proctor-orientated, enabling the aircraft to be jacked up to allow removal of the undercarriage legs. They turned out to be one of the most useful pieces of equipment we had and were still in use long after we had both left the firm. Old Bill's idea was pretty good, even if he did eschew the use of conventional measuring tools!

With a Tiger on 30-hour service on another occasion, Bill was happily checking the undercart whilst Eric carried out an oil change. The method was to wedge a short piece of guttering above the leading edge of the port lower mainplane and allow the waste oil to pour out of the drain plug into the guttering and thence drop over the leading-edge about 3 ft down into a cut-down old paint drum. A slight breeze through the hangar would cause the stream to waver but not stray beyond the periphery of the drum. Once or twice (or "twice or thrice," as Bill would have put it!) his head brushed against a length of dangling cable – as he described it. It was when he scratched his head and his fingers came away black and sticky that he remembered that Tigers did not usually have thick electric cables to dangle.

Prior to the floods and before the winter's end, Bill Tate expressed the wish to buy a motorbike. I had just stripped down the Calthorpe and was in process of giving it a major rebuild and repaint; I wished to graduate onto something more modern and better quality, but was short of cash. Bill expressed interest in the Calthorpe and we agreed a price subject to final condition when overhauled. I painted the mudguards, tank and headlamp with good quality cream cellulose (surplus from the commercial section, earmarked for finishing of baby-chairs!). The rest of the frame and cycle parts were black and I painted a black sweeping curved flash on each side of the tank. When trying to start the beast in our garden there was a sudden 'plop' and the carburetter caught fire! It had snowed about 4 inches deep and I grabbed handfuls of the stuff, ramming it all over the carb until the blaze was smothered; never before or since have I been so grateful for the presence of the horrid white stuff. No damage had been sustained on my beautiful paintwork and when I removed the cylinder head once more, I found a small crumb of carbon stuck onto the inlet valve seat sufficient to allow a flame to blow back into the carb. Rectification only took a short while and I was able to ride it to work next morning for viewing by the prospective new owner.

I got into work before Bill and when he saw me he asked the usual question: "When will you finish the bike?"

I confessed that, unluckily, it had caught fire when I was trying to start it. Immediately his face fell, but he brightened when I said that it hadn't been too serious and asked him to come and look at it outside, parked out of sight at the back of the hangar. His face was a picture of joy when he beheld the machine in all its pristine splendour, and well worth the little bit of subterfuge I had devised.

Early in 1948 another Miles Gemini arrived at Broxbourne; registered G-AJZK, it belonged to the Missionary Aviation Fellowship and was to reside for a short while for final post-delivery checks and fitting out for its proposed African tour. I was given the job of making a special lightweight toolbox of the maximum dimensions suitable for stowage beneath one of the front seats. To save weight I made it of 1/16 in ply with slender spruce stiffeners and cunningly contrived gusseted corners to add strength. Having prevailed upon their foreman, we had it painted in Wrighton's polishing shop and it emerged in splendid glossy black finish. The MAF Engineer was very pleased; Jock, however, was less happy and gave me a right wigging for taking too long on the job. Par for the course. Situation normal!

In early summer a gathering was arranged of MAF members around the aircraft in a quiet corner of the aerodrome for a short service and blessing for both aircraft and crew prior to their African mission.

Some years later, one of our bright young lads (John Chapman) joined MAF as a ground engineer and was with them for some time; he got in touch with me again through a letter I had published in the August 1997 issue of *Aeroplane Monthly*.

Our Ground Staff increased by six new members in the spring of 1948. Stan and Les Kimm returned from the Army; Reg Kent joined us from Miles Aircraft, Peter Bradbury had worked for London Aviation & Motor Services based at Stansted until they became defunct; Jack, a new general labourer, came to sweep the hangars and wash the aeroplanes; and, straight from the RAF at the end of his conscription, a 20-year-old named Ray Clapham. I think I was the first to speak to him when he arrived in the workshop looking lost and about four years younger than his actual age; he told me that prior to his RAF call-up he had started an apprenticeship with Miles Aircraft, now gone to the wall and with assets and debts taken over by Handley Page. He lived locally and had been introduced to the firm by Peter Ayles who, he believed, did so in order to ingratiate himself with Ray's sister. Ray and I hit it off straight away with much in common – aviation, music, entertainment and motorbikes, a friendship that was to endure until his untimely death nine years later.

I was callow and inhibited then and Ray helped me out of my shell. He was the youngest son of 1930s radio entertainer Charlie Clapham, of the double act Clapham & Dwyer. As our friendship grew, I looked at things with more amusement than hitherto. At the cinema for instance, he often saw unintended humour in some of the dialogue; once, he put an absolutely outrageous and unprintable interpretation on one line in the film and hung helpless with uncontrolled laughter over the back of the empty seat in front. Later, when he explained, I too fell about. Sometimes when we met in the hangar we'd go through a routine of mocking false heroics depicted in film dramas.

Effecting excruciating upper-crust accents we might say: "I say! Have you heard? Poor old Carruthers has bought it!"

"Oh, hell! You don't say?"

"Yers, 'fraid so. Silly b***** actually paid three-and-six for it!"

Or Ray might take the mickey out of the typical Hollywood war film where the hero flyer's wing man gets shot down in a spiralling smokestream and he hysterically yells out: "Joe! Joe! C'm back Joe!"

Then, with delightful dumb-show, a quick 'film reversal' to restore the buddy alongside once more with the 'star' wiping his brow in relief and exclaiming: "Gee! Ya had me worried that time, pal!"

Or we'd go through the dog joke routine.

"We shot our dog last week."

"Was he mad?"

"Well, he wasn't very pleased about it!"

Needless to say, Jock seldom found our humour as amusing as we did.

Spring, summer and early autumn that year had been a hive of activity with overhauls, rebuilds and servicing of many aircraft. Comper Swift G-ABUS arrived and was stripped and rebuilt to the requirements of its new owner, Peter Cole, and finished in silver with scarlet lettering and flashes. Jock bade me devise the flashes to emphasise its projected racing career. I painted lightning streaks on the fuselage sides to align with the registration letters and engine centreline, with an additional lightning streak on the outboard face of each wheel spat. Later, when its sponsors – *Black Magic* Chocolates – required it to be painted in the black and gold livery of their product package, I was pleased to note they had retained my original design for the flashes.

I did a fair amount of work on 'US; in addition to the woodwork, I helped with installing the engine magnetos and stripping and repainting the fairings and wheel spats.

I was at my woodwork bench in DeeKay once when Stan Kimm came in with a short length of electric cable. He jabbed the bared end of it toward my hand and exclaimed: "Look, Harry. Live wire!" Naturally I jerked back and he hooted with laughter at the reaction to non-existent live current, pleased to have caught me out. He recounted the incident to the others, including Ray, who next day brought in a cartoon depicting Stan holding a piece of wire that someone behind his back with an evil grin was joining to another length of cable hanging from an overhead light. In front of Stan, I was leaping into the air, arms and legs akimbo, mouth agape and with lightning flashes of electricity sparking around me. The caption was Stan's phrase "Look, Harry. Live wire!"

We rebuilt Miles Hawk Trainer III G-AKNA that summer for our co-director Roger Frogley; it was a 'one-off' type for, in place of the normal de Havilland Gipsy Major engine – as installed in the Service Magisters (as the Hawk Trainer IIIs were more commonly known) – this one was fitted with a Blackburn Cirrus Major. When finished and painted in the Club colours and test flown, a serious snag arose when the ARB refused it a Certificate of Airworthiness, due to it not being recognised as either a service or civilian type.

As autumn of 1948 drifted toward winter I had the opportunity to buy a brand new Triumph Speed Twin motorbike (see Chapter 6). At that time, due to export priorities, a two-year waiting list was the norm. This particular machine had become available due to a colleague of my elder brother having ordered it two years previously and, since married, being unable to afford delivery. I unashamedly borrowed from relatives and friends and arranged to take delivery on his behalf. Then, halfway through the negotiations, the blow fell; I was made redundant!

Management had grown alarmed at the burgeoning wage bill and ordered Jock to reduce engineering staff to 6 during winter. Wrighton's were asked to take any members of staff, but in the event I was the only one to join them. Ray Clapham heard of some vacancies at Hatfield in the DH Service Department and, having first told the Kimm twins about it, set off there on his bicycle. The twins on their motorbike got there first and secured jobs. Unfortunately, when Ray arrived he was told that he was still under 21, and could not be considered; it did little to enhance his peace of mind, as he had just previously met the twins on their way home and been regaled by them with enthusiasm about what a wonderful job it was going to be.

CHAPTER 13

'GEORGE' PARKER

Sydney Harry (George) Parker joined H & E as a flying instructor in 1946; he had been attached to Training Command in the RAF during the war as Instructor with many hours on Tiger Moth initial training. A keen motorcycling Sporting Trials rider, he came to work on one of the first post-war limited-edition Matchless trials bikes. I was keen to chat bikes with him and at first he seemed a little reserved, no doubt justifiably, in consideration of my tatty-looking 1935 350 cc Calthorpe; he probably thought me a bit of a 'yobbo.' Relations improved when he began building a large control-line model of a Hawker Typhoon and found that, as resident 'chippy,' I was a useful chap to know when bits of ply and wood needed machining.

In pre-war days he had been in the Design Office of Percival Aircraft at Luton, and entertained me with several enjoyable anecdotes about design and construction of the Mew Gull racers. Jock always regarded him with respect as a first-class pilot and instructor and told me that George could trim a Rapide to fly with better aerodynamic efficiency than many other pilots. With a couple of other bods I had the good fortune to fly with him in our first Rapide, 'ZU, up through the cloud layers and around the district for about half an hour. Being paid for it at the time added cream on the top. Tiger Moths were his speciality, though; I once saw him fly one upside down across the aerodrome despite it not being fitted for inverted flying, and on another occasion hanging on its prop at zero ground speed into a 30 mph wind with both Handley-Page slots fully extended!

One day he was checking out Club member and pupil Bruno Pini (later to be the proud owner of the ex-Lindbergh Miles Mohawk) and, as they were taking off on the short run, Bruno slammed the throttle shut when the aircraft was still climbing and at about 300 ft, and yelled through the Gosport: "What'll you do now, George?"

With a quick side-slipping 180° turn, George 'dead-sticked' it downwind back onto the aerodrome in a faultless three-pointer and succinctly retorted: "That!"

I once asked him: "Do you know who invented the postscript, George?" When he shook his head I answered "Adeline Moore."

His reaction was surprising, to say the least; looking a bit puzzled he said: "That's a girl's name."

Non-plussed, I asked if he knew what I meant by 'postscript'; again he shook his head. I explained that if one added an afterthought in a letter it was usual to prefix it with the letters 'PS.'

This time he nodded.

"Well! 'PS' means 'Postscript'!"

"Ah! I see!"

But he still walked away with a puzzled expression on his face.

Although subtle humour was not his particular *forte*, he was highly amused one afternoon when chatting with Jock in the hangar and I approached Jock and asked if he would care to purchase the tie I was wearing.

"Whatever for?" he asked.

"It's too tight around the neck," was my reply.

Whilst Jock stared at me in disgust, George exclaimed: "He's pulling your bloody leg!" and burst into roars of laughter, which heightened Jock's disgusted expression.

In 1951, George went back into Design Office employment, this time with the de Havilland Aircraft Company at Hatfield, although he continued to instruct at Broxbourne on a part-time basis. In later years, when I too was in a DH Design Office – but on the other side of the airfield at Manor Road – I had a job that required the installation of special equipment in a Venom drop-tank; it pleased me to note that its assembly drawing was signed 'S.H. PARKER.'

Many years later, one evening in the summer of 1986, I had a surprising telephone call. It was George. How he managed to obtain my number I know not, but we had a wonderful chat and he horrified me with tales of personal physical problems and then went on to chat about various projects in which he was involved. When I asked how he managed to cope, his reply was typical of the man.

"Well, you have to keep active, otherwise you might as well hand in your chips."

Later, he was in contact with my friend Tim Moore of SkySport Engineering concerning Tim's project for a replica of the pre-war Heston racing aircraft. He had been involved in the original design and was able to supply a lot of useful data, including aerofoil profiles and such. Tim gathered a lot of data, and was about to start building the replica when his partner Cathy O'Brien was tragically killed, whereupon the project was shelved. I have not heard any further news of George since, either.

CHAPTER 14

'TOSSER'

Throughout my school and working life there was always at least one fly in the ointment 'giving forth of a stinking savour' and spoiling an otherwise agreeable situation. Schoolmarms and bullies polluted schooldays; the original foul-mouthed works foreman at Broxbourne did the same at the start of my working life. In the early fifties a much less significant nerd bestowed his haemorrhoidal presence upon my tranquillity.

'Tosser' joined the staff at the end of 1949. He turned up in RAF-style raincoat and, as Jock introduced him, glowed with simpering bonhomie. Of rubicund complexion, he had what novelists kindly describe as 'rough-hewn features' topped with unruly crinkly black hair. Jock mentioned that he had served in the RAF and knew Ray Clapham. Ever boastful of his unremarkable time in the Service, he recalled his association with one or two RAAF members by calling all and sundry 'Cobb' – short for 'Cobber.' 'Tosser' was not his real name, the soubriquet given herewith being more printable than the nickname bestowed on him by us, his workmates.

Once employed at Thruxton by a firm operating a DH.84 Dragon, his last job had been a lorry driver's mate. He brought no toolkit, and we doubted his technical employment at the Thruxton job. Although offering no evidence of a regular female companion, he was always yacking on about girls (which he pronounced 'gurrels,'), said with a lascivious smirk on his pimply visage. Later on, Ray – an enthusiastic Shakespeare buff – dubbed him 'King Leer.'

His first job was to assemble and rig the tailplane, elevators and rudder of a Club Auster, and I had been instructed to oversee and check his work. It became obvious that he was utterly clueless how to begin and, due to the urgent need of the aircraft, we ended up with me going through it step-by-step and using my own tools. For all his help I could have done the job in half the time on my own, and I wondered what sort of CV he had presented in his application, and what questions Jock had asked at his interview!

Ray Clapham rejoined the firm later and was appalled to find him working at H & E. He confided that Tosser had been known as a sycophant in the Service, always sucking up to NCOs and trying to be photographed with them. He frequently irritated Ray by recalling their Service days, starting with the phrase: "'Ere, Cobb! 'Joo 'member when we woz on Daks at Neveravon . . . ?," tee-hee-ing with his silly grin and continuing with some tedious cameo Ray would prefer to forget.

As Tosser possessed no toolkit, Jock – unwisely in our opinion – gave him tasks that usually required no personal hand tools, for example daily inspections and spray-painting. Bob Collins, in addition to welding and plant electrical maintenance, had hitherto carried out the spraying activities, but when he left, no one else had been allotted the task, so Tosser got elected. Not that he was particularly competent: he paid scant regard to any sort of surface preparation – so long as the paint went on, he cared not a jot if the surface could double as a bit of sandpaper. And his method of cleaning the spray gun was to dunk it in a can of thinners still attached to the air hose – much to the detriment of its seals. It wasn't until Pete Jackson later took responsibility for spray-painting that the aircraft once again looked smart. Our compressor was a portable petrol-engined device that Jock insisted be operated only outside the hangar; sometimes I saw it on the apron, its air hose snaking in through the door, and its Villiers engine at full chat with the compressor safety valve blowing off at 100 psi whilst Tosser chatted to the 'gurrels' in the office.

He worked hard to ingratiate himself with Jock; that he too often succeeded we put down to Tosser's luck and a particular blind spot that Jock suffered, due, in part, to the following incident. In fine weather the aircraft were brought out of the hangar for daily inspection and parked on the grass next to the gravel road between Clubhouse and hangars. The office girls cycled in each morning later than the engineering staff. Tosser always seemed to be underneath one or other of the aircraft just as they were arriving, ostensibly to inspect the undercarriages, but in reality to craftily look up the girls' skirts as they pedalled by; a glimpse of stocking-top and suspender would have his eyeballs distended like bloodshot golfballs. If a girl looked his way, he studiously inspected the nearest bit of structure above his head. During one such voyeuristic episode, he was beneath an Auster lying between the undercarriage legs (the only ones he should lie between, and preferably when it was taxying, as some cynic observed) and, as the particular wench glanced in his direction, he looked up and, by chance, spotted a small crack in the welded joint of the steel tubes forming the Auster undercarriage leg. Quick as a flash he scrambled out from under and rushed into Jock's office to triumphantly announce that 'EI would have to be taken out of service with a cracked undercarriage leg. Jock confirmed that it was so and later remarked to Pete Jackson, who had earlier cast doubts as to Tosser's personal hygiene, that he was a good bloke to spot the snag. Pete's opinion of him was less than ours; his grudging reply was, in effect: "If you say so. But he still stinks!"

Although never attempting to buy any tools, he was never backward in coming forward to borrow from his workmates. Some of us put copies of the following little piece of doggerel on the lids of our toolboxes:

'The fellow whom we all despise,
Is he who borrows and never buys.
And a lower scrounger yet, one learns,
Is he who borrows and never returns!'

Needless to say, he did not take the hint! He boasted about passing the test to get his driving licence and sometimes hired a car to impress 'gurrels.' In those days, few of us could afford to run a car and some even thought me rich and extravagant to own a fine motorcycle! So we all looked askance at him when he turned up in a hired Ford Prefect once or twice when going out for the evening.

One day he asked to borrow my small hand drill. I had replaced the one destroyed in the fire with a novel cast aluminium 'Leytool,' no more than 7½ inches in overall length, with fully enclosed gears and well designed grippy-top handle. Not having a side handle as per the traditional ones, it was extremely useful for getting into awkward corners.

"I've got to drill this 'ole, Cobb, and your drill is the only one that'll do it," he carolled. I was delighted to inform him that it was in use and he would have to manage without. Despite his pleading, I was adamant; I had an urgent job on hand and did not wish to be disrupted. He went away crossly and returned later with a grotty loose-handled conventional drill that he had had the gall to borrow from someone else for me to use whilst he took mine ("I must 'ave it, Cobb!"), and was then quite put out when I told him in no uncertain terms that I had no intention of changing to an inferior drill borrowed by him in preference to my own. As he persisted in arguing for the arrangement, I seethed.

"Look!" I said quietly, "why not do what I did?"

"Wassat, Cobb?" he gurgled in simpering anticipation.

"Bloody well buy your own!" I shouted.

So loudly in fact that Peggy, who ran our stores, looked out to see what all the fuss was about. Somewhat shaken, he quit the workshop. How or if he resolved the problem, I never cared.

When he did some work on a Proctor, Barnie and I checked it over and had to do it all again ourselves in order to bring it within acceptable safety standards. On another occasion, when the firm was awarded a small contract to re-cover a set of wings and control surfaces for a private Auster, I was ashamed at the standard of work he perpetrated. Serrated tape crudely doped on with curled-up edges and air bubbles over the stringing were only some of the faults I noticed.

But his masterpiece concerned the replacement of a barrel-lock in the door handle of a privately owned Miles Messenger. He was duty man on his own that evening when the particular owner caught up with him in the Clubhouse billiard room as he chatted through the service hatch to the girl in charge of the kitchen. Passing the reconditioned barrel-lock to Tosser, the owner asked him to refit it to the aircraft as he would be flying to a business meeting the next day, and was at pains to point out that it should be pushed into its socket as it was – with the key already fitted – and under no circumstances should he turn or try to remove the key prior to so doing. Tosser, of course, being more interested in chatting up the woman, listened with only half an ear; consequently, when he attempted to fit the mechanism to the aircraft, he did exactly what he had been specifically warned against and twiddled the key. The resultant minor explosion strewed the assembly of tumblers, springs and bits & pieces all over the aeroplane and hangar floor.

Darkness loomed as he panicked to retrieve all the tiny parts, and finally he left the aerodrome to rake out Denis French, who lodged nearby, and pleaded with him to help to find the missing bits and put the lock back together. It was an impossible task, and particularly hard on Denis on his night off as, after fruitlessly trying to get it all together again, he had to help him to put the aircraft away for the night. Being mid-summer, it was about half past eleven before they could lock the hangars.

Next day the idiot recounted it all to me with much 'tee-heeing,' salivating and giggling. It was all a big joke; pity that Denis had been available, otherwise the joke would have been on him! Mr Turner, the owner, was far from pleased and it took a fair amount of sweet-talking on Jock's part to mollify him.

Tosser left the firm after about six months, due I think, to financial pressure. His wages were not all that great and what with paying for lodgings and hiring cars to impress 'gurrels,' he decided to return to the transport firm where he could earn more money with overtime and such. We all breathed a sigh of relief, hoping never to see him again; however, at the end of the year, we ground staff were looking forward to having a bit of a ding at the Clubhouse whilst the Members enjoyed their Annual Dinner & Dance in the West End, and who should turn up but Tosser himself! It seemed that the office girls had stupidly invited him in the belief that he was popular with us. A short while later he re-joined and was still ensconced when I left in the late summer of 1953.

Early in 1953, Major Chris Draper, a ex-WWI pilot who had gained a certain notoriety in the 1920s by flying an aeroplane through Tower Bridge between upper and lower spans, hired one of our Austers (G-AGYD) and, accompanied by his friend Joe toting a ciné camera, flew under 15 Thames bridges in London, eschewing only Tower Bridge (too easy) and Hungerford & Kew (too dicey).

He said he did it in the hope that the ensuing publicity would help him to get a job (not easy at his age), which it did; he eventually became a car salesman for Raymond Way of Kilburn. When paying his hire fee to Ted Darlow upon return, he stated that he had had his 'swansong.' Exactly what he meant by that remark was brought home to us an hour later when half of Fleet Street descended on the Club waving cameras and asking for statements. We ground staff were having our tea break in the billiard room when the *Daily Mirror* reporter came to the public payphone therein to telephone his copy to his Editor. Our mirth was hard to contain at the sound of his report which owed more to Capt. W.E. Johns' 'Biggles' than fact. Never let the facts get in the way of a good story! They paid for an Auster to be flown for photographing and next day the London dailies were full of faked-up prints of alleged 'on the spot' pictures showing an Auster, its registration carefully fuzzed out and the aircraft enlarged out of proportion to its background (in which case, if it were true, the diminutive Auster would have dwarfed even the Bristol Brabazon!). 'YD had been stowed in the hangar out of sight prior to the press boys' arrival so a cream-painted one was used for their photo session, gleaming white in the black & white pictures in the newspapers; 'YD's grubby and rather tired silver would have appeared dirty grey.

Tosser, grinning from ear to ear, went out of his way to attend the aircraft when it set out, and again upon its return. Although he denied it, he undoubtedly knew more than he would admit; giggling fit to wet himself and unable to contain his secret, he later showed me a letter addressed to him on friendly first name terms in which Major Draper thanked him for all his help and suggested a visit to his pad in town when his friend Joe would be showing the ciné film of the adventure. The letter was signed "Kindest regards, Chris," confirming, to my mind, that he was in on the plot beforehand. Had the management been aware of such complicity, he would have been thumbing a lift and clutching his P45 on his way back to the transport firm before the Auster's engine had even cooled down.

TOP: An autumn 1947 line-up of the Club fleet.
BOTTOM: The BEA Bell 47 G-AKFB visited Broxbourne in 1951 to take Lord
Rowallan, Chief Scout, to an important International Jamboree.

TOP: "To think that I would ever see a Tiger Moth up in a tree." Pete Jackson awaits the rescue crane, late spring 1951.
BOTTOM: G-AIDS is pulled clear of the trees with Jock on the guide rope.

TOP: Proctor Mk. I G-AGZM; note the bulge in the cowling for Mk. III generator.
BOTTOM: G-ALMA, the Piper Cub owned by Club member Eric Haywood which was involved in a 'close encounter' with G-AGZM.

TOP: Proctor III G-AJCX overhauled and repainted for J. Hazard by H & E (I converted it to a 4-seater).
BOTTOM: Tiger Moth ZK-BAF, with its hopper installed but with paintwork yet to be made good, awaiting its first test flight.

CHAPTER 15

INTO THE FIFTIES

I spent a miserable winter employed at Wrightons. My job title was 'sub-assembler' which involved such tasks as glueing and pinning bits of beading and members to pieces of plywood to make wardrobe shelves. That particular job was timed at 1½ minutes to glue, pin and sandpaper each component; that meant it had to be done in half that time to make 100% bonus, which I found impossible. My pay was about the same hourly rate as that paid by H & E, but reduced slightly to qualify for bonus earnings. Hourly pay means just that: no pay for sickness or extra holidays. At Christmas we were told the factory would be closing for an extra week, so at the wrong time of the year I was short of a week's pay I could not really afford; I had collected the Speed Twin and was in debt to about a third of its value!

I found the incessant machinery noise practically unbearable and dust lay thick over everything. My large replacement toolbox at the end of my bench was targeted by one 'maker' – who thought himself a wit but was only half right – and he continually chalked on its paintwork things he considered funny during my absence, for instance: "Why go home in the fog? Put up here for the night" was one example. It left chalk embedded in the woodgrain and permanent scratches on the paintwork.

The foreman allotted jobs to favoured 'makers' in a way that allowed them to earn big bonuses, his own bonus being based on the collective rate of the whole workshop. With one exception, all the jobs I had were impossible to make any decent money on. I once overheard some makers discussing other firms' working conditions and bonus rates; one of them remarked that when he worked for Co-Op Furnishing, he found it to be an appalling sweat-shop with suicidal bonus times, so he left as soon as he could. How about that for the Co-Operative Society socialist principles? Although employed on bench-work, I was interested in the various woodwork machines and their functions and applications, and that interest was to prove fruitful in later years.

In March, I was called into the foreman's office, told to collect my tools and was given two hours' notice. Unable to carry my big box on my bicycle, I carried it into DeeKay workshop (after vigorously trying to wipe off four large chalked letters – 'URA1') and asked Jock to let me leave it until I was able to arrange transport. I usually called in each night to wait for Bob Collins and we cycled home together. Jock offered me a job back with H & E and asked for a decision next day. I consulted my elder brother that evening and he advised acceptance until such time as a better offer was available and then hand in notice without rancour. The following Monday saw me back in the fold, but it was to be four years before I handed in my notice.

Whilst I was with Wrightons, Slosh had left and a new chap, Frank Wiswould, started; he was an engine man, formerly with Pan American

Airways and Handley Page. Frank had earlier given me the name of someone at HP to write to for a job after I had unsuccessfully applied at de Havillands at Hatfield and the London Aeroplane Club and RAF Reserve Flying School at Panshanger, near Welwyn; that had been no more fruitful. As a former joiner, Slosh had been doing the woodwork repairs whilst I was in Wrightons, but now Jock needed me for the task once more. Dick Ison had joined just prior to the big redundancies but, as an unpaid student from Chelsea Aeronautical College on work-experience, was unaffected by them; he now possessed a new Scott-engined Cyc-Auto autocycle that seemed as prone to malfunction as had been my 1935/6 models. Later, having obtained his Ground Engineer's licences, he stayed on for a while as a salaried member of the Club staff.

I learned much from both Frank and Dick. Dick and I worked together when he was involved in electrical jobs and radio installations for the aircraft; he always asked for me as his helper, for which I was truly grateful! Frank had been involved in a lot of motorcycle grass-track racing and was impressed by my Speed Twin; he once suggested that I might act as his sidecar passenger if he should take up grass-track 'charioteering' again. He, in turn, passed on to me many useful engineering and motorcycling tips. He drove a pre-war Morris Ten saloon and I was able to make a new sliding roof from beech and aircraft ply covered in doped fabric that we fitted to it: double curvature ply-skinning experience from Proctor repairs was useful for that. The runners we made from 'Tufnol' sheet. When he resprayed the car, Barnie and I helped to rub it down with 'wet and dry' paper between coats during our lunch hours.

Also during my Wrightons sojourn, H & E were fulfilling a contract to ferry bolts of cloth from Lille in France to the UK using the fleet of Rapides which, with the two ex-Dominies, numbered three. During one trip, an engine of one of them started to run roughly and made such expensive noises that anyone who cared to listen might well have been charged a fee. The machine was past the point-of-no-return over the Channel, so the pilot pressed on and put down at Merville as an emergency. Jock went out to assess the damage and found that an exhaust valve crown had broken from its stem and bounced around in the cylinder with dire results to head, cylinder and piston. Twenty or so air miles at 1,800 rpm with a rogue bit of hardened steel adrift inside knocks thousands of little dents in such parts and a Club member was recruited to fly out in Auster G-AJEG with all necessary spare parts for Jock to effect repairs. What should have been a couple of days' work became rather protracted for Jock when said Club member stalled whilst taking off on the return flight and fatally crashed.

It had been planned that, when the Rapide was once more up and running, Jock would fly as passenger in it whilst the Club member was to follow solo in the Auster. At the inquest some weeks later, Jock stated that as the Rapide circled to allow the Auster to catch up, he looked back and was horrified to see the Auster nose up " . . . at an impossible angle, then stall and nosedive into the 'deck'." He, of course, had to remain in France until all the official business that ensued had been dealt with and then accompany the coffin back to England.

Between 1947 and 1953 I gained much experience with Miles Geminis and Messengers. Club founder member Neville Browning had obtained an ex-RAF Gipsy Major-engined Messenger which we serviced but he kept on his farm where he had his own landing strip. He always flew with a certain panache; once, on returning from an Army co-operation flight, he looped the Messenger at about 1,000 feet and, as he pulled out, he switched off the engine and glided down to a perfect landing, rolling to a stop two or three yards from the petrol pumps. He jumped out as I approached to refuel the machine and as he made his way to the Clubhouse, I asked jokingly if he was saving petrol.

"Oh yes!" he replied, laughing.

Telling Jock about it next day, Jock said that I had better believe that he meant it! On at least two occasions he had looped Rapides.

On another day he came into the circuit slowly, made a cautious approach and very gentle landing, taxying up to the hangar very gingerly. I remarked to Jock that something must be seriously amiss with the aircraft for such circumspect handling. I was right.There were holes in the ply skin on fuselage and wings, one flap was broken and some of the formers and members had been broken away inside. Neville was in a rage; some ramblers had been through his farm and left a gate open so that his cattle were free to roam into the barn where he kept the Messenger and they had nudged and licked it and even tried to climb up onto the wing – hence the broken flap. The woodwork repairs kept me occupied for a week.

I became expert in leading-edge repairs through bird-strikes on Geminis and, on one occasion, the Airspeed Consul. It was unpleasant to remove the ornithological cadavers at such times as they always seemed to manage to spread themselves along inside the leading edge and stain the front web of the spar; it put me off poultry for quite a time.

Once, a Gemini landed badly and managed to dent the bottom of the port fin. Jock told me to check it over and get a couple of bits of ply to patch it. Reference to the spare parts book quickly indicated that the fin plywood was a preformed shell, glued glove-like onto the rib/spar assembly that only had a very thin profile leading edge member (3/4 in wide by 1/8 in thick). I reported this fact to Jock and asked if he would obtain a portion of moulded fin skin to effect the repair as there was no substantial tip member upon which one could glue ply patches.

He became enraged and said, in effect: "I told you to patch it up with a bit of ply. Now do it!"

In vain I had tried to explain that a piece of preformed skin was essential and that once I had cut the damaged area away the aircraft would be out of service until the special bit was to hand, but there was no way he would listen and, by that time, I too was ready to erupt. I went out to the machine with my small saw and cut the damaged skin away and removed the broken bits of profile member. Returning to Jock, I requested him icily to please come and inspect the opened-up fin and, when he saw it, I then asked how he wanted me to glue the said patches onto thin air! Somewhat shattered, he said he had no idea it was like that and had to admit a piece of preformed fin covering was essential.

"That," I said with heavy irony, "was what I tried to explain earlier."

Jock and I often clashed in verbal battle. It annoyed me when he bawled me out in front of others. Once, when he yelled across the hangar to me for some imagined misdemeanour, I called back: "Can you say it a bit louder! I don't think Bill in the corner heard you."

Another time, he and I were in the cabin of a Rapide accompanied by his son Roy and he remonstrated with me for not working enough overtime. We had a weekend rota among us six staff ground engineers, so that any two were on duty every third weekend. Additionally, we each worked a 'duty night' during the week whereby we took turns to be available for servicing after normal hours should any Club member require to fly or be flown. It so happened that the said Rapide had fallen due for Certificate of Airworthiness overhaul between my weekend duties and, requiring extensive woodwork repairs, I was obliged to work both weekends when I was normally off, as well as evenings in addition to my late duty night. My justified and indignant retort was embarrassing to all concerned. I never understood why he didn't just call us into the office, quietly ask the question and then allow the excuse to be heard.

Club members rarely hobnobbed with us ground staff, they preferred to socialise in the Clubhouse. In those days there was still a strong 'them and us' attitude, although there were certain exceptions. One chap in particular used to arrive in a newish Ford Prefect van to fly one of the Club Austers, and often strolled over to the hangars for a chat and to look around the aircraft. He confided one day to Barnie and me that he hoped to buy a reasonably cheap Auster, subject to selling his van for a decent price. Not so far-fetched as one might think, because then, good motor vehicles were at a premium and Austers and such were fairly cheap. A Tiger Moth in fair condition, with C of A, could be obtained for about £250! He was budgeting in the region of about £400.

He said to us: "As you know, the Republic of Ireland is a Catholic country and birth control is taboo. French Letters fetch about 15/- for a packet of three over there, six times our retail price. I propose flying in a gross or so now and then, concealed in the rear fuselage, and sell them on the Black Market."

Barnie and I thought his idea highly amusing, but we never found out if his plan came to fruition.

Battle of Britain Day, 1952, saw a grand public open day at RAF North Weald. Two of our aircraft were involved in providing joyflights for the public, one of which was Vic Ercolani's Gemini. We had recently been bothered with deflating tailwheel oleos on Gemini and Messenger aircraft, and sending them away to specialists had little success; we usually just kept them well pumped-up with a special high-pressure inflator. Toward the end of the day, the tailwheel oleo on Vic's Gemini deflated in flight and the impact on landing pulled the rear bulkhead out of position and split the rear fuselage ply skin around its periphery about a foot forward of it. I spent the following week travelling to North Weald each day on my Speed Twin (no travelling expenses but free aviation fuel) to repair the aircraft in the comfort of an excellent RAF hangar surrounded by Gloster Meteors in various states of serviceability. In order to effect the repair, the whole empennage (tailplane/elevator/-fin/rudder) assembly had to be removed. The RAF 'Chiefy' obliged with many willing hands to lift the bits as necessary. Having cut away the damaged ply skin and reglued the rear bulkhead in its proper position, I pointed out to Jock that it was thanks to Miles Aircraft's silly ideas about attaching ply skins on their aeroplanes with the major grain direction at right-angles to the length of the components that had exacerbated the damage. I've no doubt that their stressmen could have put up a very good argument for thus fitting the plywood skins, however, when it came down to practicality, the best all-round strength was obtained by directing the outer ply grain lengthwise. With the fuselage tapering into a cone at the stern, any torque load induced by the empennage aerodynamic loads were adequately catered for by its natural stiffness. Percivals did it on all their wooden aircraft and who could doubt their success? For once Jock listened to my arguments and agreed that we should replace the skins in the damaged areas with the grain lengthwise.

It was during this time whilst lunching in a nearby transport cafe, I heard the news that a boyhood hero of mine, John Cobb, had been killed whilst attempting the World's Water Speed Record on Loch Ness.

No sooner had the Gemini and I returned to base than we learned that another stern bulkhead had split out due to a deflated tailwheel oleo, this time on a Club member's Messenger in France, at Nevers, halfway between Paris and Marseille.

"How do you fancy a trip to France, Smuthie? Got a passport?" was Jock's greeting upon my return.

I fancied it very much, and replied in the affirmative to both questions. Tosser was nearby and butted in to say that he had a passport and would be prepared to go and help repair the Messenger, grinning in oleaginous obsequiousness. He had previously boasted about having a passport as if it were a prized qualification, which in his case, it probably was! For once Jock showed no enthusiasm for Tosser's eagerness.

The prospect of our 'jolly' to France was at first dismissed, it being mooted that a British itinerant repair firm were in France at the time and would deal with it. In those days, the ARB would not allow such repairs to be carried out by French repair organizations, due perhaps to the somewhat cavalier attitude they showed in using materials that the ARB would not approve of. Later, when I saw how the French maintained some of their civilian light aircraft, I realized they had a point!

However, as I was about to trade-in my trusty Speed Twin for a brand new 650 cc Triumph Thunderbird, all thoughts of damaged Miles Messengers were as far from my mind as was said aircraft from its home base. I had approached Mr Frogley to request a loan through the firm for £20, which was the balance required to add to my savings to buy the machine for cash. To my pleasurable surprise, he offered a personal loan, to be repaid to him at £1 a week via the wages office. In the week after this interesting episode, Jock broke the news that we were to travel to Nevers the following Monday and repair the Messenger on site and be flown back home in it afterwards. I know not why the itinerant repairers were not given the job; I suspect the management had been well and truly frightened by the estimated cost.

That Monday found us on our way, hung about with a large roll of 1/16 ply stuffed with strips of spruce, glue, pins, tools, fabric and dope etc. and sealed at each end with cardboard and masking tape. I was glad of the experience with the Gemini at North Weald; I now knew exactly what to take on the trip. Club member Ronnie Riches accompanied Jock and me to act as interpreter in view of his excellent fluency in the French language; also he was to act as ferry pilot when the enterprise had been achieved.

We crossed on the boat train ferry in Royal company; the Duke of Windsor was safely esconced in his special compartment on the Wagon-Lits coaches, while we second-class travellers were obliged to detrain and sleep in bunks on the upper deck. We breakfasted on board due to the fact that choppy seas were preventing the ferry from entering Dunkerque harbour until about 8 am on the Tuesday for fear of the heavy tide displacing the lock-gate. It was after 1 pm before we arrived at the Gare du Nord in Paris, missing our Marseille train from the Gare du Lyon. The next one was not due to leave until 6 o'clock that evening, so Ronnie took us to lunch at a fine restaurant in the Champs Elysées and afterwards on a lightning tour of Paris by taxi and Metro and a trip up to the top gallery of the Eiffel Tower. We caught the Marseille train with only seconds to spare; at three minutes to six we entered the Gare du Lyon, collected our left luggage and clambered aboard the train as it started to move on the stroke of six!

There were no seats to be had and whilst Jock and I guarded our goods and chattels in the train's corridor, Ronnie went off to book us into the second class dining car. This at least allowed us an hour or so to sit comfortably. Later Jock and I stood between the dining coach and the rest of the train. We noticed a waiter clearing a hamper of a pile of used table linen; he then laid a clean cloth on top and bade us to sit on it – Jock must have tipped him after our meal! It had been a long 24 hours and I dropped off to sleep.

Next thing, Jock was nudging me and shouting: "Grab the stuff, Smuthie! We're at Nevers. If we don't get off here, we'll finish up at Marseille!"

Sleepily we made our way into town from the station and Ronnie bartered with the concierge of a local *pension* to secure us three rooms with the promise of breakfast at an early hour – if you can call a small pot of weak tea made with one diminutive tea bag and a couple of rolls with butter and a spoonful of jam breakfast! I was appalled at the awful hole-in-the-ground loo and disgusted with French plumbing generally. We went by taxi to the Aéroport Nevers and set to work at once dismantling the tail assembly from the fuselage. It was by now Wednesday and we had to get cracking for the aircraft to be flyable by the weekend; I was grateful for the dress rehearsal on Vic Ercolani's Gemini at North Weald!

After helping me remove the bulky stuff in order to make the fuselage repairs, Jock, Ronnie and Monsieur Bruno (the airport manager-*cum*-engineer-*cum*-sweeper-up-*cum*-general factotum) disappeared into the aerodrome office and allowed me to proceed with the structural repairs uninterrupted. The work then proceeded much as it had on the Gemini at North Weald. A replacement tailwheel unit was needed, as there were no facilities for re-inflating the oleo. Jock telephoned to Broxbourne, with some help from Ronnie to get over the language difficulties of an international call, and arranged for Peter Ayles to fly one out to us in a Club Auster. We needed to re-solder some bonding connections and a pantomime ensued with Jock trying, in his limited schoolboy French, to obtain an electric soldering iron. It did little to help when some interested local lads came by and one of them said in perfect English: "Can I help you?"

After Jock had been gabbling away for some minutes in his best Edinburgh English, it became painfully obvious that those were the only four words of English the lad knew! Then Monsieur Bruno came on the scene and Jock tried again to explain our requirements. After another ten minutes of this, I became impatient and beckoning to Monsieur Bruno; I showed him the job, placed the offending bits together and made a dumbshow of soldering them by saying "Pftt!" This brought forth the exclamation "Ahh! Mais oui! Très bien!" and he toddled off and returned with solder, flux, a large electric soldering iron and an ancient lead light; the latter two items fitted with considerably careworn cables which connected to a mains extension lead by their bared ends! Sharing the cramped confines of the rear fuselage with such equipment was only marginally safer than with a man-eating python!

The other aeroplanes in the hangar shared with our Messenger were a small parasol-wing Potez, an ex-RAF Tiger Moth – still in its wartime camouflage but with the insignia crudely painted out, – a Fieseler Storch and a cute little silver-painted Jodel Bébé single-seat low-wing monoplane powered by a converted VW air-cooled car engine.When its owner heard that some Brits were working on the Messenger, he came to the aerodrome especially to demonstrate the machine. I think it was the first ultralight aircraft to be powered by the Volkswagen flat-four engine. Later he packed us into his diminutive Renault and drove us to the local *estaminet,* the *Auberge de la Sangsu.*

When Peter arrived in the Auster he was disconcerted to find that we still had to reassemble the tail unit. He joined us for lunch and was further put out at the way Jock was distributing H & E largesse on aperitifs and wine. After work in the evening we had hitherto repaired there for dinner and spent time and money on drinks and socializing, returning to the pension in town in the small hours. Such shenanigans were not conducive to efficient working and I, in the vernacular of my contemporaries, was 'pissed off' with the whole setup. Not only evenings but lunchtimes were also conducted in the French *laissez faire* manner.used to a quick dash across the road to Monty's Café for bangers, mash and beans with a cup of tea, I found half an hour of aperitifs prior to a leisurely lunch somewhat irksome. Do not misunderstand me, such pastimes are a treat on holiday, but when trying to get an aircraft airworthy, a half or threequarter-hour lunch break is adequate.

It was this to which Peter took exception. That evening at the pension, he took Jock to task and I suffered the embarrassment of being a spectator to a noisy altercation. Later, Peter apologised to me for the row and said: "Just think though, Harry. Can you imagine a couple of Frenchmen coming over to Broxbourne and spending a week's wages in Monty's for a couple of lunches?"

I saw his point. That evening we went back to the Pension after dinner and later explored the town.

At lunch the previous day Jock had negotiated with the proprietress of the *estaminet* to purchase some butter which was freely available in France but still severely rationed in the UK; Jock asked for 3 lb of the stuff and Ronnie explained that it was in kilogrammes and that a kilo was just over 2 lb.

"So how much do you want, Smuthie?" he asked. I did a rough count-up of those I wished to benefit from this bounty and quickly converted the quantity to about 1 Kg (250 grams to each of four people – about ½ lb each). It was unsalted and would not keep except in a fridge which none of us possessed at that time.

"That all?" he said and then asked for 3 Kg for himself. I tried to point out that a kilo was over 2 lb, but he was involved in payment negotiations and did not listen.

At that point, Monsieur Bruno arrived on his ancient Armor Alcien motorbike and offered a lift back to the aerodrome for anyone who wished. Jock elected me for the privilege in order to complete my tasks for the machine to be ready for test- and home-flight on the morrow. It was some while before the others returned in a state of some excitement and altercation. It seemed that Ronnie had disappeared into the rear of the premises with the young waitress – ostensibly to pay for the lunch. After a protracted wait, Peter became impatient and barged into the inner sanctum, surprising Ronnie who was by then in an advanced state of joyful physical intimacy with the young waitress! The incident provided a conversational topic for some days after.

Amid the bustle of pre-flight preparations next morning, the lady turned up with the butter and Jock was appalled at the number of 250 gram packs in four kilogrammes – to say nothing of the number of francs it cost. Whilst Jock was chuntering about with payment and stowing the stuff, Peter Ayles remarked sarcastically that maybe the aircraft serviceability could wait but, whatever else, we must not neglect the butter!

Peter, exerting his authority as CFI, decided he would fly the Messenger with Jock and me aboard and Ronnie would take the Auster and, with Jock's agreement, combine the test flight with the journey home.

We flew back toward Paris along the Loire and, passing over the gardens of the Palace of Versailles, saw the Eiffel Tower in dim silhouette in the distance. Onwards via Dieppe and the D-Day beaches, where Peter flew down to wave-top height, we saw remains of rusting hulks half-buried in the sand and, speculating on the noise and horror of 8 years previously, we waved to friendly beachcombers, landing at Le Touquet to refuel aircraft & occupants and clear Customs prior to heading across the Channel at its narrowest point. Peter seemed a trifle tense as we climbed to 6,000 ft, but after half an hour or so he suddenly relaxed back in his seat and proclaimed that if the engine stopped now, we could glide into Dover!

Back at home base, as we unloaded, Jock became alarmed at the quantity of butter he had brought. After some pleading on his part I agreed to take another kilo of the stuff off his hands, which gave me the task of dashing around distributing it to friends and relations lest it become rancid. Not only that, when I was totting up my cash later I found I was a whole £1 out of pocket over the week. In those days that represented a sixth of my gross weekly salary!

An amusing incident one summer Sunday afternoon concerned once again the peculiar method of plywood attachment on Miles aircraft. Pete Jackson and I were on duty and relaxing in front of the Main Hangar inbetween calls for prop-swinging and refuelling whilst the Club and private aircraft were busy flying. Club co-director Roger Frogley was strolling around inside with a tweedy-looking gent in plus-four suit and flat cap (which Ray always referred to as 'a clorf kep'). They were comparing the differences between the Club's Proctor Mk. I and a privately-owned Messenger. Roger called me over and asked if I could explain why the skin on the Messenger was rippled with minor dents and that on the Proctor was smooth and even. Leaping astride my hobby-horse I explained at some length that the rippling on the Miles aircraft was due in part to there being no internal protection and therefore dampness in the air swelled the inner surfaces, causing them to bow against the doped, fabricked and painted outer ones.

"But," I warmed to my theme, "the main reason is due to the fact that Miles, for some weird reason, always attach the ply skin with its major grain direction at right-angles to span and length, whereas Percivals have always put the major grain direction spanwise and lengthwise."

Then summoning up all the wisdom of my 25 summers, I cocked a thumb at the Proctor and pronounced: "The man who designed that obviously knew what he was doing!"

A silence ensued for some seconds, then Roger, grinning widely, asked if I knew the name of his companion. Unable to answer I shook my head.

"Let me introduce you," he said; "this is Captain Percival!" And at that they both roared with laughter. Recovering only slightly, I expressed silent relief that he was not F.G. Miles.

Later, whenever he visited the Club, Captain Percival favoured me with a conspiratorial grin.

In pre-war days famous people from the aviation and entertainment scene patronized Herts & Essex Aeroplane Club – Amy Johnson, Will Hay, the Western Brothers etc. After 1946 well-known people from motorsports seemed to favour Broxbourne: Malcom Craven and Eric Chitty, speedway stars of West Ham and other members of their team became flying members, as did racing driver Roy Salvadori. I once saw him four-wheel-drift a Morris saloon into the Club entrance drive. Peter Ayles – who worked with Alvis pre-war – joined the Steering Wheel Club when journalist Tom Walkerly visited the 'drome and he persuaded young Stirling Moss to take flying lessons with us; I swung his prop for him during an early lesson in an Auster Autocrat!

Robert Montgomerie-Charrington became a member and sometimes arrived in a splendid pre-war Hispano-Suiza; I saw him competing in the Freiburg Hill Climb when I was on a motorcycling tour of Germany with Les Kimm and Eric Soulard in 1951. I spoke to him and he was pleased that someone from Broxbourne was there. Afterwards, Les seemed a bit miffed and asked "Who was that, then?"

A well known politician also learnt to fly at Broxbourne in the late 40s and into '51; known to us as "The Barrister," he learned primarily to gain experience for a better understanding of his government post as Under-Secretary of State for Air – he was, of course, Geoffrey de Freitas MP. On one occasion during his early solo flying he brought a Tiger Moth down to earth slightly quicker than was prudent and, as he taxied it to the hangar, it leaned a bit to the left and the fuselage fabric had slackened just above the bottom wing. Peter Ayles was quick to reassure him that all was OK, but later we had to dismantle the aircraft and fit a new port forward side-frame where the fully compressed undercarriage strut had bent up the bottom longeron.

The Government had decreed that the minimum flying hours to qualify for a Private Pilot's Licence should be 40 hours, but under pressure relented to the extent that when certain flying schools obtained an Air Ministry Approval this could be reduced to 30; thanks to "The Barrister," Herts & Essex was the first approved flying school.

When Captain Fresson started an air service to the Outer Hebrides and parts of Scotland, the second aeroplane he purchased was the de Havilland DH.84 Dragon G-ACIT. When the Labour Government snatched his modest airline in 1947 and gave it to British European Airways, the Dragon was still serviceable and, as there was no place for it in the BEA schedules, it was deemed prudent to transfer it to the Combined Airways Flying Club. A Certificate of Airworthiness renewal overhaul was put out to private tender in 1949 and Herts & Essex won the contract. Only a modest amount of restoration was needed, the biggest task being to completely repaint the machine in a colour scheme that reflected its tripartite ownership. My small contribution to the exercise was to rebuild the starboard lower aileron and journey to Hatfield to study the one and only DH.84 overhaul manual available in the country in order to ascertain the proper rigging dimensions. Upon completion of the C of A and paint job of red, pale blue and silver, the owner's representative brought a whole package of Company logos to stick all over the aircraft to advertise to the world in general who owned the machine – BEA, BOAC and BSAA.

In addition to G-AGZU, H & E obtained two other DH.89s, both ex-RAF Dominies, which we converted to civilian 8-seat Rapides and painted in the Club colours of silver and green. Previously used in the Service as flying classrooms for wireless telegraphy instruction, they contained quantities of radio gubbins and the attendant *spaghetti bolognaise* of cabling, which we had to remove and replace with appropriate seats for paying bums. 'ZU arrived with an impressive radio station bolted to the bulkhead that divided the passenger cabin from the pilot's 'office' with a small swivel chair facing it for a radio operator; I was allotted this seat when I cadged a half-hour pleasure trip over London one Sunday. Denis Parsons was the pilot at the time and he bade me stand by the cockpit door to point out places of interest to the passengers.

I asked if I should tell them to fasten their seat-belts.

"No, we haven't time to bugger about like that!" he replied.

Quick turn-rounds were the order of the day as the pilots got a modest percentage on ticket sales. A couple asked if they might swap seats, and when I passed the request to Denis, he said, in effect: "let 'em please themselves."

Pleasure flights were a good revenue generator for the Club and a member from North London came every Sunday with a couple of helpers and ran the enterprise on a business-like footing. Denis Parsons mostly flew the Rapide and other pilots flew Autocrats until the Proctor G-AGZM became available – which Dave Phillips flew on a spare-time basis.

Quick turn-rounds ensured more passengers but sometimes led to silly situations. Denis would take off on a London trip and upon return would lob straight in without circling the field, in order to save time. On two occasions the wind direction changed 180° whilst he was away so that on return he landed downwind; on the second occasion a Club member in Auster Autocrat

G-AIZV followed him in and collided with a Tiger Moth (whose pupil-pilot had done everything by the book) landing in the opposite direction. A slight swerve at the last minute avoided fatalities but both sets of port wings were chewed-up by the respective props.

Denis left soon after and obtained a job flying Avro Tudors for AVM Don Bennett's company Fairflight Ltd. On 12th March 1950 he was bringing a party of rugby supporters home from Dublin in Avro Tudor Mk. 5 G-AKBY, when the machine stalled on the final approach into Llandon in Wales and 80 people were killed in the ensuing crash. Ray and I discussed the tragedy and speculated about the behaviour of the passengers at the time. Ray had a pretty low opinion of football fans in general and rugby supporters in particular. I pointed out that if passengers moved about the cabin during finals, it would not need many running aft for their off-ration goodies to initiate a vicious stall. I wondered if Denis had been as casual in passenger discipline in the Tudor as he had for the joyflights: no one will ever know.

Another minor incident with our pleasure-flying Rapide had amusing consequences. Pleasure flight boarding was located at the corner of the aerodrome where Nazeing New Road joined the old Nazeing Road and Keysers Estate. This was ideally suited to attract customers but was a long walk from the hangars. With the exception of visiting friend Rob Capper and a local schoolboy who liked to help us in order to be around the aeroplanes, I was alone one busy Sunday afternoon when summoned to this area and asked to check the Rapide's landing flaps as the pilot had reported that on the last landing they appeared not to slow the aircraft. When I arrived at the aircraft, the pilot had vacated it, presumably to indulge in a tea or wee, but it was fully loaded with mums, dads, kids and aunties. Squeezing my way through this expectant throng I operated the flap lever, which offered no resistance in a flaccid sort of way. Charlie, the joyflight king, called through the cabin door that the flaps had come down; but I realised this was due to gravity and not mechanical linkage when, having removed the quadrant cover, I fished out a couple of feet of 10-cwt control cable with a frayed end.

When told that this particular aeroplane was out of service as of now, Charlie wailed: "What about the passengers?" Glancing over my shoulder into the cabin, I remarked that they looked quite serviceable, but he did not see the funny side of that, and was even less amused by the realization that he'd have to offer them flights in the Auster or return their money.

Half an hour later I was told to fetch the Rapide from 'Joyflight Corner' back to the hangar. Pilot and ground crew had all gone home and I was obliged to either taxy it or picket it out where it stood. Summoning friend Rob Capper and young Clive to walk by the wingtips I prepared for my first experience of taxying a DH.89. I had taxied Austers, Gemini, Proctor and Tiger Moth but this was a whole new ball game for me. With the engines still warm, starting on its own battery was the easy bit. Bill Pegg, when asked if he felt any trepidation about flying the Bristol Brabazon on its initial test-flight, had replied that he would fly the cockpit and trust that the rest would follow. So, taking the controls and fast disappearing courage in both hands I prepared to follow his example but try my best to keep the machine stuck to *terra firma* – the more firmer the less terror!

Hitherto I'd found taxying the Proctor was a doddle; it had a Bendix differential brake system and with the handbrake pulled on four clicks the aeroplane would steer quite easily whichever way one turned the rudder pedals. The Rapide, on the other hand, was more of a handful; holding the column hard into my chest and trying to manipulate handbrake and two throttles, three hands would have been useful. It did not help much, having the cockpit so high off the ground: like being on the top of a see-saw and hoping that it would not swing down the other way! Giving a burst of port engine with the rudder pedals hard a'starboard and grabbing at the handbrake, she reluctantly swung to starboard but kept going despite my efforts to reverse the process. Eventually, it began to straighten but then needed a burst of starboard engine and port rudder to try to get back on course. Slowly, I began to master the situation and with decreasing oscillations we weaved our way back to 'ZU's parking area.

Arriving at the spot, another challenge presented itself; it was necessary to turn the machine 180° to present its tail to the tall hedge that bounded the aerodrome with Old Nazeing Road. But by that time I was ready: full throttle port, close starboard, full starboard rudder; at 90° close both throttles and full port rudder. Such a pirouette Nureyev should envy! Rob and Clive sensibly let go of the wingtips at that point and avoided dislocated shoulders. More by luck than skill it stopped exactly in the right position! Later, with everything switched off, young Clive helped me picket it down and tie on the cockpit cover.

I apologised to Rob for nearly wrenching his shoulder on my rapid turn.

"Not at all," he replied; "You've obviously done this before!"

As the perspiration trickling down my spine began to cool I shrugged as though to say: "All in a day's work, you know!"

Next day Jock was not in the least happy to learn I had taxied the Rapide without tuition but was less unhappy when presented with the alternative of picketing it for the night at the exposed corner of the aerodrome. He ambled away shaking his head and muttering about "the rising bloody generation," later indicating his forgiveness by asking me to go across to Hatfield on my "mooterbayk"and collect a new flap cable.

Earlier mention of Dave Phillips and the Proctor brings to mind another incident generated by hasty joyflight operations. Taxying out at the best part of a fair lick with three passengers for a quick circuit, he sliced into the rear starboard wing-strut of Piper Cub G-ALMA which had just preceded it to the take-off point, and buckled it in a way that changed the aircraft's dihedral to about 10° droop. The Proctor's port wingtip leading edge did not look too cheerful either! Thus, two more machines were put out of service for an unspecified period.

The Proctor needed about 4 ft of leading edge ply replacing and I was happy to provide it. What made it even more enjoyable was to go each day for a week and taxy it from the blister hangar to outside of DeeKay, where all my equipment was, and work on the aeroplane as I wanted, taxying it back to its normal bedspace prior to knocking off each evening. As to the Piper Cub, that was out of service for about a year due to the difficulty of getting spare parts from the States thanks to dollar and import restrictions then prevailing.

Soon after getting its Approved Flying Course status, H & E hosted a number of Air Training Corps Flying Scholarship winners who resided at the Club whilst they learnt to fly. A small room had been set aside in the Clubhouse as an Air Centre and Peter Ayles was in charge. A part-time Instructor known as 'Hitch' joined the firm and shared the training with Peter. The lads were keen and good pupils and although there were a couple of minor prangs, none of them did anything serious or foolish. One lad, coming in on the short run across Nazeing New Road, slapped the Car Park sign with his port lower mainplane knocking it from its post and breaking the front spar of the wing. In those days we merely put on another mainplane cannibalized from the RAF surplus ones we had lying around.

The other incident was a bit more dramatic and involved a pupil flying dual with 'Hitch' and attempting a landing. Having descended from a reasonable altitude with the engine throttled back, he was doing well on finals but drifted on a bit too far and had to 'go round' again. It was then he found out about letting the engine get too cool so that when he slammed open the throttle the engine merely coughed and said "What, me?" Hitch took over and stalled it neatly tail-first onto a convenient maytree in a piece of 'no-man's-land' 'twixt airfield and the River Lee. The Tiger Moth, G-AIDS, was recovered and repaired and test-flown a week later; Peter Ayles flew it and I was passenger on my first-ever open-cockpit flight. Hitch, however, was afterwards known as 'Ditch'!

Young lads were not the only Air Cadets to become pilots at Broxbourne. A couple of attractive young women also gained their wings. Freydis Leafe visited the field once or twice with Womens Junior Air Corps contingents and gave the girls flights in their own Fairchild Argus; I think our young female pilots were successful WJAC cadets.

A more dramatic pile-up that occurred a couple of years earlier involved an RAF Percival Prentice. Each Saturday that summer, a Flying Officer and two Senior NCOs arrived in the Prentice and arranged for it to be tied down a distance from the hangars whilst they went off for the weekend. Our cheeky and most junior member, young Robin, usually waited with screw-pickets and ropes to attend it, and was sometimes seen walking back with them, his pocket heavier with silver coin and a smirk on his bespectacled pug-like dial. He seldom offered 'owt for nowt.' Each Monday morning, the trio would arrive sharp at 08:00 hrs.and Robin would reverse his Saturday task and wave to them as they departed on the longest run.

One Monday, the aerodrome was shrouded in heavy mist, much to the concern of the pilot. Pete Jackson tried to persuade him to wait until about 9 am, when he was sure the mist would have lifted; he lived a short distance from the gates and was familiar with the local climatological idiosyncrasies. But the officer was adamant and would not be deterred, insisting that he had to get the aircraft back before it was missed! Despite Pete's plea to wait, he set off, Pete having advised starting from the Keysers Estate corner and aiming north-west along a line bisecting the angle of Nazeing New Road and Old Nazeing Road. Dick Ison was at the wheel of the 'bloodwagon' with the engine running as the Prentice disappeared into the mist. When the engine noise from the aircraft increased to take-off revs, it seemed to emanate a long way from where Pete suggested they should be. The roar of the Gipsy Queen and DH prop in fine pitch terminated suddenly and was followed by an immense crash of breaking glass.

At that time, Broxbourne Aerodrome was bordered at the northern perimeter by acres of nursery greenhouses, as mentioned earlier. It was part of the working routine among the Lea Valley Growers that workers started at 6.30 am and went home for breakfast at 8 o'clock; this fact was the reason no one was hurt as the machine hurtled into the gable-end of one of the greenhouses. When we arrived at the scene, a 4 in x 3 in purlin had gone through the starboard lower windscreen and exited via the port rear side window – the occupants had ducked!

Peter and Dick had to attend the subsequent Court Martial as witnesses and were complimented by the Judge Advocate for their prompt arrival at the scene. We never learned what happened to the pilot; I guess it did little for his promotional prospects. A London evening paper had carried a picture of the crashed aeroplane with the headline: 'The plane and its crew went into the Glass House!'

In February 1953, Ray emigrated to Australia. Barney and I were particularly sad at his departure as, with a couple of the other lads and some girls we sometimes went on pub-crawl outings in Barney's Dad's estate wagon – used during the working day for B. senior's upholstery business, referred to by Ray as "You folstery." These were hilarious episodes, not least due to Ray's natural showbiz clowning, but he also somehow managed to bring us all out of our shells to act the fool. He had only worked at the 'drome for two short periods but Jock seemed unable to grasp the fact that he could be a serious and useful worker. He was in digs opposite the main gate and spent his spare time with us when we did our duty stints in the summer evenings. At that time he worked for a local enamelling firm.

I too was getting itchy feet, though I had no wish to travel halfway round the world. Friend Rob Capper had obtained a de Havilland Engineering Apprenticeship when he was demobbed from the RAF, and suggested I try for a post as fitter in their SDCR (Service Department Civil Repair) hangar at Leavesden Aerodrome. I sat down one evening and carefully composed a letter to the personnel manager. I must have said all the right things because a day or two later I received a reply inviting me for an interview. Whilst awaiting the letter to confirm the date and time, Jock asked me to estimate the period needed to install new-type undercarriage retraction switches for a Gemini. I had done the job once before and knew what it entailed, so when I said "two days," Jock reeled in disbelief and said it must be a lot less. He had probably already quoted a ridiculousy short time to show himself in a good light with the management. I was about to explain that the whole fascia panel must be removed in order to modify the underneath fixed panel so as to accept the bigger switches when Barney strolled in, so Jock asked his opinion.

"Couple of hours?" he replied, without thinking.

Jock demanded to know who was right and I suggested that Barney had best do the job, but that was not on as he was already engaged in a much more urgent task.

"You'll do it, Smuthie – and not take two days!"

I replied, in effect, that it was impossible to do it in less time.

"Start now, and I want it tomorrow night!" was his parting shot.

Barney was contrite and apologized for dropping me in it. By knocking-off time the job had not progressed very far, and at home that evening a letter awaited me from de Havilland SDCR confirming an interview for the following morning.

I arrived back at H & E after lunch, having secured the job at Leavesden, and quite prepared for Jock to upbraid me for dereliction of duty concerning the Gemini switches. But he shrugged his shoulders when told the reason and accepted my resignation with good grace, merely requesting that I serve the week out.

Barney had taken over the Gemini job after all in my absence and was astonished at the difficulties presented in removing the pressed aluminium crackle-grey fascia panel from the main panel with all its conglomeration of knobs and handles sandwiching it. To his credit he did manage to complete the operation in under two days. When told of my move, he wondered why de Havilland still required woodworkers and was amazed to learn I was to be a fitter; but of course I had been trained as a fitter first. This sort of attitude is a cross borne by all woodworkers; no one believes they are capable of any other discipline and that all woodwork from rough carpentry to the finest cabinet-making is all of a piece. Jock could never understand my ill-grace when taken off an interesting aircraft job to crate up a propeller or mend a Clubhouse chair. But I shall always be grateful to Broxbourne Aerodrome for the skill and knowledge gained in 12½ years which made one so adaptable.

After congratulating me for landing the job at DH, Albert, my eldest brother, pointed out that advancement might accrue by investing in a set of golf clubs. But as I never subscribed to the erroneous belief that the pinnacle of man's achievement is attained by booting and bashing balls, I eschewed the suggestion; in retrospect, had I done so, maybe I could have retired as a Director. But, then again, perhaps not.

My valedictory week at H & E passed quickly enough, my last job being a minor woodwork repair in the cockpit of Rapide 'ZU. After the fire of 1947 the firm had supplied me with a basic kit of tools. One chisel had been lost and, in handing in the rest of the tools to Jock, I offered a replacement that I had bought.

"Keep it, Smuthie! I didn't expect to get all these back. I wish all the other b*****s were as honest!" he said as he shook my hand in a warm farewell.

A schoolteacher friend, Ralph Jones, kindly transported my heavy toolkit home in his estate car and, after filling in the final timesheet, shaking hands with the guys and kissing all the girls, I rode my Triumph Thunderbird through the gates for the last time, finally severing the umbilical that had kept me attached to dear old H & E for so long.

I had a week at home to prepare for my de Havilland adventure and spent some of it assembling my fitter's toolkit in the new purpose-designed toolbox made at woodwork classes. Some discrepancies would have to be made up in the near future as and when I could afford them.

Also, that week coincided with the Royal Coronation Review of the RAF at Odiham. It was stated in the news broadcasts that it would not be open to the public, however, Johnny Farrow and I decided to go anyway and take a chance on whether or not we could get in. We went on my Triumph Thunderbird and parked it with the thousand or so other motorbikes already there. In fact there was no problem except for the special royal enclosure; as John and I were standing near to this, we had a first-class close-up view of our new young Queen and her Consort in the royal car as they were driven in.

CHAPTER 16

THE PROTOTYPE DART KITTEN –
ITS RESTORATION AND DEMISE

Throughout the war I was intrigued to know the identity of a small aeroplane who's silver-painted mainplanes bearing the registration letters G-AEXT were stored in the roof trusses of the main (old) hangar. My curiosity was not appeased until later when Jock told me they belonged to an ultralight aeroplane called a Dart Kitten, the main components of which were stored elsewhere. He went on to say that it was hoped the rest of the aircraft would be arriving at Broxbourne to be reunited with them for its post-war C of A overhaul. Unluckily, the mainplanes were incinerated in the 1947 fire.

In early autumn that year, my interest was re-aroused when Jock confided that he was considering buying the only other Dart Kitten, the prototype G-AERP. Some correspondence between its owner and Jock brought forth a magazine clipping with a photograph – three-quarter front view – showing its quaint 'AVA' flat four two-stroke engine to advantage. As negotiations proceeded, I asked what happened regarding 'EXT. Some helpful soul, it seemed, had accepted the daunting task of making new wings; hopefully, it would fly once more. Meanwhile, having arranged with my brother Joe to hire his firm's lorry, he and I went to Leicester to collect the prototype Kitten G-AERP from a Mr Scott, with me clutching a banker's draft for what in those days seemed a large sum of money (just over half the current price of a new Triumph Speed Twin – ignoring the two-year waiting list).

Little was done to the aircraft for six months or so, because the ARB were unwilling to allow it to fly without a dual ignition system on its engine; this was a pity as I wanted to hear how a four-cylinder two-stroke sounded and was intrigued by its ingenious rotary mixture valve set in the crankcase 'twixt the opposing cylinders. The filler cap on the 10-gallon fuel tank, set in the aircraft's top decking aft of the firewall above the pilot's feet, bore the instruction: '*Use only Castrol motorcycle air-cooled oil in the petrol.*'

By the summer of 1948 Jock had struck up an acquaintanceship with a couple of DH Technical School students nearing graduation and willing to branch out on a project of their own. At that time the de Havilland Aeronautical Technical School offered two grades of training according to ambition and academic achievement: Engineering or Trade Apprenticeships. The former required a higher academic standard and allowed training in all Company departments to enable the pupil to determine where, in the aircraft industry, he or she might wish to make a career. Trade apprenticeships were for those who wished to train for a specific branch of the industry such as toolmaker, machine shop, fitter, panel beater or whatever. Engineering apprentices were usually referred to as 'Students' and trade apprentices as 'Apprentices' or 'T/A's.

Meanwhile Jock had obtained a lightweight, twin-cylinder JAP J99 engine based on an Aeronca design from America – brand-new complete with two lovely BTH magnetos. The DH students, ebullient Desmond Norman and thoughtful genius John Britten, designed, stressed and caused to be manufactured a set of first-class steel tube engine bearers that allowed the JAP engine to be installed in the Kitten airframe.

Despite its long period of storage, when it was opened up for inspection and stripped of fabric very little structural repair was required. Whilst the engine bearers were being manufactured, Des and John helped in restoring the airframe and attaching the new fabric, doping and spray-painting. The original red & silver scheme became light metallic blue & silver. Fuselage and wing centre-section were blue and, where the silver mainplanes joined, an arc of blue paint swept from the root-end trailing edge forwards and outboard to the leading edge, ending in a thin stripe at the wingtip. Tail components were similarly treated, registration letters being silver on the fuselage and blue on the wing. During their time spent helping in airframe restoration, Des and John were great working companions, joining in our tea breaks and subjecting Jock to a fair amount of friendly leg-pulling. We were all on first name terms, which in 1948 was still unusual bearing in mind that John and Des hailed from a higher echelon in society. However, due to my status as resident woodworker, Des always called me "Chippy."

Once the engine had been installed, the wingless and tailless airframe disappeared for nigh on a year to the factory of a Club member, where it was fitted up with a nicely blended set of engine cowlings. Meanwhile, Jock asked me to make a new instrument panel to carry an additional artificial horizon. What started out as a stiff ¼ in ply panel became somewhat 'wingy-wangy' by the time the requisite quantity of perforations and instruments had been added. However, once installed and with its pristine coat of glossy black paint, the decking structure contributed the necessary stiffness. When about to connect the throttle linkage, we found that the existing quadrant in the cockpit would produce a reverse effect (shades of wartime dalliance with the French Caudron Simouns!). To contrive a suitable lever mechanism to counteract this situation was a daunting and unsatisfactory solution which we wished to avoid. Later, when working on a Lycoming-powered Auster, the answer presented itself.

"Write to Auster Aircraft," I suggested to Jock, "and ask if they can supply a push-pull throttle control for an Auster Mk. V."

He favoured me with a look of withering scorn implying that I was an idiot, and promptly did as I suggested. My friend and colleague 'Barnie' quickly made a simple bracket to support the yellow-knobbed device and we were in business. I think this machine helped sow the seeds of my future as a designer.

Our next problem concerned the fuel contents gauge, or rather, its absence! Considerable lack of funds and spare time meant that frugality was paramount. To remove the forward decking structure for a protracted fuel tank modification was definitely a non-starter. Those of us involved wandered around with vacant expressions as we racked our brains trying to find a solution.

At that time, the Managing Director, Mr A.R. Frogley, owned a very early Piper Cub with a side-valve Continental engine. We had been experimenting with a simple auxiliary fuel tank to supplement the meagre tankage provided, and this consisted of a two-gallon tin in the cockpit with a rubber pipe from its base running up the side, then through a small hole in the windscreen and connected to a short stack-pipe in the filler just forward of the screen. To persuade the juice to climb uphill, a bicycle tyre valve was attached to the cap of the tin and atmosphere introduced by bicycle pump in the time-honoured way, pressurising the tin and thus forcing extra fuel from tin to tank. The fuel gauge provided in this aircraft was a stiff wire rod passing vertically through a narrow sleeve in the filler cap and terminating in a cork floating on the surface of the *'petroleum spirit – highly inflammable,'* so that as fuel was consumed the rod sank lower until it was time to seek emergency landing grounds.

"Why not," I suggested, "do the same on the Kitten?"

This time Jock became a bit cross and stamped away. A couple of days later Barnie soldered a thin piece of tube to the Kitten's fuel tank filler cap and I made a rod from a length of stout welding wire and a big cork.

"I'll only allow that until we can come up with something better," Jock decreed. We never did.

The Kitten's sailplane ancestry became apparent when assembling the flying surfaces to the main airframe. The aileron cables were rigged to a crank arrangement at the wing roots so that, when assembled to the centre-section, the cranks aligned with matching fittings secured with pins in such a way that the aileron setting was unaffected. A similar arrangement was used for the elevator actuating lever which slotted into a channel fitting suspended between the control cables. Short, tapered wing attachment pins were pulled toward one another through the joint plates situated either side and top & bottom of front & rear spars by thin studs passing through their centres and secured with special slotted nuts each end. Gaps between outer wing and centre-section were bridged with 4 inch-wide cross-grained ply strips at the leading & trailing edges and finished with a covering of 6 inch-wide fabric tape doped into position around the wing chord. Landing gear consisted of pneumatic-tyred steel disc 'builder's barrow' wheels set in forks welded to 2 inch diameter steel tubes which, at their top ends, were mounted to pairs of wishbones pivoted at their rear ends to the top & bottom of the forward face of the centre-section front spar and with a spring set diagonally from front to rear – similar to the girder forks of an old-fashioned motorbike. A crude box-like aluminium fairing covered the arrangement on the undersurface of the wing, but on the upper surface a piece of sheet rubber held in place by woodscrews through a square aluminium frame covered the hole. As the undercarriage deflected on landing, it rose above the upper surface, pushing the rubber sheet into a flattish sort of pyramid.

Barnie and I made full use of slack periods during our duty rosters when when we had to be on hand to attend the needs of the flying types. It was on such an occasion that we decided to try for the Kitten's first engine run. Having previously spent a hectic day getting everything in order on both airframe and engine, all we needed were four sparking plugs, but the only 14 mm plugs in store were screened types for the Gipsy Queens and in any case, this engine really needed motorcycle types. Barnie and I looked at my Speed Twin and thought identical thoughts.

Barnie said: "Pity there are only two."

"There are spares in the tool kit," I answered, and fished them out whilst he grabbed a plug spanner and immobilised my 'loved one.'

With no Chater-Lea terminal ends to hand, we bared the cable ends, twisted them around the plug terminals and squashed them in place with the plug terminal nuts.

"It's only for the first run," said Barnie; "it won't matter."

It took about twelve swings to get it going. Barnie ran it up and after warm-up and testing for 'mag drop,' got out and offered to let me taxi it – they were *my* plugs after all! It was fun to sit in the formed plywood seat and play hangar-pilot. Without any brakes, one had to rely on the generous rudder for lateral control and the skid for braking. However, with HRB at the wingtip and my size nines planted on the harmonium-type rudder pedals, I opened her up and let her roll. Trundling round in a 20-yard turn, we halted between hangar and Clubhouse and, after Barnie had replaced the wheel chocks, I ran it up to full revs and eased back to a lumpy tickover. Without shock mounts on the engine mounting, every 'suck-push-bang-blow' was felt through the woodwork.

Meanwhile, a Tiger had just landed and Peter Ayles emerged, grinning all over his rubicund features. He signalled that he too would like to have a go and quickly took my place; he waved the chocks away and began a rather more protracted taxying routine. After taxying to the far corner of the field, he emerged at full chat into wind and, as daylight appeared under the wheels, we realized the full import of what he was doing. Having circled the aerodrome a couple of times, he gave us a 'beat-up' and then landed. Climbing out, he came over to us, thumped our shoulders and strode back to the Clubhouse, laughing like a schoolboy. As we checked over the machine prior to putting it away, Barnie, with a horrified expression, indicated one of the plugs, which was three threads loose.

"Well," I said, "how were we to know that the silly b***** would fly it?"

Next day Jock was far from amused and berated Peter at length. To his credit he did not castigate Barnie and me, and we, in turn, played down the incident by assuring him that it was an impulse action, and in any case, he had kept the aircraft within the aerodrome boundary. We also considered discretion as the better part of valour and kept 'mum' about the loose plug! More engine runs and fine tuning were carried out with a proper set of plugs, and thoughts turned to application for C of A. Prior to that, one of the engine bearer lugs cracked, causing the engine to be removed so that the damaged bearer could be sent back to its designer for consultation and possible modification. Eventually, a diagonal bracing rod, adjustable for tension between upper and lower attachment lugs, was evolved, and with suitable repair and reinforcement to the damaged part, re-assembly of the engine to airframe allowed a fresh set of test runs to take place. All this took a fair amount of time as, up to that point, it was still a spare-time project, so it was late summer of 1952 before the ARB were called in and a Certificate granted.

Before he could fly the aeroplane himself, Jock had to get a licence and, although he could do so at 'trade,' so to speak, it was still a pricy exercise to maintain an aeroplane and pay for lessons. So a deal was arranged whereby the Club offered free hangarage and maintenance and he only paid for parts and materials, and in return the Club would allow certain specified members to fly the aeroplane on hire. Peter Ayles test-flew further sorties to build up experience to pass on to those select few members.

I was on duty with Pete Jackson in late autumn 1952 when popular Bill de Vos came to fly the Kitten; he had arrived once or twice on a spanking new Ariel Red Hunter Twin motorcycle so, as a fellow motorcyclist, I invited him to view my brand new Triumph Thunderbird before perambulating into the wide grey yonder. It was in this happy mood of motorcyclists' camaraderie that we went through the starting-up routine after my showing him where all the bits were and how the seat belt differed from the other types.

After he had taken off, I returned to the hangar and busied myself with one of those 101 mundane tasks that always need attention, and was just leaving it to join Peter in DeeKay when I saw the Kitten approaching the Clubhouse from the south-west at about 200 feet altitude and getting lower. The engine was only idling and as the machine drew nearer I fervently willed him to open the throttle (by that time he was down to about 60 feet). Much too late he did so and, as the diminutive engine burst into full life, the aircraft rolled about its fore & aft axis and I had a split second's view of its underside as it completed its rotation and dived into the Clubhouse lawn at about 5° beyond vertical with the most horrendous noise of ripping and snapping plywood.

Bill died three days later.

Two crash inspectors arrived the next day and I was interviewed at length by the senior one as he painstakingly recorded in longhand every detail I could recall. It was the first serious accident to an ultra-light aircraft since the war and they were being particularly vigilant. Following on, a couple of policemen came into the workshop and the routine was repeated ("In case the poor fella don't pull through," explained the Sergeant). The senior crash inspector returned twice more and, with the aid of a prismatic compass, asked me to show him, from where I had stood, the direction of the Kitten's approach. Apparently a Club member inside the Clubhouse had seen the aircraft approaching and was convinced it was from a slightly different direction. I was also asked how I had judged the altitude prior to impact.

"How high are those trees near the road behind the Clubhouse?" I countered.

"About fifty-odd feet."

"Well, he was level with the tops of them."

Once again I was asked to stand where I had witnessed the event and to accompany the investigator on to the Clubhouse verandah whilst he explained to me where the other chap said he saw it. I stuck to my statement: I was outside, he was in the bar.

Once the investigators departed we were allowed to move the wreckage. It was very sad to see bits and pieces we had so enthusiastically produced and fitted as just so many trampled-on bits of rubbish. Among them were the ignition switches which the investigator had found to be in the 'off' position. Bill must have switched off a foot or so from impact. Apart from the tragedy, I was particularly sorry that Jock had lost the aeroplane he had so long striven to make airworthy without having had the pleasure of even taxying it.

Called as chief witness at the inquest, I was interested to note that the advisor to the Coroner was my interviewer with the prismatic compass. Our local paper noted that: '. . . *Mr Smith, unlicensed Ground Engineer with the Herts & Essex Aero Club, demonstrated with a model how the aeroplane had hit the ground. . . . A verdict of accidental death was recorded.*'

After the inquest, Bill was buried in St Augustine's churchyard, Broxbourne. Peter Ayles flew a Club Auster and dipped its wings in tribute overhead at the time of Bill's interment.

Why did Bill de Vos head toward the Clubhouse with the engine throttled back? That was a question asked by many. I have my own theory but no good purpose would be served by airing it.

CHAPTER 17

JIM MCMAHON

Australian Jim McMahon was resident pilot instructor at Broxbourne from 1951 until I left in 1953. He had flown converted Tiger Moths for an aerial top dressing firm in New Zealand, was a good instructor, an excellent pilot and popular with all of us ground staff, particularly so with the ATC Scholarship Cadets. He was also a very good aircraft ground engineer and once sorted a problem on the magneto of my Speed Twin which had baffled me for some time.

He needed transport and, although able to borrow the odd car from the likes of the Club Secretary, really required his own vehicle for the convenience of visiting people in connection with some projects that emerged later. All cars were expensive at that time – new ones even more so and even harder to come by. In the end he bought an elderly Morris Ten of early 1930s vintage and doubtful mechanical condition. Within a short time and between his piloting duties he stripped down and refurbished all the relevant mechanical bits of engine & transmission, and stripped out and overhauled the hydraulic braking system to the extent of removing all the pipework and thoroughly purging it internally.

He found that new tyres for the car were expensive and still difficult to obtain. He said that in Australia, during the war years, tyre shortage was overcome, to some extent, by cutting the wire centres out of old larger tyres and forcing the remainder over the balding, canvas-showing originals (to form 'galoshes' to extend the mileage); he was amazed that we had never done this and scandalized that 'Authority' would not have allowed it. I boggled at the thought of the heat thus generated whilst driving in the bush; maybe the tyres vulcanized themselves together to make a sort of super retread. However, persistence won out and, with some good second-hand tyres fitted later, the car was soon roadworthy and put to good use. As good a navigator as he was in the air, the roads of London were something else; one evening he became so hopelessly disorientated in town that he found a parking place, left the car and came home by Underground and Greenline coach! Next day Peter Ayles drove him to town to retrieve his car and guide him home.

One fine summer evening he was checking out a pupil pilot in a Club Auster; they were in a climbing turn over the River Lee when the engine made a series of horrid bangs and ceased to function. Taking over the controls, and with the propeller continuing to 'windmill' whilst horrendous and expensive bangs emanated at each revolution from the engine, Jim made a splendid emergency landing in Hundred Acre Field at Amwell, with no further damage to the aeroplane. This was the third aircraft to do so, the others being a

Vickers Valentia in 1935 and a Waco Hadrian glider on the way to Arnhem in 1944.

Jim was a quiet, self-effacing chap not given to boasting. When interviewed about the incident by the local press, his attempt to play down the heroic bit was misinterpreted and it read as if he dismissed such trivialities as day-to-day events in a shoulder-shrugging sort of 'devil-may-care' attitude – not really Jim at all! The Cirrus Minor engine, when stripped down later, was found to have suffered a broken crankshaft. The front web of No. 2 crank pin had fractured across its width, allowing the prop to freewheel but depriving the magnetos of drive and thus the cylinders of the requisite suck-push-bang-blow.

I flew a couple of times with Jim, once in an Auster and also in a Gemini when we were trying to get a radio to work that I had just installed. In the first case he had time to give me an unofficial flying lesson, but due to lack of radio function in the Gemini, he got a bit cross and zoomed back to base with a rapid sideslip; my stomach arrived back ten minutes after we had landed.

In the early autumn of 1952 he started to build a plywood mock-up of a hopper to install in the front cockpit position of a Tiger Moth, to convert it for the aerial application of superphosphates for a New Zealand cropdusting firm with which he was associated. Jock allowed him to borrow a spare front fuselage frame to use for trial installation. This enterprise took place near my work station and he used my tools. I was delighted that he took me into his confidence about the project and also that he sought my opinion on one or two aspects. He was concerned at possible difficulties with loads on the outlet flap (which was to be a sort of door at the bottom of the hopper and hinged at the front), particularly with regard to being able to shut the flap when necessary without too much of a Herculean effort. I was gratified when he adopted my suggestion to pivot it in the centre like a carburetter butterfly, allowing the down-load to balance the force and lighten the lever effort. Once the mock-up had been completed to his critical satisfaction, Jim took it to an aircraft sheet metal firm for drawings and manufacture of all the necessary components.

Later, when the actual metal hopper and its functioning mechanism had been installed in the particular aircraft – converted most ably by my friend Barnie (I only hacked the wooden bits) – Jim asked me to devise a quick-action sprung lid. I made a stiff plywood cover pivoted at the front edge and held shut with aerolastics in such a way that they went 'over centre' and equally held it open for filling in a secure manner (in susbequent years, when in the design office, I learnt that such a mechanism was known as a 'bi-stable device'). He also needed a fairing underneath the machine to protect the flying controls from the ravages of agricultural chemicals. Both these items that I made were successful and helped me on course for my eventual career as a Design Engineer.

Jim went to a lot of trouble to get the project approved by the ARB, but on a visit to de Havilland at Hatfield, he was told that the loads he intended to put in the aircraft were beyond the permitted parameters and could not be allowed under any circumstances; they did, however, agree that a de Havilland Canada DHC.2 Beaver aircraft could be suitably converted as an agriculural top-dressing machine with their own design of hopper installed in the rear of the cabin: this at a price that would have frightened Paul Getty.

Dismayed by the decision, he contacted the Air Registration Board again for advice, and to his delight they replied, in effect: "We gave you permission to carry these loads in a Tiger Moth. Who the hell do DH think they are to dispute our stress figures?"

The following piece of doggerel from one member of staff appeared later:

The project of Jimmy McMahon
Is a hopper as big as a vahon;
Built to carry phosphates,
It is known to his mates
As 'That aerial watering cahon.'

Two Tiger Moths were converted at Broxbourne, ZK-BAF and ZK-BAH. Later, Jim joined up with Des Norman and John Britten, who together had set up an aviation service firm at Bembridge, in the Isle of Wight. They, in turn, went on to greater things after quite a lot of work with crop-spraying aircraft in the Cameroons and the USA.

TOP: Repairs under way on Messenger G-AISL in the hangar at Nevers (note the grotty cable).
BOTTOM: Another view of 'ISL's stern, with a Potez, Storch and Jodel Bébé for company.

TOP: Jodel Bébé F-PDHK, showing its Volkswagen engine.
BOTTOM: M. Bruno, airport manager & general factotum, allowing me to sit on his 1928 Armor Alcium with H & E Club Auster G-AIZV as backdrop.
Photo: 'Jock' Ogilvie.

TOP: Peter Ayles about to test-fly the prototype Dart Kitten G-AERP post-war.

BOTTOM: Wreckage of G-AERP prior to inspection by the AAIB team.

TOP: Jock surveys his shattered dream when the crash inspectors had gone.
BOTTOM: Roy Ogilvie taking Denis French for a spin on his customized
Corgi.

TOP: Visiting Auster G-AIZU, whose pilot forgot when landing that the wheel brakes were still on.
BOTTOM: Resident Airspeed Consul on C. of A. overhaul.

TOP: Auster Autocrat G-AJEI that was used for faking pictures of G-AGYD flying under the Thames bridges.
BOTTOM: Lunchtime TLC on my Triumph Thunderbird.
Photo: Barnie (Howard Barnes).

TOP: G-AIYO, Fairchild Argus of the Women's Junior Air Corps, on a visit to Broxbourne.
BOTTOM: John Chapman and Barnie working on the engine of Hornet Moth G-ADOT.

TOP: DH Dove repair and overhaul at Leavesden (also note Company Beaver to R. of photo).
BOTTOM: Dove stripped down for complete overhaul.

CHAPTER 18

DE HAVILLAND'S

It was 25 miles by road to Leavesden Aerodrome, near Watford, from the family home at Ware Road, Hoddesdon. On a map it scaled about 15½ miles 'as the crow flies' west-south-west from Hoddesdon. The M25 motorway was not even a gleam in some future planner's eye and there was no alternative but to go via Hertford and Hatfield, then head for Watford on the A405. My new Triumph Thunderbird ate up the distance in a very efficient and rather hairy way and, realizing that a lower cruising speed might be more life-enhancing, I aimed at an average journey time of 40 minutes each way, leaving the house at 7.10 am and arriving with about ten minutes in hand prior to starting time. A neighbour opposite told Mother that she set her clock by my morning departure time.

It is difficult now to imagine what a wonderful time it then was for anyone involved in the aircraft industry; de Havilland, in particular, were in the forefront of design innovation gained in wartime with the Mosquito, followed by the Hornet and Vampire fighters. Now, in the post-war years, all sorts of exciting projects were under way with gas turbines, guided missiles and aircraft such as the Dove, Heron and Chipmunk. And with the Comet airliner now in service, the British public were justly proud of their aircraft industry.

Leavesden Aerodrome was the headquarters of the de Havilland Engine Company, whose factory complex occupied the Garston side of the airfield. The Aircraft Company's Service Department, Civil Repairs (SDCR) was located in former wartime hangar buildings on the opposite western side of the airfield adjacent to the A41 Aylesbury Road and above the railway tunnel. There was a small gate leading off this road manned by a member of the de Havilland police force from 7.30 to 8.15 each morning and 5.30 to 6 in the evening; between times one had to enter the main gate from Leavesden village and journey about a mile around the peri-track to our hangar – a tedious chore for a latecomer.

Having left H & E in July 1953 with aspirations of getting my sticky hands on the up-to-date Doves, Herons and Chipmunks, being directed to help an ebullient character put finishing touches to a recently rebuilt DH.89 Rapide (an ex-RAF Dominie) seemed something of a let-down. The character was one "Titch" Hill, a fellow motorcyclist who quickly took me under his wing and initiated me into the de Havilland way of doing things; we hit it off at once and worked together for that first week or so until the summer holiday close-down. Being a newcomer, I was approached by foreman "Sandy" Smith, who asked if I would work with his group during the closed period; not wanting another two weeks unpaid holiday so soon after starting, I complied with alacrity. Friend Rob Capper was finishing his engineering apprenticeship at Leavesden and said I was lucky, as the group would shortly be at London

Airport to introduce a large modification programme on a BOAC Comet! Dreams were beginning to come true at last.

The DH.106 Comet, the world's first jet-propelled airliner, had been in scheduled service for over a year prior to my joining SDCR, but alas three had already been written off. A Canadian Pacific Comet 1A was destroyed when it ran off the end of a runway by getting into a no take-off, nose-high stall situation at Karachi the previous March, when all on board were killed. A similar accident had occurred to BOAC Comet G-ALYZ at Rome the previous October, but the pilot had aborted the take-off with a wheels-up termination and everyone on board had walked away unharmed, although the aircraft had proved unsalvageable. Between these events, BOAC Comet G-ALYV had broken up in the air during a storm at Calcutta. An inauspicious start for such a great step forward in air travel!

As a consequence of these accidents, investigations had shown cracks in some tailplane rib flanges and it was believed that this had initiated the mid-air break-up of the Calcutta Comet. (I had earlier heard a rumour that similar fatigue in the wing structure of the DH.110 had initiated its mid-air break-up at the Farnborough Air Display in September 1952.) By the time I arrived at Leavesden, a major repair and modification programme was under way on all Comet tailplanes; this involved removal of the rear spars to access inspection and repair of any ribs so damaged. In addition, urgent research into the fitting of 'droop-snoot' wing leading edges and engine air intakes was in progress at Hatfield on Comet 2 G-AMXA.

However, a variety of other tasks were required of us skeleton staff during the first couple of days of the closed period. One morning, a huge wooden packing case stood on the apron outside the Flight Test end of the hangar, from which we unloaded the dismantled components of the first production DH (Canada) DHC.3 Otter in the UK, later to be assembled in time for display at that year's Farnborough Air Show.

Prior to this, we were involved in moving about a variety of aircraft and equipment to generally tidy things up. A smart-looking Leopard Moth belonging to the Engine Company had just been serviced and stood in front of the hangar doors; Bill Rutland told me to rally some help to push it for refuelling about 100 yards away, and I tentatively suggested that were he to swing the prop for me, I could taxy it there. Aghast at such effrontery, he wondered who I thought I was to even ask such a thing, so I politely pointed out that in the past I had not only taxied Moths, but Proctors, Austers, Messengers, Geminis and even a Rapide. Red in the face, he told me to get help and push it, and added that no one, *but no one*, other than pilots or specially approved inspectors, taxied aircraft. A bit of a come-down for yours truly!

A session of Comet tailplane repairs followed, which involved making flanged repair plates to attach to the ribs where cracks had occurred in their flanges. The tailplane skins were 18 swg Alclad with a number of 'witch's hat' section stringers set spanwise and 'Reduxed' to their inner faces. The ribs were 20 swg pressings, flanged and with large diameter plunged lightening holes over their length. Slots were cut in them where they crossed the stringers and the rib flanges were joggled to sandwich the stringer flanges and riveted through. Movement and fretting had generated cracks from these rivets along the rib rivet lines up to two or three rivets either side of the stringers. The method of repair was to remove the rivets in the vicinity of the cracks, drill small holes to locate the ends of any cracks in the rib flanges and fit the repair patch to straddle the stringer, drilling and riveting it to rib and skin with the addition of a small extruded bracket to tie the rib and patching to the apex of the stringer section with a 'Chobert' blind rivet which, hopefully, would eliminate crack-inducing drumming of the ribs. Those nearest where the rear spar had been removed were quite easy, but as one progressed forward, it became neccessary to squeeze further and further into the tailplane until one had to rest one's knees on a box or other convenient receptacle and lay prone inside between a pair of ribs to install the requisite repair. (Finding a fitter in such a position, it was a good jape to tie his shoe-laces together and laugh as he stumbled about when he emerged – but I digress!) One therefore needed a helper to 'dolly-up' the rivet tails whilst manipulating the compressed-air rivet gun.

(The prevailing method for riveting structures at de Havilland was to pre-drill the parts and, after deburring and painting, assemble them with a minimum number of skin clips through strategic rivet holes and with rivets filling in the remainder secured in place with strips of Sellotape over their heads. A pneumatic riveting hammer fitted with an appropriately shaped snap was placed on each Sellotape-covered head in turn and a smooth, flat-faced steel 'dolly' held against the rivet tail. When the gun was operated, a shock wave passed through the rivet to the dolly which, being held firmly against the rivet, reacted by hammering the rivet-tail into a satisfactory cheese-shape due to the 20-30 cycles-per-second action of the gun. Thus the rivet head was held firmly to its seating. As a bonus, the Sellotape protected it from damage by the rivet snap. If trying to set a rivet by hammering its tail on the other hand, there was a danger of pushing the rivet back, causing a gap under the rivet head and possibly also expanding the rivet shank between the faces of the parts to be joined, especially with small rivets in thin sheet alloys.)

A pair of apprentices were in such a position one day when the riveting one of the pair suddenly ejected like a cork from a highly-charged champagne bottle and began waving his arms and gasping for air; he was swearing volubly, if a trifle incoherently., and such words as "bloody stink" and "dirty sod" emerged in a tirade. The other one came out from the tailplane more slowly with a sheepish smirk on his face; apparently, whilst straining to hold the riveting dolly, he had broken wind and the fumes – being contained within the confines of his boiler suit – had exited through his open-necked shirt into the face of the riveter!

Upon completion of internal repairs, tailplanes were taken to Hatfield for setting in the jig for reassembly of the rear spar. This was done in the evenings when the dayshift had departed and the jig was unoccupied and available. We were all required to attend in order to manhandle them in and out of the jig. Later, it was found that, by just re-riveting the rear spar in its original rivet positions, no structural distortion occurred and such expeditions became redundant. During the jig re-riveting procedure, those of us not directly involved were free to look around 'the line,' as the Comet assembly area was referred by the *cognoscenti*. I was a bit daunted by the complexity of it all but nonetheless somewhat concerned at the here-and-there way of doing things. I suppose I had expected an assembly line similar to pictures seen of bombers rolling off the production line at Willow Run in the States; instead, large sections were brought together as whole aeroplanes wherever space could be found in the limited hangarage available. Large vertical hinged flaps, each with a semi-circular cut-out, had been attached to each of the mating edges of the large sliding doors opening onto the concrete apron, and the edges of the cut-outs were lined with thick strips of felt; thus a Comet could be accommodated two-thirds into the hangar and the big doors partially closed and the gap filled by the hinged flaps fitting snugly round the rear fuselage. It looked very odd from the outside, as if an empennage attached to a little bit of fuselage had been stuck onto the outside wall of the hangar!

De Havilland's assembly plant at Chester was better equipped for production, having been built just pre-war as a Government 'Shadow' factory during the period of the 'Arms Race.' DH acquired the premises for Mosquito production and carried on with Dove assembly on cessation of hostilities; by the time I joined the firm, they were producing Comet components as well.

During the second week of the holiday closed period, we precious few were dispatched to Heathrow for a rapid 'mod' installation on BOAC's Comet 1 G-ALYY in their spanking new and wonderfully equipped Comet maintenance hangar. We all worked a 12-hour day shift for over a week including Sunday and August Bank Holiday. Another group worked a similarly-houred night shift for continuity. In view of distance from base and length of shift, we each qualified for a lodging allowance of 15/6d a night but, as we all chose to journey to and fro each day by our varied forms of transport, we pocketed the tax-free lucre. To start at 8.00 am at the Heathrow hangar meant leaving home no later than 6.30 am and arrival home no earlier than 9.30 pm, and a bit later when caught up in the wretched Bank Holiday rush. It was a case of 'bite, bed, breakfast and bike to work,' with 'bike' home again at night: my Thunderbird was getting well run-in!

I was very impressed with the way that the BOAC ground staff set about preparation of the aircraft for a major maintenance schedule. By the evening of the first day the cabin had been stripped, tanks drained, all four engines removed and every inspection orifice laid bare. Our DH gang were then able to fit in our particular tasks alongside BOAC's people without getting in each others' way. Some weeks later, with all the overtime payments in, I was bemoaning to my eldest brother how much Income Tax had been taken and was amused to note the way his eyebrows shot upwards, as though to compensate for his thinning pate; he was astutely aware of the wages needed to qualify for that amount of tax!

Upon return to Leavesden, tailplane repairs were still a priority and I, along with some of the Engineering and Trade Apprentices, was asked to work night shifts. We were tasked to assist a gang of itinerant Service Department fitters who were likely to be dispatched anywhere repair work was required at any time. There were several such gangs, controlled by a Mr J. Coppin, working wherever de Havilland aircraft were in service, and known by the base staff as "Coppin's Mob." The gang was equipped with a new Bedford Dormobile van within which was a large wooden box containing most tools and parts that might be needed for general repairs according to what aircraft type they were to service; this was usually referred to by the gang as "our 'b*****y' box." The ganger in charge was a tall, lean, mid-thirties Irishman and a great character; he organized our tea breaks in the small canteen at the end of the main hangar, and when it was ready would yell the full length of the hangar in a voice that could have been heard at Pinner: "Tae oop, yer b*****s!" A further fortnight of 8-to-8, seven days a week, followed before I had a weekend off and returned to normal dayshift.

Once the tailplane saga ended, a variety of jobs came my way and Tich, who had inherited a better 'barrow' (mobile workbench), kept his promise and endowed me with his old one; thenceforth this was always referred to as "'Arry's barrer," a most useful item when one has to travel to the task rather than when the task is set before one. Such was the camaraderie of us motorcyclists – referred to by the jealous as the "Mo'bike Mafia"!

Once again I became involved in that scourge of quality, an individual bonus system. On the tailplane and Heathrow jobs, an average 'shop bonus' had been paid; now every operation was timed to the minute and, unless a run of a dozen or so identical jobs were undertaken, it was practically impossible to make a killing. Eight hours to strip and rebuild one Dove main undercarriage leg was ludicrous. Once I had to rebuild 10 Chipmunk undercarriage legs and was given a Trade Apprentice to help me; that was the only time I made over 100% bonus.

Another time I was given a Chipmunk mainplane to repair that had suffered taxying impact damage. The front root-end attachment bracket had been wrenched apart and there was damage to the leading edge. A new bracket was fitted and much jockeying with the root-end attachment jig ensued prior to all the riveting-up. It was only after trying to fit a minor modification to the aileron differential that I noticed that on impact the control cable had pulled the mechanism so hard that the differential structure had been distorted. Strangely, this fact had been missed by the senior inspector who had written up the damage report and, coincidentally, that same inspector oversaw my repairs, so I had to summon all my tact to bring the problem to his notice without involving those above who might feel compelled to chastise him. When he realized the situation, the Design Office at Hatfield were prevailed upon to produce a repair scheme for me to incorporate. A young, pleasant draughtsman from the Repair D.O. at Hatfield came to assess the problem and draw up a scheme; his name was Derry Banks, and little did I realise that, ten years later, we would be working alongside each other as colleagues in the New Project No. 2 Design Office at Manor Road. The inspector was later very kind regarding any jobs of mine that needed his signature. Needless to say, that particular job was well and truly sunk bonuswise despite my pleas to the rate fixer, who only allowed time for the extra repair. What I was supposed to book on for all the toing & froing the task had entailed was not his problem.

The SDCR Superintendent, Ken Brown, had a select number of fitters who were employed on a weekly staff basis and were not therefore involved in bonus schemes as such. Some of them were ex-RAF Flight Sergeants or experienced long-service DH types and former DH engineering apprentices. When an engineering apprentice finished his time and needed to further his practical experience before becoming a Company Technical Rep, he was employed in this group. There was some resentment toward these types from us hourly-paid fitters doing similar work, and matters came to a head when Ken Brown summoned them all to a meeting in his office to point out that, although they were not involved in the bonus scheme, they had to abide by the times given as if they were. This did not please them very much, but the response of the hourly-paid staff in contrast was a predictable "tough!"

My wartime experience of aircraft inspectors was never to argue and just do as they asked; after all, they had the last word when it came to signing out the job, and unless they did so there was no bonus at the end of the week. It was easy to revert to this philosophy and I soon had a good rapport with them, in particular one meticulous soul referred to darkly by some as "Denis the Menace." In fact, he was very conscientious, knowledgeable and helpful once he knew your abilities. I also befriended a Staff Fitter, George (Steve) Stephenson; he had joined the RAF pre-war as a Halton 'Brat' and had been a 'Chiefie' on a Liberator squadron in the Middle East. A long-service regular, he had been obliged to leave the Service to care for his ageing and ailing parents. (In order to do so he had been forced to seek employment at home in Brightlingsea, the only suitable local job being a Hoover rep.) They had since died, and so he joined DH and lodged nearby. We attended one another's Club Dinners, his Sailing Club at Brightlingsea and my Motor Club at Berkhamsted. He also came to Broxbourne with his fiancée Audrey for a New

Year Party at the H & E Clubhouse, where I introduced them to the boys and girls – my former friends and colleagues. We had a great time!

Early in the New Year in 1954 Air France Comet F-BGNZ came to Hatfield for overhaul and the introduction of many modifications and I was among the number of fitters sent from SDCR. There was an added bonus for me as we were paid mileage allowance from Leavesden to Hatfield; I normally passed Hatfield on my way to work and so I was halving my normal journey and being paid extra for it. My first job on the Comet was to remove the valuable cockpit clocks to be stored for safe keeping. Soon after, a serious altercation arose between Denis the Inspector and the Supervisor in charge concerning damage to a bulkhead in the equipment bay when a relay panel had been removed and the fitter involved had managed to chisel through the structure. When a Repair Scheme had been produced, Denis asserted his authority and declared that it was to be carried out by someone he could trust not to make a balls-up of it.

"Get Harry Smith to do it!" was his parting shot.

The Supervisor in charge of our Group was an ex-woodworker who was somewhat out of his depth dealing with large and complex all-metal aeroplanes. He relied heavily on his special gang of three fitters who seemed a trifle privileged and appeared to some of us unable to do anything wrong – in the eyes of their mentor at least! I suspected that it was one of these three who had caused the damage and when I was given the repair job my popularity with them – never much more than ill-disguised contempt – plummeted to 'ten to the minus six'! Sandy Smith, who was a Foreman Supervisor and second-in-command, allotted me the task and was helpful and sympathetic. I think he was disliked by the gang-of-four due to his long Company and RAF service and general competence. Furthermore, he got things moving and would never suffer fools gladly! Matters did not improve when, having completed the repair to the best of my ability, Denis was heard to say that it was a satisfactory repair nicely carried out.

Sandy allotted most of my jobs and we got on very well together. Once I was struggling to remove a changeover valve from the aileron servodyne; this required some stout hydraulic pipes to be disconnected which proved to be more than a mite recalcitrant. Sandy came along to check progress just as I was taking a breather, took the spanner from me and had a go himself; exerting his greater strength, his muscles bulged and he became red in the face. When it still failed to budge, he exclaimed: "Jesus wept!" It took both our combined efforts to make it shift.

Afterwards, as we rested from our toils, he asked, apropos of nothing whatever, if I knew the definition of a piebald horse. As I began to describe such an animal, he waved me to silence and said: "No, it's a horse with testicles exactly 3 1/7 inches in diameter!" (Pi-Balled.) Weakened further by the laughter, it was some while before I summoned sufficient strength to undo another pipe joint.

A large caravan trailer parked near the aircraft in the hangar had been allotted to our group as a sort of mobile workshop-*cum*-office/stores. In it, our Supervisor held court and doled out tasks. It annoyed me to note that whenever I passed by, the three stooges were in conference with him and, I suspect, dishing the dirt on the rest of us and wheedling all the best jobs. The most pugnacious of the trio was a strutting little turkeycock to whom I shall refer as 'Jed.' One day he made a great show of clambering onto the top of the fuselage in order to assess a position for an aerial mounting, not a particularly daunting task. The Supervisor gazed up at him with a silly, adoring grin on his face and remarked to all who happened to be in earshot: "Look at dear old Jed! Always taking on the difficult jobs with a happy grin." Having just fitted a new set of special pipe clips inside the wing tanks, which entailed crawling through a manhole in the front spar and into the leading edge, kneeling in puddles of fuel and trying not to succumb to raging claustrophobia, I was not really very amused!

It was a blow when Denis the inspector was diagnosed as having a severe dose of mumps. He had called in on his way home from his doctor, and I looked out of the crew door of the aircraft down on the chaps standing in a 20-foot circle as Denis, his neck swathed in heavy scarf, stood in the centre explaining his predicament. As I watched, the circle parted widely and he left to begin his protracted sick leave; a much needed ally had departed.

Shortly before we all reported to Hatfield on the Air France Comet, a newcomer had joined from Handley Page who was by chance allotted a bench space right outside the foreman's office, where he set up his fancy little tool cabinet containing a new-looking copy of Machinery's Handbook (and precious little else), ostensibly facing the office window and where he seemingly toiled away all day doing a not very technical task to a number of Chipmunk cockpit canopies. His crafty scheme worked; he said that Ken Brown was impressed with him and had marked him down as 'staff' potential. Not wishing to be too harsh, I can best describe him as a four-eyed oily little twit whose limited technical ability was overcome by blatant crawling. Needless to say we all dubbed him "The Creep." Happily, the favoured deadly trio treated him with even more contempt than they showed the rest of us. Toward the end of our session on 'NZ, a job sheet was produced for us each to sign off any task individually completed, and The Creep asked me if I had completed any of the jobs.

"Who wants to know?" I queried.

"Well, I can sign them off for you."

"Thanks, but I have already signed."

I knew what his slimy little game was: he wanted to take credit for a lot of jobs other people had completed.

Kim Stanton, a recently graduated Engineering Apprentice, with whom I had worked on night shift, went round among us saying: "Don't forget, chaps, The Creep will sign for all our jobs, so you needn't be too fussy about them!"

Up to when we first went to Hatfield all the people working in the Service Department were kindred spirits and nicely articulate. Naturally, there was a certain fruitiness of language when things went wrong, but nothing to offend. At Hatfield, there were a number of semi-skilled operatives (sub-assemblers, riveters and personnel referred to as 'dilutees'), whose vocabulary was so limited that they scattered the dreaded 'f'-word throughout their speech in a crude attempt at emphasis. Both Kim Stanton and I found this amusing and pathetic. Sometimes, they even split up words and inserted the odd 'f' between syllables. For instance, one Saturday morning a couple of riveters were working on our aircraft and bemoaned the absence of a fellow worker who should have been present; when finally he arrived a hefty argument ensued, culminating in the bossy one exclaiming: "Why wozzen't you effin' 'ere be nine the fuggin' smornin'!"

When Comet G-ALYP was lost at Elba on 10th January 1954, a fisherman reported hearing an explosion. It was theorised that the main turbine might have shed blades, penetrating the fuel tanks. This theory generated some panic modifications to Comet engine bays and our 'NZ was the guinea-pig for first installations. As well as fitting some heavy stainless steel plates adjacent to the fuel tank walls in the engine bays, within the vicinity of the large turbine wheel, the engine bay lower doors were also each to be lined with thin stainless steel sheet and a pair of 6 in x 4 in spring-loaded 'explosion doors.' I was given the first of these to modify and discovered how vicious stainless steel sheet can be to cut, shape and rivet. Furthermore, the drawings supplied were unfinished and carried no details as to how the explosion doors were to be made and fitted. Having reported that the job had come to a grinding halt for lack of information, I was told to leave it and start another; this one also terminated in a similar uncompleted state, and when the Drawing Office Section Leader was asked why the drawings were incomplete he replied that his chaps had been working long hours and had to have a break. No one pointed out that we were all working 12-hour shifts in 7-day weeks. I was more than a little miffed when Sandy reported that JT (the Supervisor) was complaining I should have progressed much further, although Sandy, at least, realised that I had done two and the other fitters only one. I asked how we were to finish them without drawings but for some reason the D.O. were held up as faultless and not to be criticised. JT, meanwhile, began daily to get more gaunt and haggard-looking as his responsibilty weighed ever more on his shoulders.

I then moved on to fitting the engine fuel filter de-icing installation, which had to be pressure-tested to 50 lb/sq in and held for 10 minutes.This system was operated by a hand pump located on the floor of the Flight Engineer's station, drawing de-icing fluid from a small reservoir in the equipment bay adjacent to a four-position change-over cock to select for each engine. When test pressure was applied, both pump & cock leaked like sieves. Also, the pump had an estimated maximum operational pressure of about 10 psi. With the inspector's agreement, all I could do was pressure-test each pipe run in turn in isolation from pump & cock, which involved sloshing Teepol over every joint whilst under pressure to check for leaks. When the inspector questioned the draughtsman about the test pressure instruction, he waffled on about a 1½ times maximum on the pump plus a factor and went on to prove that he was totally theorising and devoid of practicalities. A colleague, Ron Carter, was given a fitting to install inside the rear pressure dome that was, according to drawing instructions, located from the layout lofting by a theoretical dimensional station somewhere in mid-air and hence totally impossible to apply. This was common practice, which saved the draughtsman having to leave the office and crawl about the aeroplane. I quickly lost faith in that particular D.O.

The aircraft was nearing completion when, on 8th April 1954, disaster struck in more ways than one. Comet 1 G-ALYY, the one we had worked on at London Airport, was lost over the sea near Naples (and with it a 2BA Terry's spanner that had slipped from my fingers, dropped between the inner and outer skins of the port inboard engine air intake and wedged into an irretrievable position). Among the major repercussions this event generated was that all Comets were henceforth to be grounded, and Air France, BOAC and UAT demanded vast sums in reparation. Sir Geoffrey de Havilland was interviewed on television and, unwise to the evil deviousness of egocentric media personnel, pilloried and made to look foolish by an overpaid programme presenter who had neither made, nor done, anything useful in his tedious little life.

Returned once more to our Leavesden HQ, I was just getting back into routine tasks when Sandy approached and asked if I had a passport; he said that urgent modifications were required to RAF Venoms in Germany and I, along with others, should report at Hatfield the following Monday. It was only later in the day, when a young secretary asked me to sign a form, that I found meant a temporary transfer to Coppin's Mob. I was not best pleased but it was too late to retract. Three more of us from Leavesden reported at Hatfield, my 'oppo' Ron Carter, Bert Hooper and a new chap who had been transferred to us whilst at Hatfield from, of all places, a Drawing Office! He was not a youngster being given experience in various departments, but a forty-something former airline pilot called Pat Rochfort. Ron, Pat, a pleasant chap called John from Hatfield Experimental and I soon found ourselves, along with toolboxes and personal luggage, being loaded into the Company's own DHC.2 Beaver, flying formation with their Airspeed Consul in which another batch of fitters & inspectors was being chauffeured by Pat Fillingham. Our pilot was Peter Bois. Bert Hooper, who had joined us just prior to the Comet job at Hatfield, was not among our number heading for Germany; he had been allocated postings to remote UK RAF stations. A pity, as he was part of a trio with Ron and myself at Leavesden and we would have enjoyed his company. The other Pat, our new colleague, claimed the right-hand seat next to Peter by virtue of his past flying experience. So for the second time in less than three years I crossed the English Channel in a single-engined aeroplane, this time going the other way. Having cleared customs at Lympne, we followed the coastline into Holland to land briefly at Eindhoven, then carried on to RAF Buckeburg for another short stop to exchange real money into 'BAFs' (British Armed Forces currency) prior to landing at our destination at RAF Celle.

We were greeted by the foreman in charge and joined the rest of the group who had just finished for the day and were in a RAF bus on its way back to the billet, a former Luftwaffe barracks block, named by the RAF "Cunningham Block." After being allotted our bed spaces, we dined in the Sergeant's Mess and next day reported to the repair hangar to start work on the Venom modifications. But first we had to be issued with our Service Paybooks in the office allotted to our foreman. Although civilians, we were officially designated senior NCOs in order to reside in and come & go from a Royal Air Force Station in a foreign country. For a short time therefore, I was a Royal Air Force Flight Sergeant! Our Paybooks were used to issue us with our living expenses (£14 per week in BAFs) whilst we were overseas. Our weekly salary of £12 was posted to our home address or bank account as we pleased. We were charged about £4-10s per fortnight for all-in meals and accommodation on the RAF Stations. Although we could receive a percentage of our allowance in deutschmarks for local expenses such as visiting town, we could not exchange the residue into normal Bank of England currency. To those of us who had no wish to blow it all on booze and crumpet, a way round the problem was to obtain large denomination British Postal Orders from the RAF Camp's own GPO Sub-Post Office and send it home by normal Service mail.

On the Venom at that time, a certain weakness to the underside wing skins had shown up where a skin butt-joint was located adjacent to the wheel wells, and this required the skin to be strengthened with large 12 swg Alclad plates riveted over this area on the outer surface and secured with a great number of 5/32 in & 3/16 in countersunk rivets. Flexible fuel tanks and hydraulic actuators for the high-speed air brakes had to be stripped out to allow drilling and riveting through the skin. Foreman Supervisor Bill (alas, I have forgotten his surname) was a great organizer and soon had his team working in a production-line technique with us working in pairs and doing one particular task so that we became skilled enough to speed up the job.

After the RAF boys had brought the machine into the hangar and drained the tanks etc., one pair of our fitters would strip out the fuel bags, another would disconnect the flap actuators, a third would drill and fit the patch-plate and a fourth would rivet it up. Similar pairs would begin to put the bits back so that as one task was completed we moved onto the next aircraft. Pairs of fitters were doubled so that port & starboard sides were worked on simultaneously. In time we were turning out modified Venoms at the rate of two a day.

Ron Carter and I teamed up and we riveted the pre-drilled plates to the wing skins. After two weeks at Celle, we were sent on to Fassberg, which had been Goering's show-piece Luftwaffe aerodrome; all the hangars, workshops, stores, barrack blocks and administration buildings in smart red brick construction were set among the pine trees around the field and it was rumoured that it was not found by the Allies until a month or two after the war's end.

At Celle, Cunningham Block had been a dormitory type of barrack block, open plan, with beds arranged in rows either side, and the bed opposite mine had been occupied by a small, self-effacing, middle-aged fitter whose nightly snore rattled all the windows! His spongy-looking proboscis was large and coloured with what my old H & E colleague 'Slosh' Saunders would have called "a fine saloon bar tan," doubtless a contributory factor to the nightly reverberations. At Fassberg, however, we were allotted ground floor twin-bedded small rooms with windows looking out through the pine trees. Ron and I, being paired up workwise, decided to share. One item of furniture we found therein was a 4 ft-high by 6 inch-wide rack-like wooden device which was later identified as a rack to accommodate a couple of ·303 Lea Enfield rifles; its *raison d'être* was made apparent at 4.00 am one morning when we realized that a platoon of the RAF Regiment was billeted on the first floor as they crashed along the corridors on their way out for a military exercise, their hobnailed army boots ringing and echoing on the concrete floors and through our fragile bonces.

Leisure time was well catered for at RAF Fassberg. Although we had visited the historic old town when we were based at Celle, we mostly patronized the Malcolm Club, NAAFI or the Church of Scotland Huts canteen. Once, we teamed up with Pat and John and went into a restaurant for dinner and a modest cabaret. It was late when we left and we missed the last Camp bus. Setting out to walk the few miles back to Camp, John found a vacant taxi and, when we had all piled aboard, we could not make the driver understand what we meant by the 'RAF Station.'

"Die bahnhof, bitte?" queried our driver.

"Nein! Nein!"

Luckily, I remembered a few words from my tour with Les and Eric in 1951, plus a bit from a phrase book.

"Wir gehen die flugplatz, bitte."

"Ach, so! Jahwöl!"

"Danke! Danke!"

The other lads seemed most impressed.

From Fassberg, Celle was still the main town but much further to travel to, so we mostly stayed on Camp in which was provided an *Astra* cinema showing the latest releases, plus Malcolm Club and NAAFI. We were advised by our longer-residing colleagues that it was frowned upon for senior NCOs to patronize the NAAFI which was mainly for lower ranks. Fassberg was a super place. The RAF personnel were well catered for in sports and leisure facilities; as well as the usual sports fields, running tracks, gymnasiums etc., some of the more affluent were able to take up gliding. Ron and I often went for quite enjoyable walks within the aerodrome boundary. Sometimes we went to the village. Ron, who had only just finished his service as an air mechanic on a carrier in the Royal Navy, had reverted to his Navy vernacular as soon as we arrived at Celle. If he fancied a trip to the town or village, he would ask: "Going ashore tonight, H?" and kept referring to "bulkheads," "decks" and "liberty hours." He also, now and then, sang the Royal Navy version of Stephen Foster's song thus:

Beautiful Dreamer,
Lash up and stow.
"Cooks-to-the-Galley"
Has gone long ago!

Our £3 to £4 per two weeks' board and lodging on the Camp included all our meals which, in the Sergeant's Mess, as well as breakfast, were listed as 'Dinner' and 'Tea' (lunch and dinner). At all meals a large jug of tea with the milk already added was set on each table. One of the more amorously inclined fitters darkly intimated that it was overly laced with bromide; it certainly had a peculiar taste – sort of liquid cardboard-ish!

Work progressed quicker than expected on the Venom wing mods – probably thanks to Bill's efficient techniques – so six of us were sent back home and the rest were due to go on to Wunsdorf. Ron was particularly pleased to be on his way back to 'blighty,' as he called it. We all boarded a long troop train at Fassberg and waved to the girl who had served us tea and wads at the C of S Huts canteen as the train passed through Celle *bahnhof* (railway station) on its long journey to the Hook of Holland. Here we embarked on the *Empire Parkstone* for our overnight sea passage to Harwich. I accompanied Ron when he expressed the wish to take a turn around deck before "hitting the sack." Next morning we disembarked to change our money when Ron, being a few quid over the limit, asked me to change it with mine; in those days we were allowed to bring in only £15. And to go through Customs before boarding the train to Liverpool Street they charged me five guineas tax and duty on my new camera, about five bob more than I had paid for it. The Senior Customs Officer who took my money assured me that it was still a bargain. I repeated his strictures to the lads but they were less than impressed – derisive, in fact, inferring that I was a mug to have declared it. A couple of years later I was glad to have done so, otherwise I could not have traded it in at a reputable West End camera shop for a more advanced one which had been a Customs-confiscated new one, sold as second-hand.

In the aftermath of the Comet disasters, many stringent economies took place, one of which was withdrawal of Company sponsorship of the London Aeroplane Club at Panshanger. All the engineering apprentices based there for hands-on experience for Ground Engineers' qualifications, plus the permanent staff (notably the Chief Engineer and his assistant) were transferred to jobs at the Hatfield site or Leavesden, so some new faces were in evidence when we returned to base.

For the rest of my time at Leavesden I was involved in all manner of different jobs, mostly on Doves and Herons but with a smattering on Chipmunk components and some work on the same DHC.2 Beaver in which we had flown to Celle. I did not earn much bonus, but the experience was invaluable, as repair schemes, trial installations and one-off odd jobs all came my way. I was asked to help the resident fabric worker who was a bit inundated, and was given a Chipmunk mainplane and a pair of Dove inner landing flaps to re-fabric and dope. With experience of fabric work at Broxbourne, I had no problem except when attaching the double zip-fastener fabric patch inspection panel (at Broxbourne, we had had little success fitting fabric zip panels to Austers); it was creased from packaging, so I approached the 'fabric man' to enquire if he had an electric iron to press it.

"Don't bother!" was his surprising answer. "Just soak it in water, wring it out and whilst still wet, lay it on a thickly wet-doped surface, smooth it out and brush more dope on top. When it has all dried, rub it down and give it another couple of coats."

Poor old Jock would have had a heart attack, but the final result was very pleasing. I recalled the incident when young Jack Davey and I doped that Tiger Moth wing fabric on a cold damp October afternoon back in 1946. Maybe we had it right in the first place.

Another odd job was some restoration of the DH.53 Humming Bird, now at Old Warden with the Shuttleworth Collection. Someone had unearthed the remains and the DH students were given it as an exercise to redraw, manufacture new flying surfaces and rebuild the whole machine for flight. The fuselage assembly was brought to Leavesden pending completion of other parts and, as work was slack at that time, I had the task of removing the engine bearer fittings and then shot-blasting and repainting them. After that, Bill Rutland asked if I had any experience of woodwork. Prior to joining, Rob advised me to play down the woodwork part of my career as DH already had a surfeit of such skills. Going against his advice, I admitted that that had been an early discipline, so with the helpful co-operation of the Inspector, Geoff Lawson, we set about stripping off damaged and worm-eaten panels and replacing them with new ply. Our resident 'chippy,' who was busy on another job, could not have been more helpful, lending me tools and equipment and showing me how to make perfect scarf joints in the ply with his windy-drill-powered sanding disc (at Broxbourne we had had to use smoothing plane and spokeshave). Many years later, when visiting Old Warden, I saw a notice saying that the DH.53 had been restored by apprentices. "Ah yes!" I thought, "but who restored those fittings and renewed those ply panels?"

As autumn of 1954 drew nigh, the prospectus of Hatfield Technical College, now known as the University of Hertfordshire, was circulated, and my thoughts were turned to 'further education.' I had expressed enthusiasm to become an Aircraft Inspector, but one of my Inspector associates thought that a better goal would be to study for a degree; that, however, with my limited academic achievements, was a non-starter! In the end, due to my total lack of qualifications, the only course I could join at Hatfield was one for Aircraft Maintenance, divided into three sections: 'Engineering Drawing,' 'Science' and 'Aircraft Engineering,' three nights a week after work from 7 till 9 pm plus homework. By working overtime there was just time to make for Hatfield and tea & a bun in the Aerodrome Café prior to joining the class and arriving home at about 10 pm for my late-night kept-hot dinner, somehow fitting in the necessary homework in any other spare time I could find. The strain of trying to catch up on years of lost school work, in addition to homework, overtime and 50 miles a day motorcycling to and fro in all weathers, was manifested by a surfeit of disgusting boils being visited upon my body that stayed within its system for two or three years.

In early 1955 I met H & E colleague Pete Jackson and mentioned these problems to him, saying that a shorter journey workwise was what I needed. He suggested that if I joined the DH Propellers Flight Hangar at Hatfield, where he now worked as a planning engineer, I could at least halve the journey, and he arranged an interview with the Flight Hangar Super-intendent, Cliff Aubrey.

Cliff's office was in a long wooden hut on the airfield, adjacent to Propellers Flight Hangar and my interview was successful despite the distraction of his sexy secretary who rolled her come-to-bed eyes at me whilst I waited to be called to his inner sanctum. He was telephoning when I entered and waved me to a chair in front of his desk whilst I listened to him explaining to his caller why it was not a good idea to belly-land a particular Canberra in his charge.

"'Look! There's a 3,000 psi air bottle mounted in the bomb bay. If it belly-flopped, the bloody thing could go off like a 1,000 lb bomb."

This was said quite matter-of-factly and entirely without rancour. I gathered there had been an emergency during a test flight when the undercart was reluctant to lower for landing and the caller was asking the manu-facturer's representative for advice.

When able to give me his undivided attention, he explained that I would be working in the fitting shop making parts and bracketry for various trial projects installed in the variety of aircraft allotted to him, for different departments of DH Propellers, plus some for the DH Engine Company, whose aircraft were also in the care of Cliff's department. Because I was already DH-employed – albeit in a separate Company – I realized there might be some reluctance to allow me to transfer. Such actions were rigorously discouraged (if not overtly forbidden) in Company traditions. When Mr Aubrey asked why I sought to change, I explained about halving my daily journey and the proximity of Hatfield Tec for the course I was taking. Suitably impressed, he said he was sure something could be arranged and, after offering me a job (which I accepted) promised to keep the position open for me.

Upon return to Leavesden I approached Bill Rutland, explaining the situation, and asked if I could tender my notice and go to Hatfield. He smilingly acquiesced and so I next put my case to Joe Porter the Personnel Officer and asked for a week's notice; he promised to help all he could.

Foreman Ollie Wood had taken me under his wing, so to speak, to assist with various odd tasks that he was wont to deal with, and I had pleased him by listening to his strictures and getting the jobs done to his satisfaction. We had to make some undercarriage parts for a Fox Moth, which involved devising a welding jig for steel tube parts and rebuilding a rubber-block-filled compression strut. Later he gave me the task of hand-fettling a Heron elevator hinge-pin extractor that refused to locate as it should. When I told him that I intended to transfer to Propellers he suddenly lost interest in me and behaved in a hurt way as though I had upset him. I probably had, and I was saddened by this as I had liked working for him and hated the thought of having injured his feelings.

Things did not improve when I went to see Bill about leaving at the end of the week. He looked at me in amazement and said that I certainly could not and that he knew nothing about my wanting to transfer! I went to see Joe Porter and asked, in effect, what the hell was going on. What was the matter with Bill? Joe sympathized and asked me to leave it to him to try and arrange things for me. Somewhat mollified, I returned to the hangar to attempt to retrieve the rivet gun and air hose that I had passed over to a new chap. A couple of days later, Joe called me to his office and explained that he had spoken to Cliff Aubrey; my promised job was in abeyance for a week whilst my predecessor worked out his notice, and I was not to worry, he assured me that the transfer would go through. I never knew what diplomatic wiles he employed, but I was extremely grateful to him for whatever such machinations he used on my behalf. I looked at the transfer paperwork and in his notes Joe had explained my wanting to halve the journey mileage and added: " . . . Keen reliable worker and never late despite long distance from home and during extreme & adverse weather conditions."

I was quite touched by this, although 'never late' was a bit of an exaggeration. When the snow lay thick, my journey to Leavesden took twice as long with slithering slow progress in low gear whilst trying to stay upright and not slide off in front of a lorry or some such. Once, when zigzagging downhill toward a roundabout near Radlett, I knew I would be unable to stop and saw a British Road Services 8-wheeler just entering it from my right. The driver realized my predicament and halted his vehicle to allow me a straight run. They were true 'knights of the road' in those days! I dare not raise my hand from the bar to acknowledge his courtesy; I just hoped that he saw my nod of appreciation.

I was giving a regular lift to a student at the time, picking him up opposite the Aircraft Company main gate at Hatfield in the morning and dropping him off there on the way home at night. Sometimes, he would be a few minutes late and come rushing from the flats, coat tails flying, a piece of toast in his hand and spraying crumbs & apologies in equal measure and, as we proceeded, crunching toast noisily in my ear. One morning, after a heavy snowfall, I was about half an hour behind schedule and when I reached the pick-up point he was nowhere in sight; I waited a minute or two to tell him to find alternative transport but he did not appear, so I slithered my way on to Leavesden alone. Shortly after my arrival he turned up in a rage and got quite stroppy that I had not waited for him.

"I waited for nearly 30 minutes!" he moaned, "and then went over to the factory Transport Section to get a lift on the Company van" (which operated a regular daily 'milk run' between Hatfield and Leavesden). I pointed out that he must have been in the Transport Section before I arrived, and added that in any case I would never risk taking him in those conditions. He thought that a stupid excuse, inferring that it was my duty to do so as he paid me a shilling or two a week for the rides. Shortly after, he told me he would not need a lift any more as his middle-aged fitter boy friend had grown concerned at him risking his precious skin on my pillion in bad weather and promised to pick him up himself each day in his pre-war Ford Popular.

"Good riddance!" I thought.

This particular student was inclined to partake in late-night drinking now and then and often seemed half asleep. When helping me rivet some stiffeners to the inside of a Dove fuselage, he was outside with the rivet gun whilst I 'dollied-up' the rivet tails inside. When I called out to him "Rivet!" he sloppily allowed the snap to slide off the shallow mush-head and chatter down the fuselage skin, leaving a line of little half-moon nicks in the Alclad. Thinking of my lost bonus due to the time needed to rectify his damage, I called him a stupid useless b***** and suggested none too politely that he might stop playing with himself at night and wake up and concentrate. He just tittered foolishly at my vented anger.

My leaving was quite touching, with all and sundry wanting to shake my hand and wish me well in the new job. Ron Carter asked me to keep in touch and to visit him and his wife & family whenever.

CHAPTER 19

DE HAVILLAND PROPELLERS
(MANOR ROAD)

On a chilly Monday morning in March 1955 I presented myself to the Personnel Office at Manor Road to begin work at de Havilland Propellers, and was impressed by the business-like attitude of the Personnel Department. By the time they had completed all my details, the tea trollies were being wheeled from the nearby canteen to various morning tea-break locations on the Manor Road Site: I followed one to the Flight Hangar.

The Fitting Shop Chargehand at Manor Road was George Smith, and when he showed me my workplace, I found that I was sharing bench space with ex-H & E colleague Alan Slade. With Pete, Alan & myself at Manor Road, and the Kimm twins and Barnie & George Parker at the Aircraft Company, Herts & Essex had become a force to be reckoned with at de Havilland!

Work in the Flight Hangar Fitting Shop was a pleasant change. All the jobs were interesting with no individual bonus schemes to worry about. Hourly rates of pay were slightly higher with a monthly production bonus based on the main factory output and as much overtime as anyone wanted. Pete, Alan and I used to visit the canteen together at lunchtimes. Manor Road main canteen was far and away the best one on site; all the canteen facilities at Hatfield and Leavesden were good, but the Manor Road one – at its peak then – was just that little bit better.

At that time, de Havilland Propellers seemed even more exciting than the the Aircraft Company. Production of the large hollow steel four-blade propellers for Beverley and Britannia aircraft were under way, and radar scanners, air conditioning, alternators and Firestreak guided missiles were only some of the many projects being developed or produced. All these needed air testing with sundry observation equipment installed on the diverse aircraft that were cared for in the Flight Test Hangar.

Aircraft involved then were Brigand, Canberra, Firefly, Hastings (with a huge spray-bar erected in front of the port inner engine for propeller icing trials), Meteor, Mosquito, Swift and Venom. The Firefly had infra-red heat sources on each wingtip for missile homing tests. I counted five Canberras, at one time used variously for engine, infra-red homing, radar and air-conditioning testing. Each of the others were also involved in a variety of experimental flight tests. One evening, just prior to leaving time, another fitter and I were required to attend the Supermarine Swift parked at the edge of the Flight Hangar apron whilst the Rolls-Royce engineer ran the engine for about an hour at a pre-determined jet-pipe temperature to enable the infra-red laboratory technicians to check its heat radiation on their equipment housed in a mobile laboratory as it drove all around the aerodrome stopping at various places.

Nobby Clark told me that some laboratory boys were once testing a Firestreak infra-red homing device at one end of the Hatfield runway, aiming along it, and were puzzled by a small heat source that appeared to cross slowly back & forth at the other end. It transpired that a tractor driver was crossing the runway for a can of fuel for his tractor and then returning the empty can: the heat source was his glowing cigarette!

I still attended Hatfield Technical College and found that Engineering Drawing was the most interesting subject – it seemed to come naturally. One thing I learnt, useful to my new position, was the British Standard for calculating bend allowances in sheet metal, essential when making 'Top Hat' section pieces. George devised a long narrow 'Vee' block to be bolted to the base of our fly-press and a number of mating tongues of thick steel in various widths to attach to the ram. Thus, one could produce perfect right-angle bends in various widths and gauges of steel and light alloy. Pete Ordway was then nearing the end of his apprenticeship and was based in our fitting shop; George gave him the task of making up the bending equipment but, as an apprentice, he was not allowed to operate the large bandsaw to cut the 3/8 inch-thick steel plate to make the tongues. George asked me to do it and, although I had never operated such a device, I went with young Pete to the machine shop and was able to perform the task to his satisfaction. The bandsaw was an awesome beast and not to be trifled with by the faint-hearted; luckily my experience with woodwork machines helped and this was similar, apart from the deafening shriek of metal. Pete got the sized pieces he required and with the task completed I spent a few moments looking at the activities around us.

A quartet of heavily masked and overalled figures were sliding a shaped section of sheet steel for forming a large hollow steel propeller blade into a furnace belching wicked flames through its open door. Various propellers were being worked on and many sorts of machine tools filled the workshop. How sad it was that in later years, after nationalisation, all this activity disappeared and the space became filled with tinwalled offices populated by non-productive, self-generating, empire-building, paperwork systems-mongers who plagued – and eventually killed – 'The Enterprise.'

That spring and summer was probably my best time in the workshops of the DH Enterprise. Our Fitting Shop, located on one side of the Flight Hangar, was about 25 ft long by 15 ft wide and there were ten of us including George Smith, our Chargehand. All my cohorts were witty and articulate and much chafing and ribaldry ensued. It appeared that at least half the workforce were either called George or Harry; there were two of each in our little enclave and several others in the hangar. I opined that if someone were to stand in the middle of the Flight Hangar and shout: "Harry? George?" production would stop as we all assembled. The following is typical of the banter that flew around at that time:

TOM FAULKNER: when he asked "Can you work with 'mike' and vernier?" I said I'd work with any b*****s if they were sociable!

PHIL RUSHTON: "Did you hear about the bloke who thought that 'Hors de combat' was a fight in a brothel?"

NOBBY CLARKE: "That's the eye-effin'-deah. We'll make it exactly free 'n' eleven seventeenfs!'

HARRY: "Should a weighbridge attendant claim to be a 'Big Scale Operator'?"

Nobby was our highly skilled sheet-metal worker and coppersmith and he had a list on the wall of funny things people had innocently said in all seriousness, for example: "This fish ain't so hot when it's cold!" or: "The engine wants doing up badly," and: "We'll dismantle the unit, get it inspected and re-mantle it." Against all quotations he added the names of each perpetrator.

Whilst continuing my course at the Hatfield Technical College, I frantically attempted revision as exams loomed. Shorter travel helped greatly. My boils were less troublesome but persistent; it was to be another three years before they finally cleared. In June I sat the exams, held in the evenings on three different days. The first one was Engineering and upon opening the envelope I was astonished to note that the first question asked: '*What is the influence of Trade Unions in the twentieth century? Write an essay.*' Although sorely tempted, I returned the envelope.

"What has this got to do with aircraft engineering, chum?" I asked the invigilator. He looked askance and crossly riffled through his pack of sealed envelopes and gave me the proper one, whilst observing that I should have quoted the appropriate code as there were two different courses in the room.

"I did!" I said, and repeated the code letters. I do not think he was very pleased with me, firstly by my showing him to be in the wrong and secondly by my addressing him in a manner that indicated I thought him less important than God. I noted a few quiet smirks upon returning to my seat.

I passed all three exams with moderate success, highest marks being those for Engineering Drawing and lowest for Maths and Science, with Engineering coming somewhere between. '*Quantum in me fuit,*' I might have thought fitting, had I been aware of such a Latin phrase (meaning, roughly: 'I did the best I could'). At that time, Dick Francis was still steeplechasing and had not then thought about writing thrillers, especially the one titled *Hot Money* from which I have shamelessly nicked the quotation.

One of my fellow students on the course was a Canadian ex-bush pilot/engineer, Johnny Dapp, a tremendous character of wit with a fund of stories. He once told us about a Canadian lakes pilot of an Avro Anson who landed at a remote airfield and, noticing that the undercarriage oleos were lower than was prudent, asked the chap in charge if he would re-inflate them for him; but as he was busy with other things at the time, he passed the pilot the keys of the tool & equipment stores and bade him use whatever appropriate air bottles were required and do the job himself. Now, all aircraft engineers are taught that oxygen combined with oil is a volatile mixture and stringent measures must be taken to de-grease all connections when dealing with the stuff. For safety's sake air and oxygen bottles are colour-coded and fitted with different connector threads. How he managed it, no one ever found out, but somehow the pilot had re-inflated the oleos with pure oxygen. Apparently he took off all right but his error manifested itself with some violence when all four oleos exploded as they compressed at the next landing.

The following autumn I applied for the second year course, and was dismayed to learn of its cancellation due to lack of support. Although the Head of Aeronautical Engineering kindly fitted me into other classes they were not really suitable and I dropped out after disastrous half-term exams.

1955 was a good summer, and we sometimes had our tea breaks outside the hangar in the sunshine. Once we were near the compound where the Venom that carried an experimental Firestreak missile was serviced. As we watched, a laboratory technician trundled the missile trolley into it to collect a test Firestreak from the aircraft. Soon after, we heard a double thud as a pair of full wingtip fuel tanks struck the ground. The particular Supervisor emerged red-faced from the compound, on his way to Cliff Aubrey's office to report the accident. It seemed that the technician had aligned the trolley under the missile, but when he signalled to someone in the cockpit to pull the release, the unfortunate therein released the drop-tanks instead.

This missile-loading compound was located near the Flight Hangar apron at the side furthest from the airfield. In line with it but at the opposite end of the hangar was an engine test building occupied by the Napier Engine Company, and its jet efflux outlet faced a piece of waste ground. Sandwiched 'twixt this and adjacent to the compound stood a small outbuilding used by the Flight Hangar electricians. At that time, Napier were testing either their new Nomad or possibly the compound diesel piston/gas turbine, the Naiad. However, the disgusting fumes blew straight into the electricians' hut and made the resident 'sparks' representative somewhat displeased. Having been instructed by their union to leave the premises each time the engine was running, urgent electrical tasks were getting delayed. Some terse remarks were, I believe, exchanged between Cliff and the Napier Supervisor and a compromise was reached whereby engine runs were restricted to times that did not interfere with the smooth running of electrical workshop projects, until a new location could be found.

In mid-August the Short Sperrin arrived for a final check-over by the Engine Company bods prior to appearing at the Farnborough Air Show. It had been designed with four Rolls-Royce Avons mounted in vertical pairs on either side, one above and one below each wing. However, the port lower one had been replaced with the vast new de Havilland Gyron encased in an enlarged pear-shaped cowling. One morning it was on function checks with the Murex Ground Power Unit coupled up. Upon checking the hydraulic system for control functioning, the flaps were lowered but no one noticed that the Murex was parked underneath one of them. A loud crunching ensued and the flap now resembled a crushed and discarded beer can.

Panic stations were manned and a select number of fitters and inspectors were recruited to work 'ghosters' until the machine had been repaired and made good to the usual display standards. Cliff began firing on all six ulcers and much telephone time was spent between Hatfield and Belfast. Thanks to everyone's combined efforts, the Sperrin reached Farnborough in time and was duly shown & flown as per programme.

Our tool and material stores were ranged along one side of the Flight Hangar contained in a wire mesh compound. I was at the serving hatch one morning when we were all startled by a loud bang that echoed back and forth around the steel walls. A Venom was being serviced at the time and someone had activated the pneumatic wheel brakes with both wheels removed. These particular brakes were full diameter internal expanding, activated by a stout rubber flattened 'inner-tube' device that sandwiched the brake lining segments between the inside of the brake drum and the brake anchor-plate. With drums and linings removed, the bags had nothing to restrain them and so they expanded beyond bursting point with the resultant minor explosion we had heard. Luckily no one was within striking distance to get hurt. When the excitement died down, rotund Bill Cowley, the Hangar General Foreman, strolled up to the stores and laconically requested a couple of spare Venom brake bags.

All these goings-on must have weighed heavily on Cliff. With so much on his mind, driving home one lunchtime he failed to notice a large pantechnicon which had halted suddenly in front of him. Although unhurt, his car was now shorter, very second-hand-looking and unlikely to be going very far. One of our long-service fitters with connections in the motor trade kindly lent him a vehicle until it was repaired. As to the pantechnicon, its robust wooden body wasn't even splintered.

To me, de Havilland Propellers were benevolent employers, with good working conditions, good rates of pay, excellent canteens and tea breaks served from mobile trolleys. But some people are never satisfied. Among the latter were numerous petty union officials, shop stewards of all the departments led by 'convenors,' trying to justify their existence by agitating the proletariat into disruption over some unimportant and half-imagined shortcoming by 'management.' What they lacked in lucid expression was made up for by pedantic and long-winded jargon, phrases such as: "It's managerial prerogative, brothers!" tripped off their tongues straight from the 'Marxist Manual for Shit-stirrers.'

Works union meetings were held at lunchtimes on a piece of waste ground just inside the gates, the microphone set up on a makeshift platform adjacent to the fence. Often, when the convenor, usually with a couple of shop steward acolytes in attendance, was in mid-harangue, some apprentices would rev up their motorbikes adjacent to the microphone as they passed along the road on their way out. The effect via the PA system was akin to a strident raspberry, which I thought hilarious. During one such meeting, a new member asked a question, but indicated his ignorance of union protocol by addressing the convenor as "Mr Chairman" instead of "brother."

Repeating the question back to him in 'unionese' for his own clarity, the convenor asked: "Is that what you mean, brother?"

"The questioner concurred by shouting back: "You've got it, sister!"

I laughed aloud but others failed to see the joke.

By attending every union meeting at the least excuse, the less skilful, technically incompetent and downright skivers embraced their respective trade unions as the only hope of hanging on to their jobs, spending hours at the local Trades & Labour Club through tediously detailed haranguing argument, getting themselves elected as minor officials and hopefully rising up the Labour ladder of command until sponsored as local councillors or even Parliamentary candidates. By these means, it could be possible for a second-rate ship's barman to rise to the rank of, say, Deputy Prime Minister! Henry Royce, R.J. Mitchell and Geoffrey de Havilland had had far more important things to worry about than to waste time with such histrionics and rhetoric.

In the late fifties, two fine British films were released. One, *I'm All Right, Jack* with Peter Sellers and Ian Carmichael, was a comedy about the utter farce of some union antics. The other, *The Angry Silence*, was a drama showing the ugly face of unionism; both were – in their own way, I think – an accurate indictment of the stranglehold of union politics then prevailing.

Trade unions in the past had done wonderful things for their members by way of wages, working hours, conditions and holidays etc., but by the mid-fifties had outgrown themselves to the point of being far too powerful, political and dictatorial. Sometimes different unions were at loggerheads with one another. In the early fifties, a northern shipyard came to a halt when woodworkers, engineering workers and electricians' unions failed to agree as to which of their members should be allowed to drill some holes in certain panels. To one brought up under flying club discipline to be adaptable and prepared to tackle any job, I found such childish behaviour bordering on the criminal. Inevitably, by savaging the hands that fed them, they perpetrated in the long run greater disservice to their members than the worst kind of management they so openly despised and which probably existed mainly in their own diseased imaginations.

Enough of politics!

Syd Neil was a hardworking Hangar Chargehand Fitter with a delightful Norfolk accent, his bane in life being a monocled and mustachioed skiver who claimed to have been an Army Major; as to which regiment, he never disclosed. He was also an active union agitator, and Syd was often heard calling his name and asking: "Ha'en't ya gartta jarb, boee?"

Syd sometimes took sundry small parts and fittings to the Aircraft Company for various forms of heat and protective treatment; he would cross the airfield in his own car around the peri-track to the appropriate department, claiming expenses for mileage. This arrangement suited everybody until curtailed by management as too costly; they then provided the head storeman with a tradesman's carrier bicycle painted bright yellow all over and with its department identity emblazoned on the panel attached to the crossbar – *NEW PROJECT No. 2*. One day Pat the storeman was making a delivery and had left his machine leaning against a wall. As my friend Pete Longland and his cohort Bill Cotterill happened by, Bill pointed to the bike and exclaimed: "So that's what they've been doing over on the other side all this while – making secret trade bikes!"

In the severe winter of January 1956, someone neglected to drain down the water system on the Hastings that was provided for the propeller spray-bar and so the aircraft was brought into the hangar for repairs to its auxiliary plumbing arrangement. Whilst in the hangar, it was decided to refurbish the spray-bar; there were some 16 nozzles in the spray-bar, each with its own little heater to avoid nozzle icing at altitude, and I was allotted the task of making 32 small contacts for these heaters, each about an inch long, in 22 swg brass sheet 3/16 in wide, slotted at one end and double-cranked (joggled) in the centre.

One thing I learned when involved with bonus schemes in the past was to perform one operation at a time on all the pieces to avoid too much shifting around of parts. All the cutting to size, drilling, filing to shape and finishing operations were carried out in turn on all the pieces and thus a sort of 'production-line' technique evolved. "Chalky" White, the other hangar charge-hand, thought otherwise, it seemed. I was halfway through the job when he began worrying about when he could have "half-a-dozen to start with." I pointed out that if he could wait an hour, he could have the lot! He came back later, but still insisted that he must have six as soon as possible. What is it with some supervisors? Can they not see that, if left alone, certain people could produce the results quicker? In the event he got his first six, then ten minutes later he got the other 26! Had he not agitated, he might have got all 32 half an hour earlier; but there you go!

Anyway, he must have been pleased, because a few days later he asked George for me in particular to do a special job for which my flying club experience doubtless fitted. For want of something better to occupy their limited outlook, the union busybodies had noted that the labourers, when cleaning the Hastings, were above the statutory minimum workshop height at which a safety harness had to be worn; so, between us, Chalky and I had to devise a suitable harness that could be worn by our amiable Irish labourer, nicknamed by our fitters as "Lemmy the Martian" from the then popular radio serial of the time, *Journey Into Space*.

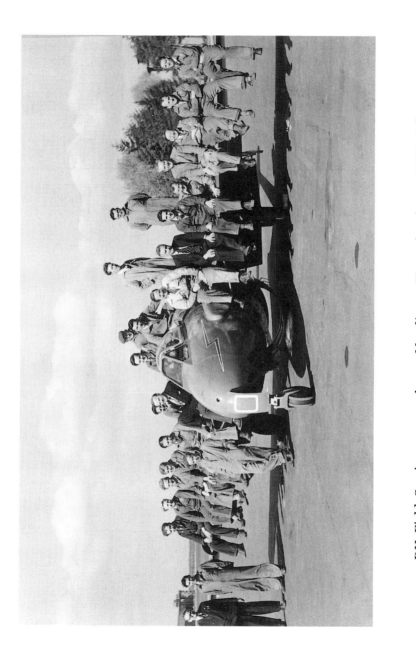

DH Field Service personnel proof-loading a Venom's wing at RAF Celle, Germany, in 1954. Bill, the foreman, is standing at extreme L. Ron Carter and I are second & third from the starboard wingtip, sitting on the wing. Photo: taken by a serving P.O. at the request of Bill, the foreman.

TOP: DH Prop's Flight Hangar fitting shop, spring 1955. L. to R.: George Atkinson, the author, Alan Slade, Harry Peacock, Reg, Gordon, Tom Faulkner, Phil Rushton, Ernie Lewis and 'Ben' Benson.
BOTTOM: George Smith (chargehand), 'Ben' and Phil.

TOP: Phil Rushton trying out his instant Groucho Marx kit.
BOTTOM: Phil and Pete Ordway lusting over an Ava Gardner pin-up.

LEFT: 'Nobby' Clarke, Phil Rushton and Pete Ordway making delicate adjustments to an equipment panel.

RIGHT: The punctured tyre, the result of sharp flints strewn on the taxiway

Chalky obtained some old parachute harness which we adapted to fit waistcoat-like, and with a crotch-strap and two additional straps from each shoulder joining above the head to a stout hook to be attached by a line to an appropriate steel safety cable. In normal wear the hook was firmly sewn with braided cord to the harness at the small of the back in such a way that, should the wearer slip off the wing or whatever, the cords would break and he would dangle from the safety line by his shoulders (like an intrepid paratrooper). We did one or two dummy runs with the unfortunate Lemmy hoisted aloft by means of block & tackle in a way that allowed the system to function. When all had been satisfactorily completed, Lemmy anxiously enquired of Chalky if he had to be hoisted up each time he cleaned the aircraft! However, in the long run, I doubt if the device was ever used. Unions had demanded and management had been seen to have responded, so honour was satisfied.

In the workshop, a bulkhead had been made for the conversion of a Canberra to carry in its nose the new experimental DH Propellers radar scanner. I thought that the standard of riveting, although adequate, would not have passed muster with Denis, the inspector at Leavesden. Later, George asked if I would help one of our leading fitters, Jack Gower, a former Propeller Service representative, rivet up some skin-work on the nose of another Canberra for infra-red experiments. Jack seemed a trifle doubtful when I offered to 'dolly-up' the rivet tails inside and let him do the business with pneumatic hammer and flat snap outside, and seemed puzzled when I took the trouble to carefully polish the riveting face of the dolly. He grew even more worried when told to give more hammering, when he thought his initial burst was adequate. However, I was trying to get the tails to the standard required of us at Leavesden. When we had completed the first run, Jack could contain his anxiety no longer and got down off his short step-ladder to look inside for himself.

Upon viewing the result, he beamed and slapped me on the back. "That's great!" he exclaimed, obviously quite pleased. For one anxious moment I thought he was about to hug me! We finished the operation in amicable accord.

One thing I liked about the Propellers Flight Hangar was that, not only were we given parts to make, but we were also encouraged to fit them to the aircraft and/or assemblies to complete the structure. For air-conditioning equipment testing, a heat exchanger, turbine and associated trunking were fitted into the rear fuselage of certain Canberras. I had to make up light alloy channels and flanged brackets to reinforce the fuselage bottom skin between the fuselage frames, and that would accept the heat exchanger with a turbine unit attached and thence connect with trunking to appropriate orifices to be cut in the aircraft's skin. I made two such assemblies on different aircraft; thus I became acquainted with the English Electric Canberra – one of Britain's most successful aeroplanes. The Americans were very impressed with the Canberra and built it under licence in the USA as the Martin B-57.

Nobby Clark, being panelbeater and coppersmith, had the task of producing quantities of hydraulic pipes needed for the aforementioned radar scanner. These pipes were of tungum alloy tube of varying diameters and with appropriate union fittings each end. (Tungum is a high-strength copper-based brass-like alloy, approved for aircraft high-pressure hydraulic tubing under the Directorate of Technical Development's specification: DTD 323.) In order to produce all the complicated bends required, each pipe had to be filled with rosin to prevent flattening or collapsing when put through the pipe-bender. To fill the pipes, the rosin had to be heated until runny and then poured into the pre-warmed pipes and allowed to set prior to bending. Nobby had a small electric heater for this purpose, upon which a gallon can of the odiferous substance was always on the simmer. Once each pipe had been formed, the job was handed over to George the welder, who played his welding torch over it till the rosin ran free into a convenient receptacle. All this activity was extremely smelly and, when George accidently pointed his torch inside the pipe, thick black smoke polluted the whole workshop. Once he overheated a pipe at its centre before the ends had properly melted and the pipe burst with a shattering bang, which blew off his spectacles and covered his face with a lot of little black spots. Such actions affected my bronchial apparatus and my absences from work with asthma attacks increased in frequency. There was no sick pay for hourly-paid staff in those days except via National Health after a week 'on the panel.' By the summer of 1956 it became obvious I would have to get a fresh-air job.

George the welder had been in the RAF in the early thirties and mustered as a blacksmith. He had served in the Middle East on a Squadron that operated Westland Wapitis. When he talked about his time with them, we younger ones thought they sounded terribly ancient and had probably been flown to base after being catapulted from Noah's Ark!

In the spring of 1955 Ray Clapham returned from Australia with a ground engineer's licence for Douglas DC-3 (Dakota) airframes; he had worked for McRobertson-Miller Airways at Perth and for a time was based at their northern airstrip at Derby near Darwin. With little else to do in Derby's sweaty remoteness, he had studied for his ticket and successfully obtained it after flying back to Perth to sit his exam.

We corresponded regularly during his absence and carried on our friendship upon his return home. With his licence transferred for use in the UK, he secured a job with Scottish Airlines at nearby Stansted Airport.

Scottish Airlines' fleet at that time consisted mainly of Avro Yorks and he was soon studying hard for a York endorsement on his Ground Engineer's Licence. Reel-to-reel tape recorders were just then becoming available, and he obtained one and audio-recorded all the technical details he needed of the York airframe to listen to in bed at night, theorising that facts were more easily absorbed into the brain during the semi-comatose state between wakefulness and deep sleep. Also, being of an artistic bent, he drew copious quantities of 'exploded' vews of York components from study of the technical manuals. Later, having passed his written paper, he presented himself to the examiners of the Air Registration Board (forerunner of the Civil Aviation Authority and seriously less bureaucratic!) for his 'oral' exam, whereupon one of them remarked: "Ah, yes! The artist!"

Ill-fated G-AMUL was the first York Ray signed out as fit for flight, referred to by its last two letters in the then-prevailing phonetic alphabet as "Uncle Love" – today it would be "Uniform Lima." (Bear with me, this point will become obvious later.) SAL were fulfilling a contract for flying Armed Services personnel and equipment to and from various bases in Europe and the Middle East. Coincidentally, as the United States Army were at that time lengthening the Stansted main runway under a NATO agreement, all aircraft were obliged to use a narrower parallel taxiway.

Fully laden with Service personnel, families and luggage, and with a full load of fuel in the tanks, the machine began its take-off from the taxiway and started to veer towards the edge. As it ran onto the grass the pilot struggled to correct the deviation, only to get into a ground-loop situation, and as the aircraft slewed sideways one of the main wheels sheared off. The kinetic energy of the wing, laden with full fuel tanks and four weighty Merlin engines, tried to roll the fuselage sideways like a piece of pastry and the loose wheel was forced into the pasenger cabin.

Two passengers were killed and a woman was trapped by the vertical member of a main structural frame that fractured at its centre and was forced sideways and down between her knees. Fuel began leaking onto the pasengers from the centre-section tank above their heads. First on the scene were SAL ground staff; Ray said he saw Wally Adams desperately trying to disconnect the battery terminals and covering the resultant sparks with his hands as fuel splashed around – tears were streaming down his face. A long struggle ensued to free the trapped woman as structural parts had to be sawn away. After everyone had been evacuated from the wreckage, the ground staff made their way back to the hangar, where Ray fell face down on the ground and began sobbing uncontrollably; there he heard 'big Cyril,' the tractor driver, say as he passed: "I wish I could do that!"

A Public Inquiry took place in London and all involved were called upon to attend. The ground engineers were absolved from all blame as the machine was proved to be mechanically sound prior to take-off. A letter was received later by the Company from the lady cut from the wreck, expressing her gratitude for the way the staff had helped and comforted her.

One minor incident during the Inquiry amused Ray; a learned counsel began his *spiel* with the words: "This aircraft, mn, ah, affectionately known as 'Uncle Love' . . . " Nevertheless, attending as a witness at the Board of Trade Inquiry was not easy for him; he took it very hard and was traumatised for some weeks.

Upon return to dear old 'blighty' Ray bought a new Triumph Thunderbird and we went out on various motorcycling trips, sometimes accompanied by our girlfriends on the rare occasions whenever all our days off coincided. Ray's girl Jean, employed in a bank, worked Saturday mornings whilst my soon-to-be fiancée Connie was a librarian and worked Saturdays until late most weeks. At Scottish they worked a peculiar rota system of six days on and two off, which meant mid-week days off more often than weekends.

Having voiced my health concerns to Ray, he suggested that if it was fresh air I needed, I should apply for a post as an airframe fitter with him at Stansted and, upon my acquiescence to this idea, arranged an interview for me with Wally Adams, who was resident chief engineer for the Scottish Airlines base there. Scottish Airlines were a subsidiary of Scottish Aviation who manufactured the Prestwick Pioneer and were in process of putting the new Twin Pioneer into production. At Stansted, the Yorks were only serviced up to 'check three' standard and when a machine required 'check four' or other major overhaul the work was carried out at Scottish Aviation's Prestwick factory.

It was a Sunday when I went for the interview and Ray, having taken me to the Chief's office, discreetly withdrew for Wally to grill me privately. Wally Adams was a diminutive 5 ft-nothing and slightly built with it, but a dynamic personality and great engineering leader with a terrific sense of humour. He was qualified on both engines and airframes and, in my view at least, commanded great respect. Having verbally reiterated my CV, I confessed to needing the change for health and fresh air. Wally offered me the job, which was at a slightly lower rate of pay but with the rota system of six days on and two off; the amount of weekend working meant a fair bit of time-and-a-half (Saturdays) and double-time (Sundays) to swell the coffers. As this system also covered Bank Holidays, it could bring in double-time-and-a-half. When I had accepted the job, Ray showed me round the aircraft and what passed for facilities. Ray's elder brother Geoff had recently joined and worked as second electrician under Johnny Sloane, an ebullient character whose experience with SAL included time with the Berlin Airlift.

Returning to Manor Road on Monday, I saw George and handed in my statutory week's notice. We both went to see Cliff Aubrey who, when told the reason, looked sideways at George and asked: "Can't he stand you any more, George?"

At that, George looked even more cast down and on our way back asked miserably if I really could not work with him. This quite shattered me, and I hastily reassured him that he was in fact the very best chargehand I had worked for, and that I was sorry to leave and was doing so only for a fresh air job to restore my health. By the time we reached the workshop again he had recovered enough to be smiling.

George was conscientious and hard-working and it annoyed me that some of the skivers ridiculed and baited him at times; they referred to him behind his back as "Puffer" due to his habit of expelling his breath in (justified!) exasperation at times.

"Where's old Puffer, then?" some halfwit would ask.

"Oh, shunted into a siding, I 'spect!' was the sort of stupidity that prevailed.

The following week I reported to the Scottish Airlines hangar at Stansted Airport where I was to be employed for the next eight months – which, later, seemed nearer eight years.

CHAPTER 20

SCOTTISH AIRLINES (STANSTED)

On the first day at Stansted I helped Ray set up the pneumatic wheel-brake differential in a York cockpit. Having spent all morning and exhausted several air bottles trying to get it right without success, we found that I had been misreading the cockpit gauges, a very poor start to a new job. "Timber" Woods, Deputy Chief Engineer (Airframes) came in next day after his weekend off and had the brake adjustment sorted in half an hour. Timber was not popular with some of the lads but I got on quite well with him, and the next day he took it upon himself to show me around the York and its systems in fine detail.

Personnel at the SAL hangar were divided into groups: Fitters (Engines), Riggers (Airframes), Electricians, Instrument Makers, cleaners (and general labourers), a sheet metal worker who spent most of his time repairing cowlings and fairings and a lone woodworker who repaired the floor panels. There were also 'Staff' personnel – a couple of office girls and the storemen. I was categorized as a rigger. Although we all collaborated one with another, certain people specialized; there was Ted, who was a wizz on autopilots, and Brian, who dealt solely with all the safety equipment such as inflatable lifebelts and rafts.

Our hangar was wartime RAF standard with fully-opening doors each end. Inside, along one wall, was a line of single-storey office-type structures which were used as follows: Bonded Stores (which doubled as General Office), Crew Room, Electricians' Department, a small workshop with a divisional cubbyhole for the tinbasher, Wally's office and, finally, a modest cabin for the safety equipment. The instrument makers and radio men inhabited a small Nissen hut a short walk from the main hangar.

Certain unattached personnel or family men who normally resided some distance away were allowed, for a small fee, to make use of Company billets; these were self-contained ex-Service huts located some distance away on the other side of the airfield. Both Ray and Geoff lived in the billets with two or three others on a self-catering basis and with a cleaner attending daily.

Ray had initiated a daily 'Service Board' which was a blackboard marked out in boxes with white paint similar to a wartime 'Ops Board' but with aircraft sections listed down the board such as 'Engines,' 'Fuselage,' 'Wings,' 'Empennage,' 'Hydraulics' etc. Three vertical columns were headed respectively '50 hrs,' 'Check II' and 'Check III.' Then, according to whichever check was due, a fitter, rigger or specialist's name was chalked into whatever task box he was allocated in the appropriate column on that day.

That first week, I was asked to help Ted German – the autopilot wizz – to install one in a York that had just arrived from major overhaul at Prestwick and, on his instruction, had to make up small-diameter pneumatic pipe runs to supply the servos. Observation of Nobby's work at Manor Road had shown me the best way to make conical pipe-joints and, when Ted was satisfied, we secured them to the floor, or wherever, with made-up aluminium clamps. My cycle and motorcycle repair experience came in useful when we had to adjust chain lengths for the mechanical operation of the servos.

When all was installed to Ted's satisfaction, he carried out mysterious adjustments and referred to 'jinking' when it was function-tested. Rudder pedals, column and control yoke jerked about in an alarming way at this stage, but Ted seemed quite pleased and Wally was satisfied. Later, in the office, Wally pulled Ted's leg (and embarrassed me) by saying that the new chap must have a good influence as it was the first time an autopilot had been installed without snags. I only did what Ted asked, and had not the faintest clue as to how the device functioned.

Apart from electric power and lighting, the hangar was completely devoid of water, heating and sanitation. For the latter, a pair of chemical closets (but without the formality of chemicals) were housed in two brick 'thunderboxes' and emptied at intervals by a couple of brave (or foolish) individuals driving a dilapidated and noisome tank vehicle known to all and sundry as "The Honey Wagon." Separate containers for urination were provided alongside the Elsans and were old Elsan inner containers, probably discarded from a York as unsuitable. For such short jobs, most chaps preferred to avail themselves of a handy secluded ditch outside the hangar. Water for cleaning the aircraft and handwashing was stored in a tank from an ex-Army water truck mounted on a platform outside the hangar and piped inside to a conveniently positioned tap over a large square tank used as a sink for rinsing decarbonized engine components. The outside tank was topped up as required by the aerodrome Fire Brigade. For casual drinking at a tanner (6d) a throw, a Coca Cola vending machine was installed at one end of the hangar; I preferred to await the tea urn.

I was now able to put into practice some of the theory gleaned during my evening classes at Hatfield Tech. The York had a low-pressure hydraulic system with enormous valves and actuators compared with the small high-pressure ones displayed at the College. We seemed to feed the system with gallons of red DTD 585 mineral oil. At Hatfield, amber coloured castor-based Lockheed fluid had been used on the Comet 1A. Routine inspections of the aircraft structure meant checking the skin covering for loose or missing rivets. (Someone described the Avro Shackleton as two million rivets flying in loose formation; we could have said the same about the York if we had thought of it first!) This invloved climbing all over the aeroplane: first, one ascended to the flat top of the fuselage through the rear escape hatch and walked aft to check the empennage components; then walked slowly forward checking the fuselage top surface; turned left and did the same along the port wing as near to the trailing-edge as one dared (no safety line here, I wonder what the Manor Road union buffs would have said!); then out to the wingtip and back along the leading edge; cross to starboard along the leading edge to the tip; then back along the trailing edge to the fuselage and down the forward escape hatch with a sigh of relief.

Now it was time to check the undersurfaces. Tailplane – easy! Checking the wing undersurfaces required a torch with a powerful spot beam to show up the rivet-lines and walking back and forth along them. This could be hazardous when looking at rivets instead of where one was walking and falling over bits of equipment and treading in oil drip-trays left about in careless abandon. Finally, inspecting the fuselage sides and keel seemed almost like a tea break after that.

The York had a fluid de-icing system whereby alcohol-based fluid was pumped through spongy metal strips set in the leading edges of wings and tail units to melt any ice that might form at cold altitudes. A 10-gallon tank of the fluid was located in the rear fuselage and distributed by electric pump via miles of pipework to the strips at the aeroplane's extremities. To inspect the system for function (having ascertained that the tank contained its required amount) one switched on the pump and slowly walked around the aircraft to make sure that the gunge was flowing freely from wherever it should, and not where it should not! Quite often it dripped on personnel engaged in other jobs who found the experience less than amusing. One of the tasks when checking the pneumatic system was to drain the oil and water trap; this unit was located behind the firewall of the starboard inboard engine and the method was to climb onto the top of the undercarriage main wheel, connect a compressed-air hose to an appropriate union and then, holding a suitable container (in our case an airsickness paper bag), undo the drain plug to allow the unit to defecate a mixture of water and oil sludge – impelled by pressure from the air hose – into it with a disgusting burping noise, then retighten the plug whilst trying not to drop the spanner into the bag before disconnecting the hose.

Inspecting and greasing the undercarriage was fairly straightforward but best done *after* the cleaners had been over it. I learned from experience that, having greased all the points, the cleaners would wash all the new grease off along with old and I'd have to do it all again.

One of the most frequent tasks was keeping the mainwheel tyres up to scratch and properly inflated. Two types of tyre were used, Dunlop square block pattern and Palmer diamond pattern; both were 60 inches outside diameter and 17 inches wide on 24 inch-wheels with detachable flanges on one side of each wheel secured with spring-steel circlips of hoola-hoop proportions. They were inflated to 60 psi; with an inside area of some 7,500 sq. in. that is an awful lot of pent-up power. Our inflators did not have a probe to depress the valve core (twice the size of a car one) so a high pressure air bottle had to be used to overcome the combined force of its spring against the inside pressure. A stock of ready-inflated spare wheels was racked at one end of the hangar with one already mounted in a special trolley to be towed to wherever a wheel change was needed. This was an 'all hands to the pumps' operation as the aircraft had to be jacked up and the wheels manhandled out and in again. Tyre changing on the spare wheels was effected during slack periods when all the aircraft were away. We had an arrangement with Aviation Traders on the other side of the airfield to use their special tyre removal equipment because, after a lot of landings and high temperature braking, the tyres were virtually vulcanized to the rims. We would load a deflated wheel and tyre assembly – with its separate flange circlip already removed – onto the workshop wagon, a venerable Luton-bodied Commer Karrier and, with half a dozen bods, trundle it off to their nice heated hangar where they maintained a modest fleet of Avro Tudors. Their tyre removal gear was a sort of capstan device with a circular flanged base bolted to the concrete floor, on which to rest the wheel, detachable-flange side down, with another large flanged disc laid on top to push the tyre bead away from the wheel rim. An acme-threaded vertical rod passed through the hub and locked in place at the base, and a big nut with a steel tube capstan bar through it was wound down by four of us on it walking round – in the same way that they raised the anchors with a capstan on Nelson's ships (but without the fiddler on top playing a jolly sea-shanty) – until the flanged disc popped the bead off the rim with a loud bang. Having first removed the wheel from inside the tyre with block and tackle, an inverted funnel-shaped piece was put in its place to push the loose wheel flange from the tyre – resting on the lower side – with the same screw-capstan device.

All this took us about half an hour with enough bods to manhandle the bits quickly as required. Aviation Traders employed a wiry middle-aged man to do all their tyre changing; he used the chain block and tackle to lift each piece as necessary, a lengthy process that took a whole day to dismantle one wheel. To reassemble with a new tyre and tube required only manhandling and compressed air – a lot of compressed air! Each wheel carried two pneumatic full diameter brake drums and these were serviced at the same time.

Engine changes rarely took place at Stansted but regular cylinder head and/or cylinder block changes to the Yorks' Merlin engines were carried out *in situ* according to engine log recorded hours.

Whilst the US Army were building the runway extension, their trucks full of spoil and aggregrates sped up and down the taxiways and, in so doing, were scattering mud and flints with careless abandon from their unguarded rear wheels. This was bad news for the aircraft tyres; once, a York was manoeuvring to its loading bay by the departure area when it ran over a large sharp flint that pierced the tyre cover and inner tube, so that as the wheel rotated another half turn the tyre burst with an explosive decompression that blew the lower cowlings from its adjacent engine.

Sometime later, a rather strained meeting took place between Wally Adams, Captain Grant (Chief Pilot SAL) and the American Commanding

Officer; someone had retained the offending flint and it was displayed trophy-like under the embarrassed CO's nose: next day fatigue parties of GIs could be seen sweeping the taxyways. Ray took a photograph of me straddling the damaged tyre with my head and shoulders poking through the hole from inside.

I arrived at work one morning to find a York in the hangar laden with three sand-camouflaged military Land Rovers. (Scottish had a contract to carry military supplies to and from Europe and the Middle East, but the carriage of Service personnel in Yorks had been banned after the accident to 'Uncle Love' (G-AMUL), thanks largely to a typically ill-informed campaign in the tabloid dailies.) Cyril, our highly skilled chief transport driver, had managed to insert them by removing the canvas tonneaux and lowering the windscreens onto the bonnets, then inching in each vehicle diagonally via an improvised ramp through the aircraft's large side-loading doors.

It was an education to watch Cyril putting a York into the hangar. With the tailwheel towbar hitched to the front of the David Brown tractor, he would skilfully drive it forwards so that the 99 ft span aircraft went in nose first dead centre with just a foot or so clearance on each wingtip – and this after turning the machine through 90° first. By doing it this way he was later able to tow it out normally and save time.

Engine runs after servicing were carried out on the aprons at each end of the hangar. Wally Adams usually ran them, propped up on half-a-dozen cushions in the left-hand seat in order to see out of the screen. He also taxied the aircraft around the peri-track to the loading and departure area. Once, I was carrying out a repair to a metal floor panel when he climbed aboard, shut the door and told me to carry on whilst he taxied around for loading. Despite the rough ride and vibration, I managed to complete the task before the boxes came aboard.

Soon after I joined, Ray went sick suffering from vertigo, brought on no doubt by the combination of pressures concerning his intense work programme to obtain a York rating on his ground engineer's licence, followed by the trauma of the crash to 'UL and the subsequent Board of Trade Inquiry. He had part-exchanged his Triumph Thunderbird motorbike for a mid-thirties Morris Ten saloon after suffering a shunt when about to pass a parked car; the cretin therein pulled out suddenly causing Ray to swerve and crash, yet another worry that had no doubt contributed to his present sickness.

He was still away when a diversion was called. One of our aircraft needed a quick turn-round when it unloaded at RAF Lyneham and a team had to be there to service it. A company Dormobile with five of us, our tools and equipment and with Wally in the driving seat, set out for Wiltshire. After an early start, a long journey with a lunch stop ensued and we arrived before the aircraft had been unloaded. I was intrigued to see at Lyneham the remains of a Hamilcar glider towering above some huts. On the way there, we had passed military convoys of vehicles painted in desert camouflage similar to the Land

Rovers mentioned earlier. The American Foreign Secretary, John Foster Dulles – who was to diplomacy what Himmler was to Zionism – refused to sanction funds for the Egyptian Aswan Dam and in consequence the Egyptian President Colonel Nasser, in a fit of pique, had snatched the Suez Canal as reparation. Great Britain and France, who jointly owned it, were more than a bit up tight about this and things were looking threatening. Israel, too, was making warlike noises.

We serviced the aircraft in time for the reload and repaired to the Visitor's Mess for a meal, and later to 'sleeping quarters,' which was a hut full of dormitory lines of Service beds. Our slumber was disturbed at about 1.30 am when an inebriated erk crashed in, turned on the lights and exclaimed loudly: "Aye oop! Yon beds is full o' blawks!"

After harsh exclamations from the hitherto somnolent occupants, he eventually doused the lights and reeled out. Next morning at breakfast, a small ginger-headed erk, very red around the eyes and identified as our nocturnal visitor, weaved through the Mess, and Wally mildly remonstrated with him.

"Oi, you! What the bloody hell was the idea of disturbing our beauty sleep last night then! Eh?"

The erk made no reply but fled with downcast rubicund orbs.

I looked forward to a bit of shut-eye in the Bedford on the way home, however the others no doubt had the same idea and got to the Dormobile first. I was left with the front passenger seat so that Wally could keep alert by chatting to me all the way home. It got even more difficult to converse and keep awake after a sumptuous lunch stop at Rickmansworth.

As autumn hove nigh, Ray returned fit and well and began to think about organizing a Christmas party. He and Geoff were also recruited in their spare time to provide sound effects and lighting for their sister's production of her Women's Institute group pantomime. I attended the performance and was invited to the champagne party for cast and friends after, a very pleasant evening.

Keeping a workforce at the ready seven days a week meant that, when the aircraft were all in use, there were periods when we had little to do. In theory such times were to be spent servicing parts & spares ready for the next checks. In reality a lot of time was spent in the crew room playing cards, reading magazines or just gassing. Some people indulged in 'homework' jobs. Geoff made a couple of electrical light dimmers for the WI panto out of discarded electric fires and was involved with one of the engine fitters in converting a Qualcast hand mower to electric power for Wally. The fitter in question, Fred Bunce, earned a spare-time crust rebuilding car engines. Others serviced cars and motorbikes during such intervals; my pair of vee-block clamps were made thus.

Scottish Airlines' lone Douglas DC-3 came to Stansted for winter hangarage and was also serviced; an engine change and replacement of a damaged port wingtip were carried out. Much swearing took place when the Goodrich rubber de-icing boot had to be refitted where the tip had been changed. The two chaps who were attempting the operation were fruitlessly jabbing about with 'icepicks' to try and align the holes with the anchor nuts. I recalled the way we'd done it at Leavesden when some rubber de-icers were experimentally installed on a Heron. I fashioned a hooked handle out of thick welding wire and, by threading a number of loops of waxed cord through each screw hole in the boot, then doubling both ends of each loop over the hook in turn, it could be pulled into alignment with the edge flashing, enabling one to insert the screws one by one and then pull away the loops just before the screws were finally tightened down. The job went well after that, but nobody seemed very pleased; maybe they wished they had thought of it first. There was an attitude of reluctance to produce a good engineering job among some staff members – perhaps engendered by the awful environment. We later had another overnight visitor in the form of the prototype Twin Pioneer (referred to by Geoff as the "Twin Pie 'n' Chips") whilst on a sales tour.

Winter began to bite in our unheated hangar as the firm's Christmas party fell due; Ray organized it with help from Geoff. Wives and sweethearts (but not both together!) were invited, and Connie and I were conveyed to and from the venue by Ray (accompanied by girlfriend) in his venerable Morris. A jolly time was had by all except when a couple of inebriates tried to gatecrash and had to be firmly ejected by one of our cleaners, an ex-policeman.

The Suez Crisis then upon us made things difficult. Petrol shortage was exacerbated by the attitude of garage attendants. "Sorry, mate, only one gallon!" changed when the price went up by a shilling (1/-) a gallon to "Yes, sir! As much as you like!" However, that changed again when fuel rationing was introduced. I covered about 200 miles a week just going to and from work, which was more than my allotted ration allowed. Social motorcycling was a definite no-no! I tried to buy a clip-on cycle motor of the type which were then in vogue, such as Cyclemaster, Minimotor etc., thereby increasing my ration by about 60%, but everyone else had the same idea and they were as rare as hens' teeth. One Esso garage near my home put up a large notice saying 'Here you get extra petrol for your coupons.' Closer scrutiny revealed the tiny word 'Esso' 'twixt 'get' and 'extra.' Just when things were at crisis point, Wally handed me a 4-gallon coupon that had been allotted by the Company for use by distant dwelling staff.

I began to feel ever more disenchanted with Stansted Aerodrome in general and Scottish Airlines in particular. Not only was the hangar unheated, but in the coldest part of the year the hangar roof was in process of replacement. Sections of it were roped off as panels of corrugated iron were changed and the old steel tie-bolts rained down like shrapnel. The contractor's supervisor walked around the hangar floor in a thick duffle coat and steel helmet. As compensation for our discomfort, two or three modern paraffin heaters were brought in and placed in those small workshops not endowed with such luxury (the Stores and crew room being already catered for in this respect). We were provided with a degreasant hand-cleaning gel, but rinsing it off in freezing cold water was not my idea of luxury. I filled a two-gallon bucket with water and placed it on the paraffin heater in the small workshop about an hour before knocking-off time; three quarters of an hour later it was nicely hot and I washed my hands in comfort to derisory cat-calls from various colleagues. However, they were soon all milling around for a wash themselves and, except for Ray, none of them bothered to rinse out and replenish the bucket with fresh water each day.

In March I saw Pete Jackson and told him I was looking for a change of job. I was now 30 years old and was thinking it time to hang up my boiler suit in favour of a clean clothes job. I had put a deposit on a house, was in process of arranging a mortgage and Connie and I were ready to set the date. I was tired of nurturing grimy old aircraft – and they did not come any grimier than Yorks, being always coated with a nasty film of oil & exhaust gunge. Also, the erratic working hours were a pain. I hoped for a liaison sort of job similar to Pete's but he suggested a better one.

Frank Jones, Chief Draughtsman in New Project No. 2 Design Office at Hatfield, wanted a draughtsman with an intimate knowledge of aircraft to work in the Aircraft Installation Group. Pete thought that I was the chap he needed and suggested I apply for the job. It would be a weekly-staff job with all the usual benefits that entailed: two weeks annual holiday, paid sick leave and an extra 'premium day' for each Bank Holiday.

Following receipt by the firm of my application, an interview was arranged; it was a security area, so I had to wait in the police box at the NP2 entrance for Frank Jones's secretary to escort me to his office. I was issued with a visitor's pass and told not wander unescorted. Whilst waiting, many people passed through the entrance and all showed a pass with their photo on it to the officer on duty.

Frank Jones, a large, jovial, balding and bespectacled man, greeted me warmly and bade me sit opposite him at his large desk. I stressed my previous limited experience – two or three sketches to apply for repair schemes from manufacturers and some radio installation drawings for the ARB surveyor etc., plus my evening classes. In turn, he questioned me concerning my practical experience; he mentioned in passing that in the previous week a draughtsman had submitted a scheme where, in order to attach a cable clip, he had called for a hole to be drilled right through the wing spar to accommodate its little bolt.

Laughing at my horrified expression he finally said: "Well, let's be honest, Harry, you are not a draughtsman as such but at least you know your aircraft. And on that point, I am prepared to offer you a post as junior draughtsman at £13 per week on six months trial. If, at the end of that six months it doesn't work out, don't worry, we'll find something else for you."

I tentatively mentioned that I planned to marry shortly and hoped that it would not be inconvenient.

"I am sure we can accommodate you," he smiled. "I have had fellows come for interview and say: 'I want £16 a week and I've already arranged my holiday!"

We walked through the main office for me to be introduced to my new Section Leader, also 'Adams'! But Bill Adams this time, and no relation to Wally. Unlike Wally, Bill was tall, bespectacled and studious; he reminded me of Michael Redgrave's portrayal of Barnes Wallis in *The Dam Busters* film and I felt a bit in awe of him. After a brief discourse, during which Frank did most of the talking, he escorted me back to the police box and said that confirmation of appointment would be posted to me, but it might be a little while as security clearance had to be arranged. He shook my hand and said that he looked forward to welcoming me into the Department.

About a week later I received an official letter from the de Havilland Propeller Company offering me the post of junior draughtsman at a salary of £13 per 39-hour week, with superannuation and sick pay benefits; if agreeable, please confirm in writing, by return. This was an offer I could not pass up; my weekly hours at Scottish were 52 plus, with my hourly rate of pay totalling about £12 for a normal week. Furthermore, it was a nice prospect to start married life by going to work each day in office clothes and working in clean – and in winter, warm – conditions.

I posted my acceptance and told Ray, hoping he would not be offended at my leaving after such a short spell. In fact he was genuinely pleased for me; he knew I was unhappy and regretted suggesting the job in the first place. Next, of course, was Wally, who was equally charming and said, jokingly: "Who knows? I might come cap-in-hand for a job myself one day!"

Whilst awaiting confirmation of starting date, without telling of my proposed move, I remarked to Timber that I thought his scale drawing of the York cabin interior very professional and queried whether he had thought about becoming a draughtsman.

His reply to that one was: "Not bloody likely! I've no wish to sit on my arse all day at a drawing board."

I grinned and let it go.

I left Scottish Airlines without regret and rejoined de Havilland Props a rung or two up the ladder. After an interview at the Personnel Reception, three of us new recruits were asked to read and sign Part Three of the Official Secrets Act and were then allotted temporary passes. Finally, at an interview with the incumbent Nursing Sister at the Medical Centre, a minor glitch presented itself with regard to my asthmatic state. The Sister scanned my records, frowned, and queried which department I would be working in.

"The Drawing Office in NP2," I said.

TOP: Ray, about to be swallowed by a SAL York.
BOTTOM: The author pretending to pilot the SAL DC-3.
Photo: Ray Clapham.

The Short Gyron-Sperrin leaves Hatfield to display at the 1955 Farnborough

"Well, I will agree to you working in a drawing office, but if you are likely to be transferred to any other department, you must first check with me to ensure that there are no hazards to your particular health problems."

Such concern did much to engender the family feeling that was so typically de Havilland's. It was great to be back and my real aeronautical engineering education was about to begin. I had been extremely lucky to experience such a wide variety of disciplines in the wonderful world of aviation, but until then I had merely scratched the surface; a new way of life stretched before me.

EPILOGUE

When Scottish Aviation Twin Pioneer G-AOEO was scheduled to embark on a North African sales tour in 1957, Managing Director David McIntyre would not allow it to be delayed for the modifications to the wing strut and attachment brackets indicated as essential by structural tests at Farnborough. The Air Registration Board grudgingly agreed to allow the machine to fly on the tour on his responsibility providing that, before each and every flight, the wing-strut fairings be removed to check that the suspect brackets were still sound.

A short time before departure, the regular flight engineer was rushed into hospital with acute appendicitis and had to withdraw. Scottish Airlines at Stansted were contacted from Prestwick to see if a suitable licensed engineer was available as substitute; Ray Clapham was and jumped at the chance.

At 7,000 feet over Libya with Captain R. Smith, David McIntyre, Ray as Flight Engineer and some oil company executives aboard, the wing strut attachment assembly of G-AOEO failed, allowing the port wing to fold upwards, and the aircraft plunged to the ground killing all on board.

Connie and I had married at Broxbourne Church a month after I joined NP2DO and Ray had been my 'best man.' We moved into a small 'semi' in Hoddesdon and Ray & Jean visited us two or three times. He last called when I was attempting to convert the couch grass-cocooned builder's plot – upon which our abode rested – into something vaguely resembling a garden. He glanced at my efforts as he left and his last words to me were: "You're beginning to knock the old place into shape, 'H.'" A week later those words echoed through my mind when trying to come to terms with the shock of reading of the disaster in my daily paper. I had assumed him to be at Stansted and hoped the newspaper had made an error, but a telephone call to the firm only confirmed the worst. Later that evening Geoff Clapham called at our house to break the news in person. It was a long time before I ceased grieving; I felt as though I had lost a favourite younger brother.

At the drawing board, I had found my niche at last and stayed in the Design Office through the many changes that occurred to the industry, firstly when de Havilland was swallowed up by Hawker Siddeley, later when nationalised by a Labour Government consumed by dogma and lacking in common sense, and finally when de-nationalised into British Aerospace plc. From time to time I called upon previous practical workshop experience when faced with design problems. I remembered the frustrations of obscure dimensioning and tried to put myself in the operator's place. Once when arguing a point with my Section Leader I suggested a solution whilst harking back mentally to my earlier hangar experience. He scorned my suggestion at first with a contemptuous "Yes! Yes! We know all about your barnstorming days!" and then proceeded to adopt my idea.

When British Aerospace Dynamics moved from the Manor Road site in Hatfield at the end of 1989, my work title was 'Senior Designer.' Upon transfer to the former BAC site at Stevenage I was re-titled 'Design Engineer.' By that time, having been involved in detail design of various projects mainly to do with guided weapons, I had now taken over the task of design support & development of the Jetstream undercarriage – probably the most satisfying job to end my career, and particularly so in view of the fact that the Jetstream was the last-ever design of Handley Page, my father's employer during the first World War; so I felt a faint family link as well.

I took early retirement in May 1990 with a monetary offer that I could not refuse. I was involved with vintage aircraft restoration as a spare-time hobby and also had joined the de Havilland Moth Club.

In retirement I still dabble voluntarily with aviation projects. I have rebuilt a number of light aircraft components in my garage and small workshop, produced some engineering drawings and, when attending the unveiling by HRH The Duke of Edinburgh of Sir Geoffrey de Havilland's statue at the University of Hertfordshire, I was proud to note that one of the aircraft in the subsequent flypast had empennage units I had rebuilt at home. Also, as an Associate Member of the Royal Aeronautical Society, I still attend meetings of our local Hatfield Branch.

Among my possessions are various items that reflect my working life: woodworker's suitcase-sized toolbox, fitter's cantilever metal ditto and engineer's small 6-drawer oak cabinet containing micrometers ('mikes') and vernier measuring instruments etc. Also within the spare bedroom is my 'AO'-sized rise-and-fall adjustable drawing board and a filing cabinet containing such useful items as Machinery's Handbook, British Standards Yearbook and Brown Brothers' Catalogue.

I still get enormous satisfaction from planing a piece of wood to a mirror finish, drilling metal with a sharp drill so that the swarf curls beautifully from each flute or filing a metal part square and smooth. People who have never had the good fortune to enjoy the satisfaction of making things must be pitied for what they have missed in life. And as to sitting in front of the telly watching football, me? You must be joking!

Harry Smith, AMRAeS, Aeroplane Mechanic (Ret'd), autumn 1999.

BIBLIOGRAPHY

Aeroplane Monthly, formerly edited by Richard Riding, now by Michael Oakey, IPC Magazines.

Air Road to the Isles by Capt. Fresson.

Bennett and the Pathfinders by John Maynard, Arms & Armour Press.

British Civil Aircraft 1919/1972 by A.J. Jackson, Putnam.

By Jupiter! by Bill Gunston, Royal Aeronautical Society.

DH: A History of de Havilland by C. Martin Sharp, Airlife Publishing Ltd.

Lion Rampant & Winged by Alan Robertson, McCorquodale (Scotland).

The Magic of a Name by Harold Nockolds, G.T. Foulis & Co Ltd.

Whittle:The True Story by John Golley, Airlife Publishing Ltd.

Hot Money by Dick Francis, Michael Joseph Ltd. 1987